RAY BRADBURY

MODERN MASTERS OF SCIENCE FICTION

Science fiction often anticipates the consequences of scientific discoveries. The immense strides made by science since World War II have been matched step by step by writers who gave equal attention to scientific principles, human imagination, and the craft of fiction. The respect for science fiction won by Jules Verne and H. G. Wells was further increased by Isaac Asimov, Arthur C. Clarke, Robert Heinlein, Ursula K. Le Guin, Joanna Russ, and Ray Bradbury. Modern Masters of Science Fiction is devoted to books that survey the work of individual authors who continue to inspire and advance science fiction. A list of books in the series appears at the end of this book.

Ray Bradbury

David Seed

UNIVERSITY OF ILLINOIS PRESS

Urbana, Chicago, and Springfield

Library of Congress Cataloging-in-Publication Data
Seed, David.
Ray Bradbury / David Seed.
pages   cm. — (Modern Masters of Science Fiction)
Includes bibliographical references and index.
ISBN 978-0-252-03894-5 (cloth : acid-free paper)
ISBN 978-0-252-08058-6 (pbk.)
ISBN 978-0-252-09690-7 (ebook)
1. Bradbury, Ray, 1920–2012—Criticism and interpretation.
I. Title.
PS3503.R167Z868   2015
813'.54—dc23   2014023778

contents

RAY BRADBURY

CHAPTER 1

OUT OF THE SCIENCE FICTION GHETTO

On June 6, 2012, the day after Ray Douglas Bradbury's death, President Obama declared that "his gift for storytelling reshaped our culture and expanded our world."[1] The many Science Fiction authors paying tribute to him included Ursula Le Guin, David Brin, and Margaret Atwood, all recalling the formative role played in their careers by his fiction. Starting with the 1948 O. Henry Award for one of his stories, Bradbury's many subsequent honors included the 2000 Medal for Distinguished Contribution to American Letters awarded by the National Book Foundation and the 2004 National Medal of Arts awarded by President Bush. In 2007 he became a Commander of the Ordre des Arts et des Lettres, awarded by the French government. And so the list could continue. In 1971 the Dandelion Crater on the Moon was named after his 1957 novel *Dandelion Wine*. In addition, an asteroid, a landing site on Mars, and a square in Los Angeles have all been named after Bradbury. When Soviet Premier Gorbachev visited the United States in 1990 he asked to meet Bradbury, and in 2002 a star in Bradbury's name was added to the Hollywood Walk of Fame during the city celebrations for "One Book, One City L.A." centering on *Fahrenheit 451*. In short, by the time of his death Bradbury had become a national institution.

Bradbury's career has been shot through with paradox. From the early 1950s, he became celebrated as the leading Science Fiction writer of the United States, a status that Thomas M. Disch commented on ironically in 2003, and yet he was the least typical.[2] His career has a historical importance pointed to by fellow SF novelist Kim Stanley Robinson (born, like Bradbury, in Waukegan, Illinois, and then a Californian by adoption), who stated that he was "one of the first break-out stars from the Science Fiction community into mainstream American culture."[3] Despite the fact that his writing career spanned over seventy years, he is best known for *The Martian Chronicles* (1950), *The Illustrated Man* (1951), *Fahrenheit 451* (1953), and other stories from his peak period of creativity over the decade following 1945. This is reflected in the organization of the present study, which first examines his creation of a kind of Science Fiction beyond the genre ghetto of the 1940s; and then discusses his writings on Mars, *Fahrenheit 451*, and its dystopian contexts; and concludes with Bradbury's writings on space.

In addition to SF, Bradbury wrote Gothic tales, murder mysteries, and Hollywood novels. In 1948 he began giving talks to colleges, and from the 1950s, when he worked with John Huston on the script for *Moby Dick*, Bradbury wrote many more screenplays, most of which remain unpublished. He was also constantly active in adapting his works for the theater; between 1985 and 1992, he hosted the Ray Bradbury Theater series on cable TV. Other media he worked on included radio drama, musicals, and opera. He wrote poetry throughout his career, from the 1960s onward campaigned for a monorail in Los Angeles, and at different periods served as a consultant for the design of city plazas. The early peaking of his creativity by no means implies that his career tailed off. On the contrary, Bradbury demonstrated indefatigable energy when working in the different media, campaigning on behalf of NASA, and promoting his interests through countless lectures and interviews.

Despite the commercial difficulties of placing collections with publishers, Bradbury's chosen form remained the short story throughout his career, attracted by its potential control of information and therefore suspense.[4] He found a recurring problem in novels of descriptive data smothering the drama of character, whereas his books were "full of people explaining themselves."[5] Bradbury played a key part in changing the emphasis in SF publishing away from novels. Surveying Science Fiction in 1951, Fletcher Pratt noted that the short story was becoming the "characteristic form in the field."[6] Bradbury's imagination was essentially scenic—the influence of film on his work can't be overstated—and his stories typically evoke situations and then explore their ironies. He became a master of concise narrative and was singled out by J. G. Ballard, when introducing his own 2006 collected stories, for praise along with Borges and Poe as the supreme practitioners in that mode. Bradbury deliberately produced stories that cut across different genres. In his 1960s recording for the University of California Oral History program, he stated: "It's very hard for me to understand the typical Science Fiction writer . . . who has simply never moved outside that field."[7] He praised writers like his mentor Henry Kuttner for working in different genres.

Throughout his career he emphasized that SF was a visual medium, paying tribute in his 1987 essay "Art and Science Fiction" (collected in *Yestermorrow*) to the artwork of N. C. Wyeth and J. Allen St. John, who illustrated the fiction of Jules Verne and Edgar Rice Burroughs, respectively; and also the cover art on SF magazines like *Amazing Stories* by both St. John and Frank R. Paul. Citing the examples of Arthur C. Clarke, Carl Sagan, and Bruce Murray (the latter two founded the Planetary Society, with Bradbury's support), Bradbury stresses the formative influence on a whole generation of readers exercised by these SF illustrators, declaring: "The world we live in today is the direct result, I think, of the artwork, the illustrations, and the architecture of only-yesterday's artists, who influenced films and comic strips as well as young writers and budding scientists."[8]

Crucial to Bradbury's childhood experiences was film-going. His middle name was given in tribute to Douglas Fairbanks, and he recalled seeing Lon Chaney in *The Hunchback of Notre Dame* at the age of three.[9] In 1928 he discovered *Amazing Stories* and other Science Fiction magazines and then the comic strips of Buck Rogers and Flash Gordon along with the novels of Edgar Rice Burroughs, whose influence will be discussed in the following chapter. Bradbury's family left Waukegan during the Depression and then moved to Los Angeles in 1934. L.A. became his home for the rest of his life, he later cribed it as a city riding the "wave of the future" and one that combined ...llywood with the "birthing of several technologies."[10]

Residence in the movie capital consolidated Bradbury's childhood memories, which were punctuated by seeing the key movies of the period. Although he was to develop misgivings about the Hollywood system, Bradbury's enthusiasm for the film medium never flagged, and throughout his career he attempted to apply cinematic methods in his fiction. In one of his first interviews, he stressed: "I try to enable the reader to *see*" without mediation; in 1998 he declared: "All of my work is photogenic. I'm a child of the cinema. . . . When you begin to write you write for the screen automatically."[11] A number of critics have commented on Bradbury's visual sense, but without exploring the close connections between his methods of narration and a cinematic attention to viewpoint and scene. Bradbury's fascination with film was complex and long-standing, which makes the critical neglect of this area of his work all the more surprising. He has repeatedly evoked a three-way interaction in his career between comic books, film, and fiction. In a 1997 interview, he glossed the techniques of his own fiction in the following way: "If you look at the average page of any of the novels or short stories, it's a storyboard, a shooting script. You can shoot the paragraphs—the close-ups, the long shots, what have you."[12]

FILM AND THE EARLY SCIENCE FICTION

The priority Bradbury gives to the visual can be seen from the very beginning of his career. "Pendulum" (1941), written in collaboration with Henry Hasse, opens with the puzzling image of a human skeleton inside the head of a huge pendulum amid the ruins of a city, viewed by extraterrestrials who supply the perspective of a first-time reader. Inside the pendulum they find a "crumbling notebook" written by the man suspended inside its head who has become a spectacle as the so-called "Prisoner of Time."[13] This is the point where Bradbury's inset narrative begins to emerge of a scientist attempting to devise a time machine. A massive explosion kills most scientists present at the experiment and the scientist becomes the prisoner not conqueror of time. The perspective in these sections of the story reverses from the spectators' to that of Layeville the scientist, who becomes a historical witness to the rise of robotics and the resulting war. Bradbury's revisions to this story reflect a gain in sophistication. The reduction in narrative omniscience, the tighter focus

on image and montage, and the use of a green winged alien observer in t'
opening all suggest a sharper attention to perspective.

Bradbury's use of a pendulum may owe a debt to *Modern Times* (1936;
sometimes described as Chaplin's only Science Fiction film), where the pendulum clock is a central image of automation and entrapment within the
machine. Walter M. Miller was to draw on the same film in his 1955 story
"The Darfsteller," whose protagonist's performance in an automated theater is compared to Chaplin's closure of the gap between man and machine.
Bradbury grew up watching Chaplin's films and later stated: "I am as much
Charlie Chaplin in Modern Times in 1935 as I am Aldous Huxley's reader-friend
in 1961."[14] The story describes imprisonment within the very machine that
was designed to release humanity from the bonds of time, and the reversals
of perspective invite the reader to speculate about the role of technology in
a society that has destroyed itself.

Bradbury's interest in SF film grew significantly from the late 1940s onward.
He recalled visiting the film set for George Pal's *Destination Moon* (1950) with
friends Forrest Ackerman and Ray Harryhausen, partly occasioned by Robert
Heinlein's participation in the project as screenwriter and technical adviser.
When the film was released, Bradbury recalled their disappointment, adding:
"since then we've learnt a lot about film making and about writing better
screenplays and doing better casting and having better effects." His disappointment was all the sharper for its contrast with his experience of the 1936
film *Things to Come*, which was formative in Bradbury's career: "I suddenly
realized that the Future, more than ever, was where I wanted to go and the
Moon was the first destination. I began to write more and more Science Fiction and put a lot of these ideas in my own fan magazine a few years later."[15]

Apart from its proximity to Hollywood, Los Angeles opened up a professional opportunity to the young Bradbury. In 1937 he attended his first meeting
of the Los Angeles Science Fiction Fantasy Society ("Fiction" was dropped
from its title in 1940), thus gaining entry to the SF community in general and
for the first time meeting professional writers and the promoter Forrest J.
Ackerman. Bradbury immediately got involved in the group's activities and
by the following year had become a regular. The editor Charles D. Hornig
recalled that Bradbury "spent eight hours a day writing," but had published
nothing at that stage.[16]

This situation was to change quickly, however. Bradbury's newfound contacts supplied him with a series of mentors who were to kick-start his career: Henry Hasse for cutting; Ross Rocklynne (a regular contributor to the pulps with stories of alternate worlds and space opera) for plot ideas and style; Jack Williamson for reading drafts; Edmund Hamilton and Henry Kuttner for introducing him to a range of English literature.[17] Robert Heinlein gave detailed criticism to Bradbury about his stories, evidently more impressed by the latter's determination than the quality of his work, though Bradbury later acknowledged that Heinlein was the "agent of my very first sale."[18] Hasse collaborated with him on his stories, revising Bradbury's first drafts, and helped him place "Pendulum."[19]

In addition to advising on his stories, Kuttner's themes would have been congenial to Bradbury. "The Proud Robot" (1943, cowritten with C. L. Moore), for instance, describes a near-future America where television has totally changed national viewing habits. The story focuses on the commercial struggles between the two main film promoters as complicated by the invention of a robot, which turns out to be absurdly narcissistic. Kuttner thus blurs the human/mechanical distinction, partly by showing humans in behavioristic terms as merely responding to stimuli. "Don't Look Now" (1948) relates to Bradbury's Martian fiction (both stories are collected in *The Best of Kuttner I*, 1975). Here, the Martians have taken over the Earth but are largely invisible to human eyes. The story takes explicit bearings from H. G. Wells to set up its paranoid vision of a world and of minds controlled by apparently all-powerful aliens. Kuttner helped Bradbury place "Chrysalis"—a story about metamorphosis during a scientific experiment—with *Amazing Stories*, a work that Jon Eller sees as introducing the recurring tension in Bradbury's SF between evolutionary hope and fear of the alien.[20]

The other writer whose help Bradbury long remembered for her tuition in "basic writing" was Leigh Brackett.[21] Over some five years they would meet on Sunday afternoons to discuss each other's stories, Brackett supplying openings, or "hooks," as Bradbury would call them, for "Tomorrow and Tomorrow" and "The Scythe," while Bradbury wrote a conclusion for her own *Lorelei of the Red Mist*. The latter opens as a hard-boiled thriller narrated by a fugitive from Terro-Venus Mines, Inc. ("The company dicks were good. They were plenty good.") and then segues into a swords-and-sorcery adventure on Venus. Brackett's own acknowledgment of Bradbury's progress came when she felt he had fully assimilated her style.

Throughout his subsequent career, Bradbury expressed gratitude to these mentors and he helped younger writers such as Charles Beaumont and William F. Nolan in their careers. The latter became one of Bradbury's most devoted bibliographers in addition to writing his own fiction, producing a series of studies starting in 1952 with the *Ray Bradbury Review* and including his 1975 *Ray Bradbury Companion*. For his part Bradbury showed his appreciation when introducing Nolan's first collection, *Impact-20* (1963); he stated that he was prouder of him than "any other young writer I have encountered over the years."[22] Bradbury singled out for special mention the lead story, "The Small World of Lewis Stillman," which describes the experiences of the sole survivor of an alien infestation of Los Angeles. After the mid-1940s Bradbury restricted his reading of SF to a few favorites, though he devoured the works of contemporaries such as Heinlein and Arthur C. Clarke.[23]

An important development in Bradbury's early career was editing the fanzine *Futuria Fantasia* from 1939 to 1940, which carried contributions from Ackerman and Kuttner among others. The first issue declared Bradbury's new enthusiasm: "I think Technocracy combines all of the hopes and dreams of Science Fiction."[24] This movement, proposing a gospel of technological efficiency, had peaked by the time Bradbury was writing, and his interest quickly passed. His reading of Lewis Mumford's *Technics and Civilization* (1934) would have suggested a far broader vision of the place of technology in culture, where Mumford explains machine age film as offering a new form of narrative: "not plot in the old dramatic sense, but historic and geographic sequences is the key to the arrangement of these new kinetic compositions: the passage of objects, organisms, dream images through time and space."[25] By the second issue of *Futuria Fantasia* (Fall 1939), Bradbury had turned his back on technocracy and even issued a challenge to John W. Campbell to a "duel of words" on the subject. In view of Bradbury's shifting relation to SF, it is revealing that this same issue should carry an essay by a supposedly disenchanted SF fan ("I'm Through!") attacking as naive the perceptions that the fiction was instructive and predictive and taking most SF magazines to task for their "frightful smugness." The following number of the magazine carried a "rebuttal" by the author Henry Hasse to the essay, which had actually been written by himself under a pseudonym. Right from the beginnings of his career Bradbury was concerned to debate the nature of SF.[26]

TRIALS OF OTHER GENRES

During the 1940s, as Bradbury's career developed momentum, he tried writing detective fiction and horror as well as SF. He contributed a number of stories to *Detective Tales*, *Dime Mystery Magazine*, and similar journals. Introducing his retrospective collection *A Memory of Murder* (1984), Bradbury honestly admitted that these stories were apprentice work distracting him from the fields of weird, fantasy, and Science Fiction: "the detective tales, because they required hard thinking, prevented my flow, damaged my ability to use my intuition to the full. They were, as a result, quite often walking wounded."[27] As was to become usual with Bradbury's work, however, generic boundaries blurred, and from this writing he produced his classic "The Small Assassin" (1946), where a mother's postnatal conviction that her baby wants to kill her can no longer be read as psychological fantasy after she is found dead. And from the same period "Corpse Carnival" (1945) describes the experiences of a conjoined twin after he is surgically separated from his other half. Although the surface plot involves the surviving twin's hunt for his brother's killer, a powerful psychological tension is set up between his loss of spectacle appeal as a "freak" and the isolation that that brings with it.

As early as 1940, Bradbury saw the Gothic as an antidote to old-style SF cliches. That year he wrote to John W. Campbell, then editor of *Unknown* [*Fantasy Fiction*], to express how that journal acted as an "antidote" to *Astounding* [*Science Fiction*] (also edited by Campbell): "when you get tired of feeding molecules to Martian fuddy-duddies and your brain is so full of mechanics and theories that it squeaks, it is a simple task to open up *Unknown* and get air-conditioned via the old Salem witchery way."[28]

Even when Bradbury was successfully placing stories with *Weird Tales* in the mid-1940s, he was expressing unease at the editor's resistance to "child fantasies," and he complained that "the pressure was there all of the time to turn me into a hack."[29] In his autobiography *The Way the Future Was* (1978), Frederik Pohl remembered Bradbury's productive energy (and shrewdness at identifying what sort of stories would sell) but admitted that in their formulaic pattern "horror stories were the dregs of the pulp market."[30] Indeed, Bradbury later recalled that his first stories for *Weird Tales*, *Planet*, and *Thrilling Wonder Stories* were all "using familiar plot, stock characters, and a predictable climax."[31]

Throughout the 1940s Bradbury struggled to move away from the formulaic methods of the pulps. As he explained to Richard Matheson in 1951, he constantly received letters from editors telling him not to write "off-trail stuff." Then two pivotal SF journals were founded: The *Magazine of Fantasy and Science Fiction* (*F&SF*) in 1949 and *Galaxy* in 1950. Bradbury declared: "there are only two intelligent editors in the field today . . . these people are H. L. Gold [*Galaxy*] and [Anthony] Boucher-[J. Francis]McComas [*F&SF*] who I lump as one person."[32] In addition to benefiting from these journals, toward the end of the 1940s Bradbury placed stories with mainstream magazines like *Mademoiselle* and *Harper's*, moving him yet further from genre publication. Here, a general characteristic emerges of Bradbury's writing in the first decades of his career. Again and again, he revised his texts for publication in new journals or for new editions. Often he changed his titles or took great pains to assemble and then revise his different collections. We shall see how this process worked in *The Martian Chronicles* in the following chapter, but the status of Bradbury's texts is a whole complex subject in its own right, admirably explained in Eller and Touponce's *Ray Bradbury: The Life of Fiction* (2004), especially as some changes were not from Bradbury's choice but introduced by his publishers.

The late 1940s were formative years in Bradbury's career. In 1952 he explained to Anthony Boucher: "I never intended writing in the weird field." The reason was the number of rejections he was getting for his Science Fiction stories. By 1946 he had reached a turning point: "my vein was run dry and I would have to *force* it to keep going. Only then did I turn my full force around and point it at s.-f. where I had originally intended to go."[33] Even here, however, he defined his field with care. It was "philosophical Science Fiction" or even "mood" or "evocative Science Fiction."[34] In the meantime, however, his first collection of stories in this field, *Dark Carnival* (1947), was coming out and received a very positive review by Boucher, who declared of Bradbury: "he's not only a fantasy writer; he is also a writer, period."[35] In 1949 Boucher founded the *Magazine of Fantasy and Science Fiction*, which was to figure Bradbury as one of its lead writers.

Despite his reservations about weird fiction, that was to remain an important second strand to Bradbury's writing. The print run of *Dark Carnival* was soon exhausted so Bradbury reprinted fifteen of the stories in *The October Country* (1955), which, like its predecessor, frames the narratives around carnival. In the opening story, the dwarf Bigelow uses enlarging mirrors to compensate for his stature. The sadistic ticket officer substitutes a mirror, which distorts by reduction, inducing a crisis in Bigelow, pity in the carny vendor Aimee, and revulsion when he sees himself reduced to a "horrid, ugly little man." This story introduces a theme running through the whole collection and much of Bradbury's fiction generally, namely the importance of seeing. Thus in the opening line we are told: "Aimee watched the sky, quietly." In contrast, the "managers of the various carnival pitches stood, like melting wax dummies, eyes staring blindly."[36] The showmen themselves have become exhibits, just as Bigelow has become a spectator, not a spectacle. Bradbury complicates our sense of vision in this mirror maze and thereby introduces the transformation of the mundane into the alien, which takes place in the succeeding stories. Seeing is immediately linked with introspection in this story, more widely with the inflections given to reality by Bradbury's subsequent characters. "The Dwarf" (1954) clearly shows how far Bradbury was to move from the formulaic pattern of weird stories described by Pohl earlier. It replaces the supernatural, which he had already taken far afield from the norm, with the psychology of seeing and avoids a resolving conclusion that merely reinstates normality.

Despite his impatience with its formulaic patterns, Bradbury never lost his interest in the Gothic. *From the Dust Returned* (2001) assembled a series of uncanny stories, several of which had already appeared in *Dark Carnival*. The series is unified around a frame situation where a young boy, Timothy, hears the tales from a mysterious grandmother-figure whose identity seems to extend into the distant past. He hears these tales in the attic of an old house, which Bradbury uses as a container for the fabulous. In a rephrasing of Winston Churchill's famous description of Russia as a "riddle, wrapped in a mystery, inside an enigma," we are told that the house "was a puzzle inside an enigma inside a mystery," and throughout the volume Bradbury uses the trope of opening—doors, lids, windows—to evoke the emergence of stories of spirits.[37] The sequence is full of allusions to earlier Gothic stories, to Dracula, "A Christmas Carol," the Oz stories, and those of Poe. In short, it is a novelized story cycle, which makes reading the Gothic an important part of its subject, and we are thus never allowed to forget the conventions of the genre.[38]

BRADBURY'S EARLY SCIENCE FICTION: THEMES AND TECHNIQUES

As Bradbury's fiction evolved, his early SF stories show him experimenting with methods and subjects like the nature of language in "Frost and Fire" (1946). From an idea inspired by Henri Bergson, the story describes a world where the life span has telescoped down to eight days.[39] In describing the consciousness of the protagonist, Sim, Bradbury confronted a double problem of how a character could think without language and how he could know the brevity of life if that was the norm. For the first, Bradbury projects a kind of eidetic thought through images, glossing over the speed with which Sim learns language; for the second, he attributes to a race memory Sim's capacity to think beyond his situation, although this does not remove the tension in the rhetoric between psychological process and commentary. The latter is used as a convenience for introducing the backstory of humans crashing their spaceships on the present planet. The rationale is tortuous and Bradbury's original title, "The Creatures That Time Forgot," helps to explain the weaknesses of the story in echoing Burroughs's lost-world romance. Bradbury's tale is no action adventure though it contains a combat sequence. Nor, despite its use of monosyllabic "primitive" names and flint weapons, does it belong in prehistoric SF, which as Nick Ruddick has shown, was a staple of American SF between the wars.[40] Instead, it describes a growth in consciousness, the pursuit of knowledge by a local remnant of scientists, and the use of a rocket as a vehicle of hopeful change (a "metal seed") when Sim leads a group toward liberation at the end of the narrative. The narrative is unusually long for Bradbury and lacks the tight situational ironies of his mature stories.

Where the problem in "Frost and Fire" is excessive explanation, "A Blade of Grass" (1949) suffers from the very explicit nature of Bradbury's narrative perspective.[41] Probably influenced by Arthur Koestler's *Darkness at Noon* (1940), which was to feed into Bradbury's conception of *Fahrenheit 451*, the story opens with a verdict against the protagonist: "It had been decided already that Ultar was guilty."[42] This immediately establishes an opposition between the regime and the protagonist, which is heavily reinforced by references to the officials as machines. Indeed, the state is named Obot (robot) and characters are presented as mindlessly mechanistic in their beliefs and actions. In that sense, robotics supplies an extended satirical analogue for political conformity. Against this ideology, Ultar has discovered the last surviving blade of grass, a Whitmanesque image of vitality, and has used it to devise a new form of human being. Much of the story is expository as he narrates a counter-history, questioning the state version of timeless technological stability. The story closes with the seizure of Ultar, presumably to suffer his fate. While the subject of the story anticipates *Fahrenheit 451*, the story states a confrontation without ever dramatizing it.

Bradbury wrote the difficulties he was finding with expression into the subject itself of "Forever and the Earth" (1950), where a would-be writer reflects on the impossibility of Space-Age fiction: "My mistake was in ever trying to picture this wild world of A.D. 2257. The rockets, the atom wonders, the travels to planets and double suns. Nobody can do it. . . . All our modern authors have failed."[43] In desperation he turns to a writer whose works Bradbury discovered in 1939—Thomas Wolfe. Bradbury was so frustrated by the latter's prose that he would cut up passages from Wolfe's novels and planned to paste them into his stories, later paying tribute later to Wolfe's narrative gusto. "Thomas Wolfe ate the world and vomited lava," he declared, though he recognized his shortcomings: "not much plot, but he was wild about life and tore into it."[44]

"Forever and the Earth" appeared in an issue of *Planet Stories* containing five other pieces. The first, about the perils of rocket men, was billed as a "thrilling space-adventure novel"; the others variously describe a murderer on the Moon, star wars, the perils of space travel, a Martian's experiences in Indiana, and a voyage to Mars to discover why the Martians called off their plans for invasion. In the latter, the rocket flight will be used to test a new device called the Harrigan Unimodulate Subetheric Telepathic Interspatial Communicator. In contrast with these stories' emphasis on adventure and technology, Bradbury's story focuses on the problems of authorship and writes Wolfe into the text from the title onward. The latter is taken from the preamble to Wolfe's *Of Time and the River* (1935), which opens with a phrase within ellipses: "*of wandering for ever and the earth again*" (italics in original).[45]

Field, the aspiring author, calls Wolfe back from the dead, thanks to a convenient time-travel machine, and asks him to describe a voyage to Mars in his own style. The logic behind this lies in a rather crude identification between the immensity of space and the largeness of Wolfe's style and physical stature, as well as a thematic link between wandering in his novel and time travel. Wolfe duly appears and agrees to fly to Mars, from where he transmits his Space-Age writing, which includes titles like "The Space War" and "The Long Midnight." In due course, Field's fantasy has to end and Wolfe returns to the scene of his death in 1938, but not before he has become enlisted in the cause of space. In one of the last scenes we hear Wolfe whispering to himself: "Mars, Mars. . . . My best, my very best, my really fine book, yet to be written."[46] By this point, Wolfe has become transformed into a fantasy precursor figure transmitting SF narratives over an ethereal teletype, a unique writer whose prose can do justice to the grandeur of space.

Unlike the other pieces in *Planet Stories*, "Forever and the Earth" is a futuristic space story about the difficulties of writing such narratives. Bradbury stated repeatedly that he drew on realist writers for his SF, as we shall see with *The Martian Chronicles*, and he was sometimes careful to remove their traces from his stories. A character in "Death-Wish" (1950), the original title of "The Blue Bottle," was called Steinbeck, for instance, before his name was revised to Beck. Bradbury's inclusion of a re-created Thomas Wolfe was a bold polemical move in resituating a major figure from the realist mainstream within the new context of SF to imply that the two traditions were not mutually exclusive. He was to make a similar move in describing a Bernard Shaw robot in "G.B.S.—Mark V" (1976).

Despite their unevenness, Bradbury's early SF stories already show signs of his trying to escape the constriction of stereotypes. In "I, Rocket" (1944), for instance, which appeared in *Amazing Stories*, the narrative of a war-rocket being sent into space to combat Martian aggression is conventional enough, but Bradbury weaves the unusual variation of making the rocket sentient and its own narrator. Unlike Anne McCaffrey's *The Ship Who Sang* (1969), Bradbury does not evoke a cybernetic entity part organic and part technological, but simply makes the rocket itself the carrier of the main perspective, the articulator of the crew's collective spirit—that is, except for two human "microbes," who (unsuccessfully) plan sabotage. The mission to Mars is successful, but the rocket later crashes on a planetoid, from which point the story is told as the rocket's "memory."

Similarly, "Tomorrow's Child" (originally carrying the Wellsian title "The Shape of Things" in 1948), sidesteps the emerging subject of mutant births, which were becoming increasingly common as fears grew of nuclear war, by describing how a young woman gives birth to a small blue pyramid. The doctor explains that it is no mutant, just "born into another dimension," though the mother finds it progressively more difficult to adjust to her situation. Bradbury briefly humanizes "Baby" by shifting the perspective round to its perceptual field of inchoate forms, and then the doctor offers the parents the possibility of joining the pyramid in its own dimension. Since the initial problem was caused by a malfunctioning of the birth machine, however, how can we know that the transformation of the parents will succeed? When he undergoes this change through a futuristic machine, the father experiences a loss of self through his inability to reconcile the alien with familiar humanity: "He began to melt like running wax."[47] By the end of the story they have turned into White Rectangle and White Oblong, respectively. Bradbury thus produces a bizarre parable on perception, which plays surrealistically with a potentially emotive family situation.

"Tomorrow's Child" gains much of its power from using geometric forms, which make it virtually impossible to project humanity onto the "child," who is named Py (after pi). Bradbury unnecessarily adds a concession to the conventionally monstrous in giving it "snakelike appendages" and three eyes. Throughout the story there is a fantastic disconnect between appearance and behavior starting from the hospital staff rushing to see Py. This bizarre spectacle highlights a central theme in Bradbury's fiction."Fantasy has filled my life," he declared in 1952, "I have always loved carnivals, magicians, circuses, mind-readers and skeletons."[48] He recalls how he studied the dialogue of a radio program about a magician and the methods used generally by these performers. The coincidence of studying their technique and the beginnings of Bradbury's career as a writer suggests that one was an analogue for the other. His notion of carnival was more complex than Bakhtin's counter-humor in his theory of the carnivalesque, incorporating notions of performance and display that appeal to characters' unconscious desires. In their seminal 2004 study, *Ray Bradbury: The Life of Fiction*, Eller and Touponce explore the different dimensions to masking in Bradbury's work, relating it to notions of authorship as well as narrative method.

THE ILLUSTRATED MAN

Carnival was to frame Bradbury's major SF collection *The Illustrated Man*, published after *The Martian Chronicles* in 1951 by Doubleday as part of their two-book deal, but containing the best leftover material from the same period. In the 1950 story with that title (initially not included in the collection), Phelps has his body covered in tattoos for his circus by a mysterious witchlike old woman. On the day of his "unveiling" his body is revealed as collage of narrative images spreading across time: "The Tyrannosaurus rex reared up along his leg. . . . Rockets burned across spaces of muscle and flesh."[49] Bradbury went on to elaborate this spectacle in the framing device of *The Illustrated Man* (1951), where the tattooed man is an anonymous itinerant outside any institutional context. His body is now used as a living trope of authorship. He literally brings into being a body of work, animated by his audience, the narrator who meets him by chance. The illustrated man supplies a holistic frame giving the stories a common origin rather than supplying narrative links, as Bradbury would use in *The Martian Chronicles*. The frame also evokes the folk tradition of oral narration transformed into film—the narratives are there to be *watched*, as James Anderson has pointed out—and gives the reader no direct hint of the SF sequence to come.[50] In that respect, it could have been a marketing strategy on Bradbury's part; he strongly requested that Doubleday remove the *Science Fiction* label from its cover and title page of *The Illustrated Man* for fear of distracting reviewers.[51] As early as 1948, when he was first planning the collection, Bradbury expressed anxieties about its generic mix "with layers of s.f., weird, fantastic and realistic fiction bunched together."[52]

The combination of genres can take place within individual stories. "The Veldt" (1950) opens with a domestic situation located in a near-future Happylife Home, a "miracle of efficiency" constructed to satisfy every need automatically, and yet one of the main ironies of the story is a reversal. As Bradbury later explained, "these people are letting the house own them."[53] The visual perspective focuses tightly on domestic interiors although there is an ingenious twist here. Unlike the automated house in "There Will Come Soft Rains," one of the key locations is the nursery, the place where the children Peter and Wendy can play by wishing up whatever fantasy location they choose. In J. M. Barrie's story, Peter and Wendy fly to Neverland, a place of adventure, and finally return to the security of their home. No such closure occurs in "The Veldt," however. When the parents enter the nursery to check out a possible malfunction, the walls radiate the colors and temperature of an African landscape. Lydia shrieks to her husband when lions seem to be running at her, only to be chided by him: "Walls, Lydia, remember; crystal walls, that's all they are. Oh, they look real, I must admit—Africa in your parlor—but it's all dimensional super-reactionary, super-sensitive color film and mental tape film behind glass screens."[54] His attempts to contain the force of the device by flattening it out as 2-D totally fail to account for the simulated reality being projected. Bradbury's story first appeared in the *Saturday Evening Post* with the more explicit title "The World the Children Made," whereas its revised title allows Bradbury to pace the ambiguities of control more tightly. The father worries that the room is "not responding" to his commands and both parents are deceived into entering the nursery. The story ends by implying that they have been killed by African lions.

"The Veldt" begins as domestic realism, shifts toward Science Fiction in its futuristic technology, and incorporates fantasy through allusion. It satirizes the consumerist ethic of the automated house, which displaces the parents from any active functions in the household. In a 1960 essay, Bradbury comments on the irony that he was "actually criticizing many of the advertisements" they carried in the *Post* since he was mounting an attack on the TV generation. However, if he had used a realist method it would have been totally different: "try to do this story in a conventional framework with conventional people, with a conventional approach and suddenly you're on a podium, the whole thing is self-conscious, and nobody wants to read it."[55] When dramatizing this story for the theater, Bradbury carefully avoided the use of screens, using the audience space itself as the veldt.

The title of one story of space travel, "Kaleidoscope" (1949), suggests Bradbury's method of counterpoint in *The Illustrated Man*, which can be viewed as a counterpoint between partial narratives revolving around the connections between technology, space travel, and the human imagination. The story opens with the worst case of a "concussion," probably with a meteorite, slicing open a rocket and hurling its crew out into space. From that point on, every astronaut drifts toward death. Hollis, who supplies the story's main perspective, figures death in filmic terms: "When life is over it is like a flicker of bright film, an instant on the screen, all of its prejudices and passions condensed and illumined for an instant on space, and . . . the film burned to a cinder, the screen went dark."[56] The story sets up a stark contrast between the immense scale of space and tiny human actions, tracing out the thoughts of Hollis in the last moments of his life.[57] Because the men communicate through their radios, they are reduced to disembodied voices, their dialogue and even the textual space of the story both giving us an illusion of proximity as they drift apart. Space for Hollis becomes a mental field, interrupted by stark reminders of his physical actuality as limbs are sliced off by passing meteorites. This reduction to abstraction also informs "No Particular Night or Morning" (1951), a dialogue sequence examining the total loss of spatial and temporal perceptions in space but without much attention to the physical bodies of the speakers.

Just as we move between voices in "Kaleidoscope," so perspectives constantly shift from story to story in *The Illustrated Man.* In "The Veldt" a household frames a kind of virtual reality technology, exposing a tension between parents and children. Disintegration actually takes place in "Kaleidoscope" as a spaceship breaks apart, with the ironic coda of a boy on Earth seeing what he thinks is a shooting star as an astronaut falls to his death. "The Other Foot" (1951) sets up a racial inversion when black Mars colonists prepare a Jim Crow system for incoming white rocket men, and "The Highway" (1950) distances us from nuclear war through a contrast between rustic Latinos and rich travelers. The pursuit of a messianic figure, possibly pure fantasy, on an unknown planet in "The Man" (1949) opens up space exploration as desire, which suddenly reverses in "The Long Rain" (1950) into Venus as a place of death and displaced jungle. From the imminent demise of that protagonist, we return in "The Rocket Man" (1951) to child/adult contrasts of perspective as a son's ambition takes shape to become an astronaut like his father.

"The City" (1950) is one of the grimmest stories in *The Illustrated Man* for its reversal of the hopes of space exploration. The opening line, "the city waited twenty thousand years," briefly evokes a huge time span and, unusually for Bradbury, sets up a narrative perspective beyond that of its human characters. The city is evoked as a technological consciousness somehow functioning long after its inhabitants have died out. The arrival of a rocket from Earth triggers a sequence of quasisensory responses to the astronauts' presence, resulting in the seizure of the captain. On analysis it is revealed that he is human like the previous colonizers of the planet who had wiped out the inhabitants by disease. The backstory motivates the transformation of the captain's body into that of a cyborg: "A heart was attached, and into the skull case was fitted a platinum brain. . . . In a moment the body was sewn tight, the incisions waxed, healed at neck and throat and about the skull—perfect, fresh, new."[58] This pivotal moment reveals to the reader a process that the astronauts don't see, while leaving the agency of the transformation unspecified, but the purpose of that technology is to wreak revenge on Earth. Originally given the more paranoid title "Purpose," the story balances arrival and final departure, but in the latter the rocket has become a vehicle for attack carrying bacteria bombs and humanoid aggressors.[59] As happens in many SF invasion films of the 1950s, the crew is indistinguishable from humans.

Throughout *The Illustrated Man* we thus read across perspectives, which shift according to the age or ethnicity of protagonists from colonizer to colonized, from travel as bliss or as hell, from adult astronauts to children's games. The dominant theme is space travel, but apparently unrelated stories are tied in through technology. "The Highway" centers on Hernando, a Latino farmer living just off a concrete highway who wears shoes made from the tires of a car that crashed into his land. Bradbury sets up a symbolic opposition in the landscape between the static countryside and the disruptions of technology embodied in the black cars that stream by Hernando's home in an accelerated funeral cortege. When a passerby announces that nuclear war has broken out, the full extent of Bradbury's symbolism becomes evident as a final cataclysm of technology. In the final line of the story Hernando, however, remains blissfully unaware, wondering: "What is this place they call, 'the world'?"

In this story travel is evoked as flight. In "Marionettes, Inc." (1949), the technology of robotics offers a character psychological escape from a loveless marriage and the possibility of time-out in Rio de Janeiro.

The dominant narrative trajectory is that of a voyage or a flight of the imagination, many of the stories thus realizing in concrete terms one of Bradbury's most recurrent metaphors. "The Rocket" thus opens with Bodoni, who yearns at night for release from poverty: "for a silent moment he would let his heart soar alone into space, following the rockets." His youthful enthusiasm is countered by the jaundiced cynicism of an old man who warns him: "this is a rich man's world."[60] Bradbury then sets up the main visual opposition in the story between the exciting openness of rocket technology (future) and Bodoni's junkyard (the past). He is offered a mockup of a rocket and takes his family on a fantasy voyage, which is described in terms of virtual reality: "let there be no flaws in the color film," he yearns.[61] Bodoni's desire for flight is enthusiastically endorsed by his children, and *The Illustrated Man* has a secondary frame in the first and last stories, which focus on the reach of the imagination outward: to a virtual Africa in "The Veldt" and the illusion of space travel in "The Rocket." As has been noted many times by Bradbury's critics, there is scant attention paid to the technology in these stories, but much more emphasis placed on their social and psychological effects and on their reification of human desires.

The interplay between childhood and adult perspectives is central to *The Illustrated Man*. In "The Playground" (1952), the final story in the British edition, a father has such an alienated view of a playground that in his eyes it becomes an "immense iron industry," churning out sadistic monsters.[62] More importantly, the penultimate story in the U.S. edition, "Zero Hour" (1947), suggests that children's play at invasion is becoming real.

"Zero Hour" follows a similar trajectory to Bradbury's other narratives of children, where their presence becomes stronger and stronger, building up to a point of threat. While the game called "Invasion" is being played, adult life goes on: "parents came and went on chromium beetles. Repairmen came to repair the vacuum elevators in houses, to fix fluttering television sets or hammer upon stubborn food-delivery tubes." It seems to be an idyllic world of order and stability without any threat of war: "the perfect weapons were held in equal trust by all nations."[63] Against this background of complacent adult inactivity, the children are acting out an energetic game of disruption, claiming that they have been guided by an extraterrestrial called Drill.[64] Zero hour comes with a climactic series of explosions and an ominously loud buzzing sound. The parents take refuge in the attic, their place of memory, but nowhere is safe, hence the concluding image of the tale where their daughter seems to be leading the invaders: "the attic lock melted. The door opened. Mink peered inside, tall blue shadows behind her. 'Peekaboo,' said Mink."[65]

Bradbury skillfully plays off the actuality of sophisticated technology against the continuing vocabulary of games, closing the story with the suspense of a threatening but ambiguous image.

The subject of alien landing was emerging as a recurrent SF subject in the late 1940s and would be used in the first film where Bradbury took an active part, *It Came from Outer Space* (1953). One year after Bradbury's story, an episode in *The Mysterious Traveler* radio series carried the same title of "Zero Hour," scripted by Robert A. Arthur and David Kogan. It evokes an emergency discovered by a professor in Montana that "advanced" Martians have infiltrated this community and many others, masquerading as humans and preparing for a "preventive" conquest of the world, which will take place at zero hour. The subject of an invasion from Mars is mentioned within Bradbury's story, only to be qualified and then dismissed by the adults as children's fantasy. The topicality of the subject is reflected in the story's inclusion in Orson Welles's theme collection *Invasion from Mars* (1949), which also included stories by Asimov, Heinlein, and others, as well as Bradbury's "The Million-Year Picnic." "Zero Hour," however, avoids potential clichés by never describing the invaders and never confirming that they are from Mars. All the information on them is supplied through the children's speech and the story carefully layers an adult perspective over the children's game in order to question the latter's status as fantasy. Indeed, it seems at the end as if events are realizing the game and the "tall blue shadows" could be taken as half-images of the aggressive alien suppressed by a culture of security.

Whereas children act as a vehicle for disrupting adult complacency in "Zero Hour," "The Long Rain" displaces its human characters into an alien situation and clearly reflects how Bradbury was distancing himself from conventional SF. Under the title "Death-by-Rain," it first appeared in *Planet Stories* for summer 1950, a journal particularly promoting swords-and-sorcery narratives (its subtitle was *Strange Adventures in Other Worlds*). That issue carried an image of a warrior/model brandishing a huge scimitar, advertising Alfred Coppel's "Warrior-Maid of Mars." The clear suggestions of physical combat, however, never feature in Bradbury's story, which describes a group of rocket men battling through the Venusian jungle in search of a refuge called a Sun Dome. Bradbury keeps traces of Burroughs's Venus in the jungle landscape and single sea and mention of Venusians and monsters, but the real antagonist is the weather. We are given no hint of why the men are there. The narrative is entirely situational, describing the psychological pressure of the endless rain through the visual reduction of scenes to monochrome. The rain bleaches men and land alike into an "immense cartoon nightmare," where the Sun Dome functions as an image of desire, promising refuge from the climate. One dome is reached but it proves to be disused and derelict. After the physical and mental collapse of his group, the sole surviving lieutenant finally reaches a dome offering company, food, and clothing. Above all, he has found refuge from the rain: "He was looking at the sun."[66] Here, the ambiguity of the ending becomes marked. Because there is no companion to confirm the lieutenant's experience, it is as if he has stepped into hallucination like the Western protagonists of Conrad and Kipling's empire stories. A purist could object that there is no rain on Venus, but Bradbury is using that planet as a site for severe psychological alienation.

At the center of *The Illustrated Man*, two stories shed particular light on Bradbury's fictional methods. In "The Exiles" (1949), a voyage to Mars results in astronauts rediscovering the spirits of fantasy writers like Poe whose works have been banned on Earth. In this way, Bradbury draws a sharply ironic contrast between his own medium and the rationalist technological ideology supporting space flights. "No Particular Night or Morning" has only a minimal narrative, depicting two astronauts discussing the nature of space. It is no coincidence that the characters should be named Hitchcock (after Bradbury's favorite film producer) and Clemens, after Mark Twain. Their very names raise questions over the relation between their two chosen media, and indeed the epilogue to *The Illustrated Man* depicts his back in cinematic terms as "the vague patch began to assemble itself, in slow dissolving from one shape to another" until his face is finally revealed like the author illustration on the back of the book.[67]

Bradbury wrote an outline and screen treatment for an adaptation of *The Illustrated Man*, but nothing came of it until finally in 1969 Jack Smight directed a movie with Rod Steiger playing the lead. Bradbury was not consulted on the script and the result was poorly received by the critics and by Bradbury himself. "It's too long," he declared. "It's filled with clichés. It gives away climaxes too soon."[68] In its poor release of information for Bradbury it made a disappointingly sharp contrast with Hitchcock's movies, and he resolved from that point on to keep artistic control of any material he sold to Hollywood.[69]

By the time of *The Illustrated Man*, Bradbury had created his own form of Science Fiction, which was largely shaped by his attitude toward Science Fiction and technology, but also by his continuing interest in non-SF writers. Thus according to Sam Moskowitz, Bradbury produced an unusual hybrid of "mainstream theses and mainstream writing in a Science Fiction setting."[70] Bradbury reacted strongly against the cruder forms of SF in his childhood as "nuts and bolts fiction" and computers rarely figure in his fiction. Indeed, in later life he was scathing about their overvaluation and the internet.[71] Critics have noted repeatedly that his fiction contains very little technical description. John W. Campbell Jr., who rejected most of his submissions to *Astounding*, observed to Anthony Boucher: "When Bradbury discusses a space-ship, it's strictly a fairy ship; it has no hardware at all. It's actually a symbol of a space-ship, not a mechanical, operable device."[72] Bradbury always minimized circumstantial description in his stories, but that does not imply hostility or indifference to technology. His emphasis always falls on the latter's human consequences.

Indeed, when Bantam published a paperback edition of *The Martian Chronicles* in 1951 with a statement that Bradbury did not "care for" science, he was furious and used William Nolan's 1952 *Ray Bradbury Review* to make a position statement. Here, he expresses ambivalence about possible futures: medical advances could lead to bacteriological war; the failures of radio to live up to its promises could be repeated in television. In short, he concludes, "technological Science Fiction, as put in motion by human beings, can either shackle us with the greatest totalitarian dictatorship of all time, or free us to the greatest freedom in history. I mean to work for the latter in my Science Fiction stories."[73] Bradbury conceived his early SF as a cumulative early warning system against unforeseen consequences. He constantly requoted his assertion that his fiction was designed to prevent rather than predict futures and, like Marshall McLuhan, saw machines as extensions, "symbols of [humanity's] own most secret cravings and desires, extra hands put out to touch and reinterpret the world."[74] Throughout his career Bradbury paid special respect to authors like Loren Eiseley and Aldous Huxley for their skill at mediating between different cultural fields, stating of the latter: "Huxley inspired the scientist to put down his contraptions and attend humanity, while simultaneously teaching your plain field-beast human to lean into the Science Fictions for browsing."[75]

A number of Bradbury's stories satirize future technological environments. In "The Murderer" (1953), a young man named Brock is interviewed by a state psychiatrist over why he has been sabotaging a whole series of electronic "conveniences" like the telephone, speaking watch, or prerecorded background music. Brock's frenzy is triggered by a perception that all time and space has been invaded by the electronic media as if the consumer is being monitored and directed constantly toward projected orthodoxies. The listening psychiatrist interprets Brock's acts of sabotage as a pathological refusal to "accept the simplest realities of his environment," but Bradbury satirically fades out his narrative with the formulaic repetition of a noun sequence: "telephone, wrist radio, intercom, telephone wrist radio, intercom, telephone, wrist radio, intercom, telephone, wrist radio, intercom, telephone, wrist radio, intercom, telephone, wrist radio."[76] The supposed diagnostician proves to be totally controlled by his technological system, which his daily routine imitates as a fixed pattern. The syntax of his day becomes truncated as objects replace thought or chosen actions.

Brock's environment has become totally electronic and the story exemplifies Bradbury's 1964 situational definition of SF as "man lost in the maze of his machineries and how to find a way out to light again."[77] In "The Murderer," the authorities rationalize dissidence as pathological, an ideology we shall encounter again in *Fahrenheit 451*. Bradbury's concern with the gradual erosion of human movement by technology is debated explicitly by two men in the sketch "Wind-Up World" (2009, but written earlier). Here, items of clothing have taken over their respective functions, transforming consumers into figures of passivity. Because every place can be simulated electronically, there is no need to go anywhere. And then in a final ironic twist, one of the men realizes that even his companion was a mechanism: "Hogan, walking down the road, had a large mechanical key protruding from his back."[78] It is a cartoon image, but carries the disturbing implication that the other speaker is the last nonmechanized human, dystopian possibility similar to that explored in "The Pedestrian." Bradbury repeatedly targeted a Science Fiction–based rationalism in his writings. In his 1968 essay "Death Warmed Over," he declared: "We have fallen into the hands of the scientists, the reality people, the data collectors."[79] His 1961 teleplay *The Jail* dramatizes a cybernetic future where the protagonist is tried by machines whose testimony is delivered at high speed as an incomprehensible whine. Virtually all human functions here have been reduced to electronic data.[80]

Throughout his career Bradbury examines the implications and consequences of technological innovations rather than describing those devices themselves. The very flatness of title to "A Piece of Wood" (1952) suggests its contrast with SF gadgetry, and it initially lulls the reader into assuming that the dialogue over the arms race between a young sergeant and his superior—the Official, as he is called—will make up the story's subject. Facing down the young man's anxieties over weaponry, the Official ultimately convinces him that no reduction or sophistication of arms will eradicate war—one has been waged for sixteen years—despite the fact that the sergeant possesses a device which will start what he calls the "Rust," nothing less than the death of metal. Like a latter-day Tom Swift, the sergeant claims to have a calibrated little machine, which can be set to destroy a specific kind of steel and which he hopes will set the world free from war. It is merely described as "just as impossible as the atom bomb."[81] Or just as likely, to the postwar reader. And sure enough, after the sergeant leaves the Official's office, the latter discovers that his pen has disintegrated into "yellow-red rust." The SF supergadget has become transformed into a fantasy remedy to the arms race. The sergeant has no memory of how he devised his machine and only uses it out of desperation. Bradbury ends with an ironic coda showing the furious Official rushing out of his office in pursuit of the sergeant with a piece of wood. The irony of this parable works against both the inventor, who thinks he has devised an ultimate antiweapon, and against the Official's incorrigible aggression in the coda.

ROBOTICS

Bradbury's description of the replacement of humans by machines in *The Jail* marks an extreme case of robotics, which was a major SF theme throughout the 1940s. During that decade, Isaac Asimov produced a series of stories about benign robots in an attempt to get away from their clichéd description as evidence of the "overweening arrogance of humanity."[82] Thus in "Robbie" (1939) a robot acts as a child's guardian and in "Evidence" (1946) an extended dialogue demonstrates the impossibility of identifying a "humanoid" robot. Asimov's robot stories represent the benign end of the spectrum. At the other extreme, the "mechanicals" in Jack Williamson's *With Folded Hands* (1947; collected in *The Best of Jack Williamson*) are introduced "not to punish men, but merely to serve their happiness and security," a utopian purpose that lapses as they take over American society.[83]

Bradbury's own treatments of robotics are, in contrast, localized and related to the consumerism of the period. "Marionettes, Inc." (1949) describes how Braling takes his friend Smith (both unhappily married and unremarkable) into the city to reveal his "secret," which turns out to be an exact duplicate of himself, manufactured from "new humanoid plastic" by the company of the title, which has been secretly in business for the last two years. The main identifiable difference between Braling 2 and the original is that the former ticks, a sign of mechanism like that in Asimov's stories. However, Bradbury's choice of title suggests manipulation rather than futuristic technology. Braling plans to use his duplicate to keep his wife happy while he goes on holiday to Rio. Smith is predictably excited by the idea and plans to make one for himself, but discovers that his wife has withdrawn a suspiciously large amount from the bank. When he tries to wake her, he experiences a sudden surge of "terror and loneliness" as he hears her body ticking. This is Bradbury's first twist. The second comes when Braling 2 claims to be in love with the wife. An absurd dialogue follows between the two Bralings where the simulation seems more feeling than the original. The coda to the story nicely focuses the ambiguity of agency in its final pronoun:

> Ten minutes later Mrs. Braling awoke. She put her hand to her cheek. Someone had just kissed it. She shivered and looked up. "Why—you haven't done that in years," she murmured.
> "We'll see what we can do about that," someone said.[84]

Bradbury introduces his SF subject into a conventional situation of marital dissatisfaction. Equally avoiding Asimov's didacticism and Williamson's lengthy backstory, Bradbury stays with the ironies of the immediate situation, dramatizing the confusion of the two men's desires.

In "Punishment without Crime" (1950), the opening situation is established through a bizarre mismatch between the routine interview and the stated subject in the opening line: "you wish to kill your wife?" The husband being questioned supplies details for a replicant, but when "she" is created, the duplication is so perfect that the husband assumes he's addressing a new version of his wife. However, "Katie" insists: "I am her. I can only act as she acts. No part of me is alien to her."[85] His fantasy of a new beginning is deflected by her deliberate provocation in rhapsodizing (by quoting from the Song of Solomon) about her lover, until he finally shoots her down. Bradbury planned a screenplay of this story, in his treatment describing the act as "facsimile murder," and the story veers skillfully between the real and the simulated.[86] The Katie robot appears after a montage of memory images of George's wife, clearly realizing his fantasy of recapturing lost youthful happiness. The shooting thus emerges as a ritual purging of George's anger, but just as he imagines that he has avoided an actual crime, he is arrested in a government clampdown on the use of marionettes. George is thus caught in a process that chimes in with his guilt, and in the last scene he observes his wife and her lover departing for fresh adventures before he is led off to his execution. The climax in the story comes with him screaming, in the film treatment, with the door of the execution chamber slamming shut.

"Changeling" (1949) similarly uses SF to dramatize a young woman's suspicion that her older lover is a "faker"; she has read about Marionettes, Inc., and puts two and two together. When confronted, the man tries to laugh it off by saying that he's created as many simulations as he has had affairs and pleads with her to keep his secret. The climax comes with a burst of violence:

> "I love you," said the man's mouth. She struck it with the hammer and the tongue fell out. The glass eyes rolled on the carpet. She pounded at the thing until it was strewn like the remains of a child's electric train on the floor.[87]

Bradbury is using the theme of robotics not for futuristic speculation so much as to dramatize different states of alienation. The story's title glances back to the folklore of human substitutes, but the new technology of replication is used to give grotesquely concrete expression to the woman's estrangement from her lover. The machinery of his innards becomes a metaphor of his serial adultery.

Bradbury's most famous robot story grew out of his meeting in 1958 with Rod Serling, who was then planning his groundbreaking television series *The*

Twilight Zone. Bradbury recommended books by Charles Beaumont, Richard Matheson, Roald Dahl, John Collier—and himself. When the pilot episode was broadcast, Bradbury realized that it had made unacknowledged use of his story "The Silent Towns."[88] Nevertheless, Bradbury wrote three scripts for the series (which included a number of episodes featuring robots), but only one was broadcast: "I Sing the Body Electric!" which went out on May 18, 1962. Bradbury was bitterly disappointed by the broadcast, later complaining that "they cut out the most important part of the story . . . the moment of truth in the story when the grandmother tells them that she is a robot."[89] He then wrote up the story from the script, describing how a family copes with the premature death of the mother by ordering a human replicant. One is ordered, delivered, and comes to life, impressing everyone except Agatha, the youngest child, who fears a fresh repetition of grief. Distressed, she runs out of the house and is only rescued from a speeding car at the last minute by Grandma, who survives the impact. After this crisis the robot is accepted as a surrogate guardian.

"I Sing the Body Electric!" takes its title—chosen as the "motto for our robot-dominated society"—from Whitman's celebration of the human body where electricity is used to designate the mysteries of the life force.[90] In the story, however, electricity has become swallowed up in the commercial process of simulation, culminating in the "first humanoid-genre mini-circuited, rechargeable AC-DC Mark V Electrical Grandmother."[91] In Bradbury's early robot stories, the promises of advertising promotion are always framed ironically and indeed the name of the company, Fantoccini—which translates from Italian as puppets moved by string or wire, in other words as marionettes—implies manipulation. Indeed, in the TV episode when the company salesman makes his pitch to the family he comes across as a showman producing new features against a dark background. Here, however, one of the story's first ambiguities emerges. The narrator was a thirteen-year-old boy at the time of the action, therefore participating in and reinforcing the children's collective desire to reverse the loss of their mother.

When Grandma is delivered by helicopter (an "Apollo machine"), the episode is carefully paced as a double revelation. The crate is opened to reveal a simulated Egyptian mummy case bearing an ornate gold mask and, within that, the replicant. When the gold key is inserted and turned, the language suddenly shifts to mechanism in a familiar moment from Frankenstein movies, this time displaced away from horror:

> The Electrical Grandmother's eyes flicked wide!
> Something began to hum and whir . . .
> Grandma suddenly sat up.
> We leapt back.
> We knew we had, in a way, slapped her alive.
> She was born, she was born![92]

Bradbury's careful paragraphing assembles a montage of shots that would alternate between the children and the grandmother, preserving the latter's ambiguity in that she is never seen as a total visual image, whereas in the teleplay the grandmother is visually indistinguishable from humans.

"I Sing" is one of Bradbury's longest stories and suffers from his visible desire to maximize the significance of its subject. Grandma not only becomes a member of the family. She takes on the role of an author surrogate in defining herself in relation to other dream machines like film.

The children's need for a substitute mother is established so directly in the opening that the rest of the story repeatedly confirms how the robot satisfies that need. The narrative hardly fits in with the pattern of *The Twilight Zone*, whose series statement declared: "you are traveling to another dimension," in that the tension between replicant and human lapses completely.

From the same period between 1955 and 1964 Bradbury wrote seven scripts for the CBS TV series, *Alfred Hitchcock Presents*. Bradbury would visit studios and sound out producers and then go and write scripts.[93] One episode relates to robotics. Broadcast in February 1956, "And So Died Riabouchinska" (from a 1947 radio drama and 1953 story), establishes a claustrophobic atmosphere through its basement setting where a ventriloquist is being questioned about a murder. However, the focus shifts dramatically onto the performer's dummy once "her" box is opened: "The face was white and it was cut from marble or from the whitest wood he had ever seen. . . . She was all white stone, with light pouring through the stone and light coming out of the dark eyes with blue tones like fresh mulberries."[94] The close-up on the features generally and specifically on the eyes as a light, and therefore life source, dominates the story and introduces the enigma of the doll's nature: is her effect of humanity simply an illusion? As the questioning proceeds, her voice gets more dominant and she admits the guilt of her manipulator. The psychological symbolism is clear: the doll verbalizes the ventriloquist's suppressed thoughts. In the final climactic moment of confession, the detective's perspective suddenly distorts the image expressionistically: "Krovitch stepped back as if he were watching a motion picture that had suddenly grown monstrously tall."[95] Bradbury's careful alternation between organic and inorganic details of the doll is totally lost in the TV dramatization where the doll's image and therefore nature is never in doubt. Bradbury's use of the detective as focalizer in the story ingeniously suggests that the ventriloquist's fantastic projection of vitality has "leaked" into his consciousness. As in Bradbury's other robot stories, the manipulation of perspective is crucial in setting up its ambiguity.

By 1964, Bradbury had become convinced that "this is a Science Fiction era we live in and the cinema is a Science Fictional device." He continues: "It follows that any invention is a means to power and therefore, since we live among robots, one would imagine we would be curious about the ideas embodied in our machines."[96] David Wolper's TV documentary about Bradbury from the previous year describes and part-dramatizes his story "Dial Double Zero," which raises the possibility of machine sentience embedded within a telephone system.[97] Bradbury's preoccupation with the machines of American culture was shaped by his friendship with one of the iconic figures of the mid-twentieth century. He first met Walt Disney in 1963 but had started defending Disneyland even earlier. In 1965 he drew on SF imagery to contrast the mechanistic gamblers of Las Vegas with Disney's robots, who are "people, loving, caring and eternally good."[98] He idealizes these creations as straddling technology and humanity, linking Disney to figures like Karel Capek and arguing that he has discovered a unique way to animate American history.

The previous Christmas, Disney showed Bradbury the prototype of a Lincoln robot, which fascinated him: "I watched the finishing touches being put on a second computerized, electric- and air-pressure-driven humanoid that will 'live' at Disneyland from this summer on [1965]. I saw this new effigy of Mr. Lincoln sit, stand, shift his arms, turn his wrists, twitch his fingers, put his hands behind his back, turn his head, look at me, blink and prepare to speak."[99] The immediate result of Bradbury's visit was his 1969 story "Downwind from Gettysburg," where a character has a dream of making a film of

Gettysburg with the help of the "Lincoln mechanical, the electro-oil-lubricated plastic India-rubber perfect-motioned and outspoken dream."[100] A namesake of Lincoln's assassin envies the machine, but is ridiculed for seeking vicarious publicity through a reenactment of the assassination. The story dramatizes the capacity of robots to dramatize history in its opening scene where the protagonist literally believes that a fresh assassination is taking place.

TIME TRAVEL

Robotic reenactment offered a possible form of time travel into the past, another staple SF theme that Bradbury explored through a series of dinosaur stories. When Bradbury discovered the works of Edgar Rice Burroughs in 1930, not only did he learn these works by heart, he even started imitating Burroughs's creatures: "I was making noises like a tyrannosaurus rex and behaving like a Martian throat, which, everyone knows, has eight legs."[101] Introducing his 1984 theme anthology, *Dinosaur Tales*, Bradbury declared: "dinosaurs started me on the track to becoming a writer."[102] One of the formative films from Bradbury's childhood was *The Lost World* (1925), which directly influenced his 1951 story "The Fog Horn," where a primeval creature is summoned from the depths of the sea by the sound of the horn. The story is narrated by one of the two keepers of a lighthouse who hears from his companion of a mysterious creature that approaches the lighthouse at a certain time every year. The narrator hears the other's stories about the mysteries of the deep before the main event occurs. Through him we are predisposed to accept the fabulous possibility of a creature emerging from primeval time ("millions of years") and from an unimaginable distance ("thousands of miles").

Bradbury offsets the huge size of the creature with the projected pathos of its situation. He later explained: "The foghorn itself was a super metaphor of all the melancholy funerals and sad remembrances in history."[103] The final appearance of the creature is a piece of finely paced revelation. From a ripple in the sea surface we get a bubble, froth, "and then a neck. And then—not a body—but more neck and more! The head rose a full forty feet above the water on a slender and beautiful dark neck. Only then did the body, like a little island of black coral and shells and crayfish, drip up from the subterranean."[104] The moment-by-moment drama of the emergence and the use of the term "beautiful" distinguish the description from the clichés of monster movies.

Despite the fact that his vulnerable position on an isolated rock would justify a perception of danger, the narrator/observer is too moved by the creature to register threat. The image makes only a prelude to the dinosaur's destruction of the lighthouse, but even then the dominant note of the story is sadness as if the creature has gone from loneliness back to loneliness.

At the age of eighteen Bradbury had met a young experimenter with dinosaur models called Ray Harryhausen, who was to become one of his closest friends. Even at that age, Bradbury promised to write a screenplay for his new friend and Harryhausen later recalled: "we wanted to make a great dinosaur movie together."[105] That chance came with *The Beast from 20,000 Fathoms* (1953), which constituted the first solo special effects work by Harryhausen, who had until then worked under Willis O'Brien, the creator of the dinosaurs in *The Lost World* and in *King Kong* (1933), another of Bradbury's favorite films. He described the latter as "pure mythology" and saw it as the prototype of subsequent monster films.[106] Bradbury visited Harryhausen in the studios, was called in as script doctor, and pointed out its similarities to his story.[107] The producers then bought from Bradbury the rights to his story, discarded their title "The Monster from beneath the Sea," in favor of the original magazine title, and encouraged him to participate in the screenwriting. Though not participating in its making, Bradbury must have been gratified when the trailer announced the "importance and impact of the *Saturday Evening Post* thriller that held millions spellbound." *The Beast from 20,000 Fathoms* is now generally acknowledged to have introduced the monster movie genre that flourished throughout the 1950s and frames its narrative with the nuclear fears of the period. The opening shot of an H-bomb blast in the Arctic is the trigger to the creature's revival and emergence, and it can be killed only with a weapon firing a toxic radioactive isotope. The associations between the monstrous, the bomb, and the Arctic were topical. The 1952 issue of *Collier's Weekly*, which carried Bradbury's other dinosaur story, "A Sound of Thunder," also carried an article about the Arctic Alert signals base watching the skies for nuclear attack.

Bradbury's primary emphasis in his dinosaur stories fell on visual spectacle. The making of monster movies became the subject of Bradbury's 1962 story "Tyrannosaurus Rex," which opens with a trial film viewing before a diminutive but dismissive producer. The Harryhausen character here is an animator named Terwilliger, whose skill is either dismissed or under-recognized during the story. He focalizes the viewing of the first film, not as a simple spectator but as a creator well aware of the care that has gone into each sequence using the laborious stop-motion technique. Bradbury gives pride of place to the composition of the creatures:

> Fuse flexible spine to sinuous neck, pivot neck to death's head skull, hinge jaw from hollow cheek, glue plastic sponge over lubricated skeleton, slip snake-pebbled skin over sponge, meld seams with fire, then rear upright triumphant in a world where insanity wakes but to look on madness—Tyrannosaurus Rex![108]

This description mimes out in close-up the assembly of the creature, which suddenly shifts scale and implies vitality in "rear upright" and which is signaled through the climactic grandeur of the species name. Bradbury satirically points to the generational gap between the older viewer who finds the film beautiful and the jaundiced younger producer. The original title, "The Prehistoric Producer," draws unnecessarily explicit attention to this irony, whereas the primary subject of the story is habits of viewing. The producer, like most viewers, is interested only in the finished product, which carries a clichéd title (*Monster of the Stone Age*), but Bradbury invokes a more subtle response, which is sensitive to the miracle of creation through models.

The time travel implicit in Bradbury's dinosaur stories was a prominent theme of SF being exploited in the late 1940s. C. L. Moore and Henry Kuttner's "Vintage Season" (1946) describes travelers who visit the present as time tourists. CBS's radio drama series *Escape* (1947–1954) included two adaptations of Wells's *The Time Machine* (in 1948 and 1950) as well as two adaptations of pieces by Bradbury himself: *Mars Is Heaven* (1951) and *The Earthmen* (1951). Bradbury himself experimented with the theme in stories like "A Touch of Petulance" (written ca. 1950), where a young man meets his older self on a commuter train and learns to his horror that he will kill his wife. *The Time Machine* is explicitly cited in relation to the story's subject.

Bradbury's most explicit story of time travel, "A Sound of Thunder" (1952), takes his characters back into the primeval past, explicitly names their vehicle as a Time Machine, but characteristically does not describe it at all. As in Bradbury's marionette stories, the new technology is privately owned by Time Safari, Inc., whose advertisement promises to take travelers back to their beginnings. The perspective character Eckels signs up for the expedition; he is warned by the guide not to deviate from the company path because the smallest act could have unpredictable consequences. His group travels back sixty million years to a wilderness where Eckels hopes to shoot a tyrannosaurus—one that will die soon and no longer impact the time line. But when Eckels actually sees one, his terror leads him to step off the path. After the time machine returns the group to the present, strange differences are noted: spelling has changed and, more ominously, a totalitarian presidential candidate who originally lost the elections has now taken office. As Eckels scrapes the primeval mud off his shoes he finds embedded a butterfly, "very beautiful, and very dead."[109] Bradbury's delicate image coincides with that used by Edward Lorenz in defining the Butterfly Effect, i.e., the disproportionate consequences of minor ultimate changes within a system.

Bradbury's visual climax occurs when Eckels finally sees a tyrannosaurus. Like the sighting of dinosaurs in Conan Doyle's *The Lost World*, this takes place in a jungle setting:

> It came on great oiled, resilient, striding legs. It towered thirty feet above half of the trees, a great evil god, folding its delicate watchmaker's claws close to its oily reptilian chest. Each lower leg was a piston, a thousand pounds of white bone, sunk in thick ropes of muscle, sheathed over in a gleam of pebbled skin like the mail of a terrible warrior. Each thigh was a ton of meat, ivory, and steel mesh. And from the great breathing cage of the upper body those two delicate arms dangled out front, arms with hands which might pick up and examine men like toys, while the snake neck coiled.[110]

Eckels resembles the spectator of a monster movie. He knows roughly what to expect and the description incorporates an awareness of the creature's weight and strength, but this in no way prepares him for the spectacle of the tyrannosaurus within his field of vision. As the perspective pans slowly up the creature's body different analogies hint at its extraordinary nature: it is like a god, a warrior, a machine. And as it approaches, a close-up focuses on its shiny scaled hide, simultaneously organic and metallic. Eckel's "safari" collapses in blind panic at his helplessness. Bradbury later cited this description as an example of prose poetry, and its use of metaphor surcharges the visual impact beyond what Eckels can consciously register.[111]

Bradbury's title carries the same metaphorical breadth as the description just examined. The first time the phrase is used, it suggests at once a weather feature and the distant roar of the creature, which is named the Thunder Lizard, a literal translation of brontosaurus. At the end of the story the safari leader has cocked his gun as if to shoot Eckels, so the title could come to mean the imminent killing of the perspective character. This suspense was completely lost by the ending imposed on Bradbury by *Collier's* where Eckels complains to his companion: "Can't we start over?" The other simply shakes his head. John Cheng has suggested yet another possible significance to the title. Arguing that older time-travel narratives tended to locate themselves within a linear historical continuum, he finds a crucial difference in Bradbury's story. In Wells's *The Time Machine*, for instance, the present moment of narration supplies the secure base to which dangerous excursions into the future can return, whereas Bradbury situates the reader between a distant past and imminent future, which has changed during the story. Thus for Cheng the future has become destabilized, and the title expresses "metaphorically the force of history, of past events' cascading effect rushing to meet the present like the sound of thunder rushes to fill the air to signal a lightning strike."[112] The simple fact of Eckels traveling into the evolutionary past indicates Bradbury's distance from conventional time-travel stories. Similarly in "A Scent of Sarsaparilla" (1953) the protagonist has imagined a "unicycle," a Wellsian device for riding through the past. Here, his attic has become his real time machine, packed with objects that give him refuge from an intolerable present, just as in "The Dragon Who Ate His Tail" (2006) and its 1950 prequel "To the Future," time tourism in the past reflects a desire to escape from the threat of nuclear war.[113]

A story from 1984 steps back from narrating in order to examine time travel as a cultural issue. The title of "The Toynbee Convector" links technology (a heating or cooling device) with the famous British historian Arnold Toynbee, who surveyed the rise and fall of nations in his massive multivolume *A Study of History*. He became the subject of an editorial, "Toynbee and the Future," in *Life* magazine for November 8, 1954, where his commitment to religious faith was stressed, and both Toynbee and Bradbury contributed to a 1972 symposium in *Rotarian* called "Reflections on My Own Death." The other two contributors were Kurt Vonnegut and Jessica Mitford; Bradbury supplied a poem with a title reminiscent of Emily Dickinson, "If I Were Epitaph." In this symposium Toynbee sees death as a merging of the self with the universe, in other words not as an ending.

Bradbury's story uses Toynbee to signal the larger sequences of human history and also describes a character called Stiles who recoils from contemporary pessimism by building himself a time machine, explicitly under the inspiration of Wells. The latter's 1895 tale describes in now dated mechanical terms the time machine, but more importantly it describes how the time traveler himself was attempting to convey a message of skepticism toward the grand narrative of human progress. An immediate difference between "The Toynbee Convector" and *The Time Machine* lies in the media. Wells describes a scientific inventor working within a group of male friends. Bradbury sets up his narrative through the perspective of a journalist who is going to interview Stiles.[114]

In short, Stiles has become a celebrity who "had reported by Telstar around the world to billions of viewers and told them their future." And the future is bright indeed. He declaims to his audiences: "The future is ours. We . . . stopped the wars, tossed solar stations across space to light the world, colonized the moon, moved on to Mars, then Alpha Centauri. We cured cancer and stopped death."[115] Conflating political hope with messianic "illumination," Stiles shows his media savvy by proving his insights with pictures, tapes, and film cassettes. His good news comes via communications satellites, perhaps a rather ambiguous nod by Bradbury toward his friend Arthur C. Clarke; and the revelation of his time machine will be nothing less than a "miracle in the sky." When Stiles's machine lights up, it takes on a kind of spiritual significance to the impressionable journalist as if it were alive.

"The Toynbee Convector" gradually builds up to a climactic moment when the machine and Stiles will be revealed to the waiting crowds. To set a Space-Age tempo of suspense, the narrative counts down, as if to a launch. A celebratory bottle of wine—1984 vintage—is opened. But then comes the real twist. Nothing happens and, as if that wasn't enough, Stiles admits to the journalist that he lied about everything. He gives as his reason the negative temper of the culture from the 1960s to 1980s: "Everywhere, I saw and heard doubt. Everywhere, I learned destruction. Everywhere was professional despair, intellectual ennui, political cynicism."[116] The triumphs of the Space

Program are as nothing. In the final scene, Stiles dies before the journalist's eyes, ironically contradicting his claim of future humanity conquering death; in yet another twist the journalist decides to preserve his illusion by not divulging his confession.

"The Toynbee Convector" has clear satirical implications for a gullible public, which accepts Stiles's "evidence" of future success, and in the story's criticism of a modish pessimism. When Bradbury was asked about this in a 1982 interview, he became very indignant and attacked pessimism as a national betrayal, declaring: "We have to learn to be proud of ourselves, we have to be confident. . . . I just can't understand this attitude of just looking for faults—it's anti-American."[117] In an essay from the same year Bradbury attacked the symbolism of the year 1984 as an "intellectual fraud," declaring his commitment to a positive future: "We will do everything, we will solve everything."[118] The stridency of his insistence connects implicitly with his ambivalence toward the future in "The Toynbee Convector." Because the title is also the name of the time traveler's machine, Bradbury implies that exploration of the past and future should be done through the medium of literature.

BRADBURY'S COMMENTARY ON SF

Bradbury's best SF stories engage in implicit dialogue with the genre norms of their period, characteristically working through understated ironies. While producing this fiction Bradbury also produced a serial commentary on Science Fiction through a series of essays and interviews, still largely uncollected. Throughout his career Bradbury insisted on SF's centrality in American culture. In a 1976 interview he explained how it supplied his education with "radio coming into existence when I was two years old, and films began to speak when I was seven, and television on the verge of being invented and there was talk of space travel. . . . As a result of reading Science Fiction when I was eight, I grew up with an interest in music, architecture, city planning, transportation, politics, ethics, aesthetics on any level, art . . . it's just total!"[119] Bradbury took justified pride in being a self-taught writer and, as the statement above suggests, he saw the shaping of his sensibility as a growing out of his national cultural witness. He literally lived Science Fiction. His overstatements should be read as strategic, part of a polemic he waged, especially in his early career, against an elitist disregard of Science Fiction.

Bradbury's relation to Science Fiction has shifted constantly throughout his career. In his later years it was not at all unusual for him to deny writing SF, but rather modern myths or fantasy. However, his positive statements on SF's capacity to distance us from familiar reality among other functions outweighed disclaimers. In 1972, for instance, he declared: "I keep coming back to the field because Science Fiction is the fiction of *ideas;*" and, after naming a range of figures from Plato through Wells and Verne, he continued: "My work follows on a direct line from such men as these, and I'm very proud of my literary ancestors."[120] From the very beginning of his career the genre label was an issue. When asked for an introduction to Theodore Sturgeon's story collection *Without Sorcery* in 1948, he reportedly produced a "study in esthetics, devoted to the problem of why American Science Fiction had not to date produced a single definite and unquestioned work of art."[121] A replacement had to be hastily supplied when Sturgeon expressed his dissatisfaction with Bradbury's piece, but the event reflects the debate attendant on SF's gradual emergence into the mainstream.

When *The Martian Chronicles* was published in Doubleday's new Science Fiction series, he was unhappy about the "s-f shadow," primarily because he was well aware of the low status of the SF label in the literary marketplace at that time.[122] Bradbury was well aware of living through a gradual revolution in the status of Science Fiction that was taking place throughout the 1950s and beyond, but the issue of the label persisted right into the 1970s. As he wryly pointed out, "when Michael Crichton publishes *The Andromeda Strain* or Romain Gary writes *The Gasp* or Brian Moore puts *Catholics* in print, the editors are impeccably silent as to the SF content therein, thus insuring front page review."[123]

Bradbury constantly tried to position himself between the outdated expectations that the SF label might carry and his conviction of extending the genre into new areas. In a 1951 interview, when asked about the emergence of Science Fiction, he explained: "in Science Fiction there are the space operas, a Western in space; you herd rockets instead of cattle. But there are some Science Fiction writers who are trying to think in human terms of real human problems. The form has a bad name because of the space operas. You say Science Fiction and people think of Buck Rogers and Flash Gordon."[124] Bradbury left his interviewer in no doubt where he belonged.

Bradbury's 1953 essay "Day After Tomorrow" (collected in *Yestermorrow*) represents one of his most considered statements about the nature and status of Science Fiction and articulates positions that he consolidated throughout his career. His central strategy is to universalize the genre: "It is, after all, the fiction of ideas, the fiction where philosophy can be tinkered with, torn apart, and put back together again: it is the fiction of sociology and psychology and history compounded and squared by time."[125]

Bradbury identifies a grand tradition from Plato to Orwell and proposes an analytical role for SF in examining the delicate balance between technology and society. Its speculative energy is one of its main strengths and it reflects his social emphasis that two writers named in the essay are Koestler and Orwell. Bradbury's only reservation lies with the outworn label, which has dealt too long with "bug-eyed monsters and half-naked space women."[126]

By 1974, when introducing a college anthology of SF, Bradbury could reflect on the revolution in reading that had taken place since the late 1940s. Over those decades SF had become central to American culture, appropriately so because Bradbury related the emergence of the genre to a national tradition of experiment and speculation. Thus the United States has always been a "country of ideas," obsessively concerned with improvement. In that sense SF is engaged, ancient (as old as Plato), and uniquely suited to engaging with contemporary issues. Bradbury's insistence that SF was the "most important fiction ever invented" by writers' attempts to maximize the genre's accessibility to his college readership.[127] We all have ideas; SF is the ultimate literature of ideas; therefore we are all SF authors.

Bradbury's surge of creativity in the late 1940s and 1950s coincided with the last years of the Golden Age of Science Fiction. In tandem with the publication of the fiction itself, more and more writers examined the nature of the genre. Reginald Bretnor's pioneering 1953 symposium, *Modern Science Fiction: Its Meaning and Its Future*, included essays by Isaac Asimov, Arthur C. Clarke (who as early as 1949 had recognized that Bradbury was producing a poetical form of SF), and Philip Wylie, as well as by editors John W. Campbell and Anthony Boucher.[128] Broadly speaking, these contributors all agreed that Science Fiction had emerged from its ghetto and taken up a socially central role as the literature of speculation. It was a sign of its emerging status that the 1956 NBC program "Ticket to the Moon" should have been broadcast at all. In addition to contributions from Campbell and Asimov, Bradbury related prewar SF to contemporary movies and advertising, declaring: "we are so enamored of effects, of surfaces, of gimmicks."[129]

Already, Bradbury's name figured among the perceived leaders in the field, although with some reservations. L. Sprague de Camp grudgingly admitted his powerful appeal to the "child-mind" buried in everyone's psyche; Fletcher Pratt complained that his descriptions of Mars tended to "strain credulity"; but Asimov had the biggest problem with Bradbury. Complaining that his Martian stories "reek with scientific incongruity," he nevertheless admitted that "among the general population, he is by far the most popular Science Fiction writer." The only explanation Asimov can find is that Bradbury is a "writer of social fiction," dealing ultimately with contemporary Earth.[130] Asimov never lost his sense of Bradbury's anomaly, but did recognize his broader mediating role as "Science Fiction's ambassador to the outside world. People who didn't read Science Fiction, and who were taken aback by its rather specialized vocabulary, found that they could read and understand Bradbury."[131]

As Bradbury's reputation grew, critical discussions of his work divided; one of the most hostile accounts came from SF author Damon Knight, who admitted that Bradbury was a "superb craftsman," but then launched into a sweeping attack on his fiction for being derivative, inconsistent, and sentimentally attached to childhood.[132] At the opposite extreme, the political theorist Russell Kirk saw Bradbury as a creator of moral fables, constantly questioning materialism and technology. In that sense he shouldn't be thought of as a futurist so much as a critic of contemporary society.

Bradbury himself constantly debated generic labels and his 1952 anthology, *Timeless Stories for Today and Tomorrow*, assembled stories by Steinbeck, Isherwood, and other writers associated with social realism. He linked this disparate selection as a collective demonstration that realists could write fantasy and also, in the process, open up the "essential mystery in everything." Their practice thus showed their perceptions of the "unreality of reality" and implicitly blurs the supposedly sharp distinction between Science Fiction and realism.[133] Indeed, several of the subjects in these stories resemble SF themes such as sentient technology and time travel. From the same decade, when introducing *The Circus of Dr. Lao and Other Improbable Stories* (1956) Bradbury categorically denies that they are works of Science Fiction, declaring: "Science

Fiction is the law-abiding citizen of imaginative literature, obeying the rules, be they physical, social, or psychological . . . predictable, certain, sure." He overstates the predictability of SF in order to set up the rule-breaking practices of fantasy, which he sees as refreshingly anarchic and liberating. In fact, he later admits that "all writing of any quality releases us from conformity," by which point his initially sharp distinction between the genres begins to blur. His selection of authors reflects this continuity.[134] He includes pieces by the pioneer of British SF television drama Nigel Kneale; the naturalist Loren Eiseley who strongly influenced Bradbury's own prose; his former mentor Henry Kuttner; and Nathaniel Hawthorne, who Bradbury sometimes cites as a precursor of SF.

The composition of these anthologies reflects Bradbury's unease about brand label of Science Fiction in the 1950s and his general hostility toward conventional realism. He made the latter unambiguously clear in his introduction to Edwin Abbot's 1884 mathematical satire *Flatland*, where he states: "Realism rarely works. Realism is for many, including myself, a turnoff. . . . Metaphor is everything. . . . The Something New is always Metaphor. Turn reality inside out or wrong-side-to, and we'll sit up and blink!"[135]

THE GREEN TOWN STORIES

Bradbury's lifelong fascination with speculative and fabulous fiction relates to his constant privileging of childhood and his repeated claim of a continuity between his childhood reading and adult writing. Thus of Burroughs he stated: "I went home to Mars often when I was eleven and twelve and every year since"; and in a 1984 tribute to Superman declared: "I once loved and still love Kong, John Carter, Flash Gordon, and all the rest. Superman came a trifle late in my teens."[136] Introducing a 2001 edition of *The Wonderful Wizard of Oz*, he cites his own story "The Exiles" as fantastically imagining the last copies of classics like Baum's as part of his on-going polemic against censorship and admits that the "fight between the dreamers and the fact-finders will continue."[137]

Bradbury's drive to preserve the vitality of his childhood imagination informs a body of his fiction that isn't SF but connects with it. His Green Town stories are set in an idealized version of Waukegan. Throughout the later 1940s, he was working on a novel to be called *Summer Morning, Summer Night*, a title that was eventually used for his final 2008 collection of Green Town stories. The first result of his labors was *Dandelion Wine* (1957), which assembles a series of stories around the young protagonist Douglas Spaulding. Despite some reviewers' arguments otherwise, *Dandelion Wine* is not a Science Fiction novel but rather an exploration of how stories—SF included—are created. In fact there is an SF theme running through the novel that centers on technology. "Seems like the town is full of machines," Douglas reflects shortly after the would-be inventor Leo's Happiness Machine goes up in flames.[138] This device is never described except as a utopian project. Douglas is then introduced to a living Time Machine—Colonel Freeleigh—one of the oldest townsfolk, whose memories stretch back into the nineteenth century. He is only one embodiment of the novel's central theme of time and change, and the machines of the town variously suggest the past (trolley), the innovative present (electric runabout), or an illusion of timelessness, as Douglas finds in the town arcade.

Reading the Green Town stories within Bradbury's oeuvre, we never lose our consciousness of stories to come. As Bradbury himself stated in the afterword to *Farewell Summer* (2006; originally planned as the second part of the novel from which *Dandelion Wine* was extracted), the ravine in Green Town was key to his earlier self: "There I imagined myself in Africa or on Mars."[139] Similarly, *Something Wicked this Way Comes* (1962) falls outside the SF genre in exploring the boundary between dream and waking, life and death, dramatized through two boys' responses to a visiting carnival, but Bradbury's preamble establishes the boys' receptivity to the fantastic through Science Fiction. The town library, a key location here and in Bradbury's writing generally, is a place of imaginative possibility, a "separate 20,000-fathoms-deep world."[140]

The allusion to Jules Verne references a whole body of writing having its impact on the boys and, indeed, Bradbury later named Verne as his favorite SF writer.[141] In 1955 Bradbury published a fictional interview with Verne, where he draws an analogy between the ocean and space, which Bradbury was to develop, and where he suggests substituting the label "geographical romances" for "Science Fiction." Verne declares that the basic motive of his fiction was to "clear the Wilderness for Man" and he stresses that space travel is the logical outcome of human evolution.[142] Bradbury's interview is an exercise in self-validation, using his famous precursor to authenticate themes he developed in *The Martian Chronicles* and his writings on space.

THE HOLLYWOOD TRILOGY

Bradbury's Green Town fiction then concerns itself with beginnings, whereas later in his career he wrote a trilogy of novels about Hollywood that focuses on death and endings. Once again, these novels are not SF but repeatedly throw up links with famous SF movies. In *Death Is a Lonely Business* (1985) a young writer looks into the mysterious death of an old man, which gives him a pretext for examining the local landscape for the physical and human traces of an entertainment world that is dying out. From the opening line with its reference to Venice Beach "in the old days," every detail displaces the reader into a lost past that the narrator is trying to recapture. In *A Graveyard for Lunatics* (1990), set in 1954, Bradbury's composite narrator has moved further into his career, working on a screenplay for an SF film to be called *Return of the Beast*. The narrator is defined through his Science Fiction reading as the "bastard son of Edgar Rice Burroughs and *The Warlord of Mars*—the illegitimate offspring of H. G. Wells, out of Jules Verne."[143] The trilogy concludes with *Let's All Kill Constance* (2002), set in 1960 and opening with the arrival at the narrator's bungalow of an aging film actress clutching two "books of the dead"—ancient phone directories, with her name included among the dead. As in the first novel, the narrator's discoveries extend outward from the initial mystery into a surreal montage of scenes commemorating the lost splendors of Hollywood, where the narrator seems to be moving among ghosts and trying in vain to communicate with the dead.

THE LATER SF

Although Bradbury's output of SF dropped off considerably by the 1960s, it never ceased to feature in his later writings and projects. When writing his script for the Federal Pavilion in the New York World's Fair (1964–1965), he linked Melville and Verne to underpin the space program.[144] In 1976 he was hired to consult on the Disney geodesic sphere, "Spaceship Earth," at the Epcot Center in Florida. The result was a script, "Man and His Spaceship Earth," constructed on SF lines, which celebrates the progress of humanity over the centuries as an evolving capacity to produce and transmit information. The film, cyclorama, and projected symbols are all seen by Bradbury as a collective time machine showing evolution from the "fire apes," as Loren Eiseley would put it, to contemporary humanity. Earth itself is figured through the central image of SF as a construct heading into the future. Taking his cue from Kennedy's 1961 declaration of a space program, Bradbury presents contemporary humanity as the "new pioneers, searching uncharted seas by the light of uncounted stars' globalizing the heritage of American discovery."[145] In a 1982 interview, he declared that people will visit Epcot because "they want to look at the world of the future."[146]

From the same decade in 1982, Bradbury was brought in by Gary Kurtz to write a script for a Japanese-American film of *Little Nemo: Adventures in Slumberland*, based on Winsor McCay's comic strip, which ran between 1905 and 1914. The script was never used, but Chris Lane's illustrations inspired Bradbury's 1998 fable, *Ahmed and the Oblivion Machines*. Bradbury's screenplay *Nemo!* was published in 2012 and demonstrates his skill at visualizing a child's fantasy world. The original cartoon follows a tight alternation between the security of Little Nemo's bedroom and his excursions into other realms. The set number of frames always contains his adventures, whereas Bradbury constructs a more fluid narrative, initially showing Nemo's excitement at visiting the St. Louis World's Fair (1904) through a montage of future scenes rushing at Nemo. Indeed, time is one of the strongest themes running through the screenplay, partly as a motif of chronometers. Bradbury sets up surreal spaces where Nemo encounters dinosaurs, endures chase sequences, descends through a "mind shaft" into a subterranean forest of mushrooms, and echoes his own Martian landscape in a sandy terrain of ruins. In the final episode, Nemo finds himself in the City of Sleep, a dreamscape of flowing shapes, where we are constantly reminded of the complexities of his visual perspective.

By the time of his late stories, SF tropes are used by Bradbury as narrative devices for reviving the past. Thus "The Laurel and Hardy Alpha Centauri Tour" (2000) describes those comedians' performance two hundred years in the future and on another planet, moving them beyond the constraints of time and place. The logic is that they exist in a media virtual reality, whereas "The F. Scott/Tolstoy/Ahab Accumulator" (2000) concerns itself more directly with recall. A friend of the narrator modifies a time machine so that they can experience a series of encounters with famous writers. "Quid Pro Quo" (2000) is more self-conscious about the metaphor of the time machine, which the narrator describes as a mental and technological construct: "I built my Far Traveling Device with fragments of wired-together ganglion, the seat of invisible perception."[147] He jokingly merges technology, physiology, and perception to express the tortuous working of memory, whereas "Zaharoff/ Richter Mark V" (1996) describes historical recall. The title glances at arms and earthquakes, burlesquing the names of devices in earlier SF. The journalist-narrator is taken by a business hustler down into an underground complex where the disasters of recent history are stored in "three-dimensional virtual reality."[148] The facility resembles a film archive where Bradbury ironically suggests how such disasters become converted into spectacle. In all these instances tropes associated with the future are deployed with reference to the past or the alternative courses human development might take. "The Other Highway" (written ca. 1950 but published 1996) makes this explicit when a father drives his family off the freeway into a green countryside packed with memories. This meandering route is contrasted with the linear freeway taking them to the "iron cities" where the driver speculates on archaeologists of the future inferring the course of technology from the monstrous ruins of his present.

Bradbury's ambivalence over the role of technology in history is here located in a landscape that combines different time periods. The unification of a story cycle around a location combining fantasy and dystopian speculation was to inform Bradbury's first major publishing success—*The Martian Chronicles*.

CHaPTER 2

THE SUBJECT OF MARS

THE MARS TRADITION

Since the late nineteenth century Mars has tantalized the literary imagination with the possibility that life might exist on that planet, a possibility given famous embodiment from 1912 onward in the Barsoom novels of Edgar Rice Burroughs. Bradbury discovered Burroughs's fiction at the age of ten and has stated repeatedly in interviews how the Mars novels caught his imagination, so much so that in the early 1930s he wrote comic-book panels of them.[1] Although Bradbury later classed Burroughs as belonging to "very primitive authors," the latter's John Carter novels must have suggested the possibility to him that Mars could function as a fantasy terrain where scenes from different eras could be juxtaposed.[2] Burroughs's hero moves rapidly from neomedieval settings to futuristic cities powered by radium, from one human species to another (helpfully color-coded), and from dangerous apes to primeval monsters. Barsoom even contains waterways and derelict cities. In other words, Burroughs's

Martian landscape assembles elements from different chronological periods and his serial hero takes the reader through encounters with creatures from actual or speculative points on the evolutionary spectrum. The appeal that the Mars stories must have had for the young Bradbury is that they opened up a landscape of possibilities without limits and, despite their notional dangers, without any real threat to John Carter.

At the same time as discovering Burroughs's fiction, Bradbury also read Percival Lowell's *Mars as the Abode of Life* (1908), which consolidated the emerging myth of Mars by discussing its canals (and "oases") as evidence of intelligent life.[3] Applying his principles of planetary evolution, Lowell argued that Mars was an old planet that, because of its similarities with Earth, showed us our future. He cautiously drew back from any attempt to describe the appearance of the Martians, arguing that we can know them only through their traces, which suggest the working of the mind. Lowell's abstract discussion complements the heightened visual detail of Burroughs's novels and their minimal attention to science.

Later in life when comparing Burroughs with Verne and Kipling, Bradbury admitted: "Burroughs stands above all these by reason of his unreason, because of his natural impulses . . . because of the sheer romantic impossibility of Burroughs's Mars and its fairy-tale people with green skins and the absolutely unscientific way John Carter traveled there."[4] In fact Carter transports himself to Mars by sheer will. Eric Rabkin has described *The Martian Chronicles* as situated in a "landscape of longing," though this is more applicable to Barsoom.[5] As we shall see, Bradbury makes the nature of longing his subject rather than the objects of that desire. As a conscious choice he discarded the use of a superhero and Burroughs's sensational action: "I began to think that there had been too many Science Fiction books written, in hasty first drafts, with no emphasis on the human equation, with too many rocket guns and bug-eyed monsters."[6] Ironically in view of Bradbury's comment on the unscientific nature of Carter's space travel, he himself was to be taken to task because of his refusal to describe that very process in *The Martian Chronicles*, one critic complaining that Bradbury "sends a single-family unity by rocket to Mars without taking the slightest account of such problems as navigation and the handling of the machine, which would be quite a job for one man plus a woman."[7] As we shall see, the short story form allows Bradbury great selectivity of information and his characteristic emphasis tends to fall on perception not the practicality of movement.

Counterbalancing Burroughs's dramatization of Mars as adventure landscape would be, of course, Wells's account of invasion in *The War of the Worlds* and also the accounts by Clark Ashton Smith of space travel as estrangement, dramas of consciousness where travelers' perceptions of space/time get radically disturbed. In "Master of the Asteroid" (1932) Mars has been visited several times but that doesn't lessen its impact: "The effects of the Martian climate, and the utter alienation from familiar conditions . . . were extremely trying and even disastrous."[8] These statements frame a journal found in a ruined spacecraft that describes how bacteria, radiation, and gravity change and all induce a collective psychosis culminating in death. In a commemorative tribute on the occasion of Smith's death, Bradbury recalled two issues of *Wonder Stories* (July 1931 and October 1932), where the imagery of Frank R. Paul's cover illustrations had meshed with Smith's stories to suggest, in "Master of the Asteroid," a "fearful blend of isolation and loneliness."[9] If Smith suggested to Bradbury the psychological cost of space travel, he was to receive explicit guidance from a fellow SF writer who served as his primary mentor and whose fiction suggested the golden eyes that were to become an imagistic signature of his Martians.

Leigh Brackett, Bradbury's mentor and fellow member of the Los Angeles SF circle, shared a common enthusiasm. In an interview she declared: "all my Mars stories came out of Burroughs," and in her foreword to *The Coming of the Terrans* (1967) she reflected on the persistent appeal of Mars as offering a template for speculative narration:

> To some of us, Mars has always been the Ultima Thule, the golden Hesperides, the ever-beckoning land of compelling fascination. Voyagers, electronic and human, have begun the process of reducing these dreams to cold, hard, ruinous fact. But, as we know, in the affairs of men and Martians, mere fact runs second to Truth, which is mighty and shall prevail.[10]

Despite Burroughs's influence, Brackett's own evocations of the Red Planet were more complex and varied than the former's imperial triumphalism. Her earliest tale about Mars, "Martian Quest" (1940), evokes a failed attempt at local terraforming, where Martian settlements are on the verge of being totally wiped out by gigantic predatory lizards. The economic impetus behind these settlements, Terrans's hopes of a better life, are central to this story, which narrowly avoids being an account of destruction thanks only to the ingenuity of the scientist-protagonist who offers a way to resist these creatures.

Brackett's evocation of Mars also varies strikingly from story to story. Sometimes it functions as the location of a lost city adventure. In "The Sorcerer of Rhiannon" (1942) an explorer named Brandon seems to be heading for death in the middle of a Martian dust storm.[11] Even in his extremity, Brandon imagines the ancient Martian ships that would have sailed on this sea before it dried up, but then fantasy apparently becomes actuality when he discovers the hull of a vessel, with a door that leads him into a cabin where two figures seem to be sitting opposite each other in suspended animation. Brandon's discovery triggers a fantasy image of himself as the "dashing explorer" gaining access to the hidden ancient culture of the planet with an excitement similar to Howard Carter's on discovering the Tomb of Tutankhamen in 1922. Although Brandon stumbles across a whole archive from this culture in a cavern, the story demonstrates the psychic costs of such discoveries when his consciousness is invaded by the spirit of a creature from the past.

Brackett's revised version of the mummy's curse in this last story shows ambivalence over the ethics of uncovering these ancient sites. Indeed, there is considerable variation in her descriptions of Mars over whether to evoke it as alien terrain or to situate it within an interplanetary system of trade. The narrator of "The Veil of Astellar" (1944) tries to point to a moral of perceptual habits when he declares: "You planet-bound people build your four little walls of thought and roof them in with convention, and you think there's nothing else. But space is big, and there are other worlds, and other ways."[12] The veil of the title signifies a threatening light source that makes objects and people disappear, but also suggests the blinkered worldview of the colonists from Earth. A dramatic demonstration of the otherness of Mars takes place in "The Beast-Jewel of Mars" (1948), when a spaceman, jaundiced by years in the service, attempts to see the real Mars. He is taken from the homogenized safe environment of a modern trade city to an ancient city far from Terran experience. There, he is not only taken on a tour of the city but even subjected to prolonged humiliation by being dragged through the streets as if he were an ape. The story describes the revenge of the colonized on their colonizers, a revenge so disturbing that Winters virtually loses his sanity. Ironically, his futile attempts at communication with the Martians only succeed in estranging him from his own cultural area. In that respect, the story marks a major difference from Burroughs's Barsoom tales, which never threaten his hero's presumptions of reality and only present physical challenges to his survival. Brackett's stories, in contrast, repeatedly dramatize the psychic threat of Mars and in stories like "Shadow over Mars" (1944), set up ironic perspectives on exploitation by colonizers from Earth.

BRADBURY'S EARLY MARS STORIES

Bradbury's own first attempt at a Mars narrative dates from the same year as Leigh Brackett's—1940—with the difference that Bradbury's tale was extensively rewritten the following year. "The Piper" takes its title from William Blake's introductory poem to *Songs of Innocence*, where the piper is a version of the poet projecting his songs on to an Arcadian landscape filled with responsive innocent children. Bradbury inverts this innocence, in the 1940 version constructing a dialogue between an old man and a wondering Martian child, where natural fertility has been lost through the economic depredations of colonists from Earth. The third figure in the tale is the mysterious piper, whose music expresses opposition to this process in a symbolic counterpart to the old man's condemnation of mining: "The men from Earth move about among the buildings [of the colonial cities] like ants enclosed in their space suits. They are miners. With their huge machines they rip open the bowels of our planet and dig out our precious life-blood from the mineral arteries."[13] The body here functions as an image of organic wholeness where violence against the terrain becomes synonymous with that against individual bodies. The tale's austere structure almost entirely through dialogue gives this image a potent vividness rather lost in the 1941 revision, which complicates the us-them opposition between colonized and colonizer. Now the colonizing force is from Jupiter as well as Earth, and the inhabitants of Mars include a humanoid Dark Race. New emphases are placed that look forward to *The Martian Chronicles*, however. In the 1941 version, focalized through a returning Martian exile, the piper's music displaces him into a lost past of garden cities and a character draws a comparison between Martian colonization and the

Klondike Gold Rush of the 1890s. Allusions to American history were to punctuate *The Martian Chronicles*, giving the reader cues for speculative comparison.

Throughout the 1940s Bradbury was producing a whole series of Mars stories, in 1944 even briefly planning a novel to be called *Earthport, Mars*.[14] The earliest of these to feature eventually in the 1950 cycle was first drafted in 1943 as "Family Outing," published in 1946 as "The Million-Year Picnic." To convert it into its final form as the concluding story in *The Martian Chronicles*, Bradbury made a number of revisions that highlight the isolation of the family, deleting references to other rockets and introducing memory sequences on the family's preparations for Mars. When two loud detonations are heard, in the original the father announces that "they just blew up our rocket," implying a malign hostile agency, whereas in the *Chronicles* the destruction is chosen and explained.[15] The revisions strengthen the story's psychological dimension, but even the 1946 version shows that Bradbury was already experimenting with the history of settlement as a broad frame to his Mars stories.

CONSTRUCTING THE CYCLE

The problem of how to assemble these narratives was eased in 1944, when Bradbury was given a copy of Sherwood Anderson's *Winesburg, Ohio* and immediately began planning a similar cycle. This marked the first step toward composing *The Martian Chronicles* but was problematic in that Bradbury could not unify his series around a single location. By the late 1940s Bradbury was using his final title in planning, but for an anthology of stories by different authors.[16] Steinbeck offered him another model when constructing his own sequence: "In *The Grapes of Wrath*, every other chapter is a description, a metaphor, prose poetry, it's not plot. I read that book and I learned to ponder, to philosophize, to make images. . . . I subconsciously borrowed that structure from Steinbeck when I wrote *The Martian Chronicles*. Every other chapter in *The Grapes of Wrath* describes the land, or the highway, or the individuals. . . . The bridge chapters in *The Martian Chronicles* are pure Steinbeck."[17]

Steinbeck uses interchapters to distance the reader temporarily from the local detail of what is happening to his protagonists, the Joad family. By interjecting passages of general and historical commentary he anticipates the potential objection that this family is not typical and reminds the reader of the sheer scale of the migration that is taking place as the farmers head west. Bradbury's link chapter "The Settlers" clearly demonstrates an influence from Steinbeck by starting with an arresting generalization: "the men of Earth came to Mars." By excluding any national specifics Bradbury gives the temporary impression of an interplanetary migration, just as Steinbeck frequently suspends our consciousness of the main wave of migration coming from Oklahoma. Again like Steinbeck, Bradbury hints at a variety of dreams impelling the migration and also at commercial exploitation through posters promising: "THERE's WORK FOR YOU IN THE SKY: SEE MARS."[18] In *The Grapes of Wrath*, Steinbeck repeatedly stresses the exploitive role of the big landowners who promise far more work than they can guarantee. Bradbury's emphasis is less commercial. Far from inducing hope, the flights to Mars bring on the "great illness," an intense loneliness resulting from a severe alienation not only from travelers' home states, but from Earth itself, which shrinks down to a "muddy baseball." The cinematic image conveys enormous distance through the rapid reduction of the Earth's image, but its implication is pointedly psychological in that the travelers literally lose their familiar bearings and are left in a void when they arrive on Mars.

Although *The Martian Chronicles* is sometimes described as a "fix-up," i.e., a volume constructed out of short stories that might have been published individually, the term can carry connotations of a makeshift publishing convenience. A more useful term is the *composite novel*, which has been defined as "literary form that combines the complexities of a miscellany with the integrative qualities of a novel."[19] The term serves better to describe the complex unity of the volume, which is constructed around three main themes. First, like Steinbeck, Bradbury saw American expansion as a history of land seizure. In a 1991 interview, he declared that "the history of the world is a history of people going to places where they're not wanted . . . Cortez in Mexico and South America, the white man across America. Our history is full of terrible stories."[20] Such stories, offset by nostalgia for the closure of the frontier, are woven into fears of nuclear war, a deep anxiety in 1950. Both themes merge into space travel, which functions as the basic rationalization of the whole sequence.

The definitive account of the genesis of *The Martian Chronicles* has been given by Jonathan Eller, where he shows the painstaking care that went into Bradbury's rewriting and constant revision of the structure during the late

1940s.[21] Eller demonstrates the intricacy of the composition, while Edward J. Gallagher has persuasively explained the book's final structure as falling into three groups or acts: accounts of the first arrivals on Mars, descriptions of the rise and fall of the settlements, and the aftermath of a nuclear war.[22] He further shows that both between and within stories, perspectives constantly reverse, and that Bradbury understates important events like the outbreak of war by placing that information in bridge passages or giving it only passing mention in the stories.[23] Although Gallagher only touches on this, the very title of *The Martian Chronicles* foregrounds time. The stories were originally dated in the millenarian years 1999–2005, with a coda in 2026, but these were revised in 1997 to 2030–2057. Time units range from era to year, month, season, life span, and beyond, in every case inviting the reader to place events within greater and smaller chronological sequences. Bradbury's narrator stresses in his stage script that the chronicles "tell tales of futures forgotten and pasts that are soon to happen."[24] The paradoxes helpfully alert us to the complex interplay between expectations and memories that runs throughout *The Martian Chronicles*. Recurrent landscape features are sand and dust, traditionally evocative of the passage of time and the dissolution of matter.

REVISING THE ALIEN

In his notes on *Chronicles*, Bradbury describes his efforts to move away from clichéd images of extraterrestrials: "I at least knew what it was *not* going to be about. It was not going to be about bug-eyed monsters or rockets or intricate inventions."[25] And he went on to explain his emerging vision of the Red Planet as follows:

> I decided that Mars could be a symbol of haven to old people, riches to young bucks, beauty to philosophers, adventure to adventurers. . . . I decided that Mars would be nothing more nor less than a mirror in which Earth Man would be reflected, twice as large as life, with all his wonders, beauties and terrors, his petty politics, his ravening greeds, and simple faiths. He would find no more and no less on Mars, than what he brought in his pocket and in his heart.[26]

Bradbury would have been familiar with Stanley G. Weinbaum's "A Martian Odyssey" (1934), which depicts a different form of intelligent life on that planet rather than a hostile monster, and we shall see throughout *The Martian*

Chronicles how Bradbury avoids projecting a specific appearance on to the indigenous beings.

By 1949 Bradbury's friend-to-be and fellow SF author Arthur C. Clarke had already begun praising the former's Mars stories for their "brilliant" use of the freedom from elaborate explanations.[27] Though using a different strategy, a similar revisionist purpose informs Clarke's 1951 novel *The Sands of Mars*, where the protagonist is a Science Fiction writer making his first voyage into space. An important part of the action consists of problematizing his and other writers' accounts of space and Mars. Clarke's writer-protagonist Gibson is warned by the captain of his spaceship that Science Fiction is unusually vulnerable to scientific developments:

> "Up to 1960—maybe 1970—people were still writing stories about the first journey to the Moon. They're all quite unreadable now. When the Moon was reached, it was safe to write about Mars and Venus for another few years. Now *those* stories are dead too."
>
> [Gibson interjects] "But the theme of space-travel is still as popular as ever."
>
> "Yes, but it's no longer Science Fiction. It's either purely factual—the sort of thing you are beaming back to Earth now—or else it's pure fantasy."[28]

As Gibson flies through space to Mars, he experiences the disparity between his fictional accounts and actuality. In effect he goes through a career change from novelist to journalist as he revises his perceptions, a process continued when he encounters living creatures on Mars: "In that moment centuries of fantasy and legend were swept away. All Man's dreams of neighbors not unlike himself vanished into limbo. With them, unlamented, went Wells's tentacled monstrosities and the other legions of crawling nightmare horrors."[29] In their place Gibson sees kangaroolike animals, neither humanoid nor malign, and this revision is symptomatic of the whole novel, which makes a point of deglamorizing every aspect of Mars.

Between the extremes of naively romantic fiction and journalistic reportage, of course, there stands the novel itself whose self-invention Clarke is clearly trying to weave into its very narrative. The result is a rather awkward attempt to balance three factors: generic revision, an educative explanation of the experience of space travel, and the political tensions between Earth and Mars that result in the secret "Project Dawn" whereby the moon Phobos is ignited so as to give nourishing heat for the nascent Martian vegetation and thus help to create a viable atmosphere on Mars. Ultimately Clarke tries to pack too much information into his novel and as a result he misses the subtle ironies and reversals that run through *The Martian Chronicles*.

One of the main issues to be confronted by Clarke and others was how to depict alien beings visually. When Burroughs's John Carter first lands on Mars his first encounter with indigenous creatures is through a hatchery where some creatures have newly emerged from their eggs. Their appearance is disturbing: "They seemed mostly head, with little scrawny bodies, long necks and six legs, or, as I afterward learned, two legs and two arms, with an intermediary pair of limbs which could be used at will either as arms or legs."[30] The presentation of these creatures as a grotesque spectacle is premature in excluding danger. Nevertheless, Burroughs establishes a pattern followed by much subsequent SF of depicting the inhabitants of other worlds as an alien species neither quite human nor animal. At the other extreme of the representational spectrum, the astronauts in Gustavus W. Pope's *Journey to Mars* (1894), on landing, encounter a "crowd of yellow, red and blue complexioned men" apparently otherwise indistinguishable from Earthmen.[31]

Bradbury avoids the physically grotesque and such race coding of Martians by making his first contact psychological and by narrating the experience from a Martian perspective not that of the space travelers. In "Ylla" (close to Latin "illa," i.e., "she") a Martian woman's domestic routine is disturbed when songs from Earth seep into her consciousness.[32] Her appearance is only minimally evoked through "fair, brownish skin" and "yellow coin eyes," the latter displacing an ancient artifact onto facial features. She is defined through domestic stability rather than action: "Mr. and Mrs. K had lived by the dead sea for twenty years, and their ancestors had lived in the same house, which turned and followed the sun, flowerlike, for ten centuries" (14). Every piece of information about this couple constructs them as different but in ways similar to Earth-dwellers. They set out for an "entertainment" just as an American couple of the period would have gone to the movies and their "name" could be read as an initial. These letters are duplicated in "The Earth Men," where the Martian characters comically resemble human stereotypes, totally undermining the drama of the astronauts' arrival. In short, far from being lurid aliens, Ylla and her husband resemble a terrestrial couple whose life has sunk into monotony. Ylla dreams of the newcomers' arrival in romantic compensation, while her husband goes hunting with his "long yellowish tube."

Bradbury repeatedly uses space travel as a Science Fiction premise to set up situations where the alien can be evoked or suspended according to the ironies of the situation. Thus in "Night Meeting," which takes place further into the cycle after settlement has taken place, one Tomas Gomez meets a Martian riding his "machine like a jade-green insect" (108) with six legs. Bradbury ingeniously displaces alien appearance off the Martian, who is not described at all, carrying the implicit message that the Martians have a technological culture sophisticated enough to have produced such a vehicle, no different in function from Tomas's car. For the duration of the event, Bradbury suspends the appearance of the Martian so that the encounter becomes a meeting of voices which is initially comic from the speakers" incomprehension despite the fact that their utterances mirror each other:

> They did not understand each other.
> "Did you say hello?" they both asked.
> "What did you say?" they said, each in a different tongue.
> They scowled. (105)

The synchronization of the questions and the identity of paralinguistic features like facial expression and gesture undermine the otherness of the Martian so completely that it seems perfectly natural for the two men to continue conversing in a shared language this time that they can understand, until they attempt physical contact. When their hands pass through each other, the dialogue shifts into a bizarre argument over each other's reality, where every feature of Mars is subject to a contradictory interpretation. Even here, however, there is no hostility. The speakers agree to disagree, the Martian departs and Tomas is left wondering whether his experience was a dream or vision.

SPIRITUAL THEMES

Bradbury's emphasis on a seepage between the consciousnesses of his Earthlings and Martians, as if through possession, reflects one aspect of Mars fiction that has tended to be forgotten, namely the connection between the Red Planet and spiritualism. Burroughs's hero John Carter is transported to Mars by a kind of willed teleportation as if to suggest that the planet is a site for wish fulfillment. More elaborately, the American naturalist Louis Pope Gratacap's *The Promise of a Future Life on Mars* (1903) argued that after death, the souls of the departed fly to Mars in a stream of "ethereal fluid" and then gradually take on shape through light or through "consolidation" into material beings on that planet. In his history of Mars fiction, Robert Crossley discusses Gratacap and many other writers whose works show the inhabitants of that planet as higher beings leading a spirit life which inspires visitors from Earth.[33] Bradbury may be drawing on such narratives when he evokes Martians as "ghosts" or floating blue forms, vestigial presences in an ancient landscape. His use of telepathy, a characteristic of Burroughs's ancient race of Lotharians, further elides their physicality and repeatedly blurs the boundary of consciousness between his settlers and the Martians. When participating in the 1971 forum "Mars and the Mind of Man," Bradbury himself declared that *The Martian Chronicles* was "very much akin to the childhood influences on me of the Old and the New Testament."[34] He stressed throughout the panel discussion the psychological symbolism of Mars and in his 1976 poem "Why Viking Lander/Mars?" he attributed the desire for Mars as a working of the Life Force.

Bradbury explicitly engages with religion in "The Fire Balloons" (not included in the first U.S. editions), where a group of missionaries encounter mysterious "blue globes of fire," which appear to possess sentience and which miraculously save them from an avalanche. Above all, they present a cryptic image: "the fiery spheres only burnt like images in a dark mirror. They seemed fixed, gaseous, miraculous, forever."[35] They also enter the story after a memory image of Fourth-of-July celebrations has been lodged firmly in the reader's consciousness and after an extended dialogue on sin has been led by Father Peregrine, who functions as Bradbury's surrogate here. With his name suggesting both "alien" and "pilgrim," he explicitly questions the superstition of shape, arguing that the globes are in no way inconsistent with Christianity. Fired by faith, he starts a dialogue with them, where the globes' voice quotes Christ's message to his followers that he will only be with them "for a little while." In his open-minded conviction that God could take on any form and location, Father Peregrine expresses a viewpoint close to Bradbury's indignation at conservative missionaries: "How *dare* we consider ourselves God's only true children? In this era of deep-space exploration we have no room for blind ego. A giant spider on Venus may be born of God, as we are."[36] Despite their similarity of attitude, this is not to suggest that Peregrine is exempt from the main irony of travel to Mars, namely projective delusion. It is possible that his sheer desire for revelation makes him imagine that the globe carries a Christian message.

Bradbury returned to the issue of religion in a later Mars story, "The Messiah" (1971), where members of different religious communities gathered on Mars are discussing their mission. They reject the implications of the 1965 *Mariner* photographs, which seem to reveal a dead landscape. Despite these, the missionaries accept that there are intelligent beings on Mars, although Bradbury carefully excludes from the story any descriptive details either about these creatures (beyond mentioning briefly their masks and telepathy) or about the Martian landscape.[37] The first part of the narrative consists of dialogues about the Messiah and draws directly on Bradbury's own screenwriting experience. In 1960, while working at MGM on a script for *The Martian Chronicles*, he was asked to help with the script for *The King of Kings*, Nicholas Ray's film about the life of Christ, which was released the following year. Bradbury turned to the gospel of John and wrote an extended treatment, which ended with the resurrected Christ meeting the disciples on the shore of the Sea of Galilee, where they are cooking a meal of fish. In Bradbury's words, "in the half-light before dawn, Christ lifts his hand above the fire, and we see the mark where the nail had gone in, the stigmata that would never heal. Blood from Christ's palm drips down upon the white coals. Thus, he proves his identity. He then leaves them, and in my script, I had Christ walk along the shore of Galilee toward the horizon. Now, when anyone walks toward the horizon, he seems to ascend, because all land rises at a distance."[38] In the event Bradbury's screenplay was never used, though, he did supply a voice-over at one stage in the filming. In the story Bradbury introduces a projection of himself in Father Niven who tells his companions how he himself drafted an identical screenplay, and the 1983 interview just quoted repeats passages verbatim from the story. It is possible that both story and interview were quoting from Bradbury's original treatment.

As in "The Fire Balloons," the discussions in the first part of "The Messiah" set up a context for the climactic scene where Father Niven seems to have an encounter with a Martian taking the form of the resurrected Christ. The priest wakes in the middle of the night and hears mysterious sounds in his church. This sequence is so closely cinematic that Bradbury's paragraphing corresponds to shots in a screenplay, tightly pacing the action: "In the midst of glancing at the crucifix above the main altar, he froze. / There was a sound of a single drop of water falling in the night." There in the half-light he sees a "figure" who extends a hand, in the middle of which he sees a terrible image: "there was fixed a jagged hole, a cincture from which, slowly, one by one, blood was dripping, falling away down and slowly down, into the baptismal font."[39] The evocation of nocturnal space with all its ambiguities, the shifts in perspective, and this final shocking close-up all give the scene its powerful visual intensity, and yet the whole figure is suggested rather than described. Christ's display of the stigmata was originally a verifying act to prove his identity, but in Bradbury's new context the wounded hand emerges from a whole pool of Christian imagery within a heavily subjective context.

Initially referred to simply as a "figure," Bradbury modulates his designations to coincide with the priest's incredulous recognition of a displaced messiah. Once this takes place, the presence becomes a capitalized "Man," "Spirit," and "Ghost." By the same token Father Niven is de-individualized into the "Priest," and an exchange takes place where the visitant explains that "he" is a Martian—given shape but also trapped by the priest's thoughts. The latter allows the other's release only on condition that he promises to return. By the end, the story's ambiguities have become complex and ironic. On one level it seems as if the priest has simply projected a wish fulfillment in his church. The encounter weaves an unusual variation on the power theme running throughout *The Martian Chronicles*, which arises from the colonization of the red planet. The priest seems to have imprisoned the Martian in his spiritual fantasy but might be imprisoned within it. The encounter follows the pattern of biblical revelations, but the priest can never communicate his experience with anyone. This positions the reader as a unique witness to an ambiguous spiritual event, which has already become estranged by its transposition on to another planet. Bradbury increases the ambiguity of "The Fire Balloons" by framing it in some editions between one bridge passage ("The Shore") on the U.S. dominance of the space program, and another ("Interim"), which stresses the material conditions of settlement on the new planet. Further ironies emerge when the self-designation by the globes as the "Old Ones" is revised in a later bridge to mean the older migrants from Earth.

The Martians in these stories emerge as projections or distorted mirror images of the human settlers. "The One Who Waits" (1949) is unusual in presenting a Martian as a disembodied being living in a well, which migrates from one astronaut's consciousness to another. Bradbury offsets this threat with the Martian's language, which awkwardly humanizes the speaker as a solitary Romantic: "I live like smoke in a well. Like vapor in a stone throat."[40] In a displaced image of introspection, the crew members peer down at their reflections in the well and then drop one by one into the water, losing their consciousness in the process.

Though this last story was not included in *The Martian Chronicles*, its imagery reflects a major theme of that collection. "I decided that my book would not be a looking crystal into the future, but simply a mirror in which each human Earthman would find his own image reflected."[41] Mirroring and doubling undermine our presumption of difference between Martian and Earthling, putting into practice an effect Bradbury described in 1952:

> A man who is unfamiliar with the mores of his own civilization is usually enlightened and re-focused by a journey through some foreign country such as Mexico where he sees his own customs through the Looking Glass, brought into an astonishing clarity so they suddenly become ridiculous or understandable, or both.[42]

For Mexico read Mars, and we have a clear explanation of how Bradbury was using that planet as an estranging device for setting up ironic perspectives on American culture of the period.

Bradbury's reversal of the most obvious association of Mars with militarism can be seen in his 1949 story "The Concrete Mixer," which was subsequently incorporated into U.S. editions of *The Illustrated Man*. Here, the perspective character is a young Martian male named Ettil, who refuses to support the glorious cause of invading Earth. This puts him at odds with the social norm and embarrasses his family until the authorities compel him to join the Legion of War. In the rocket to Earth, Ettil registers a sense of dehumanization from this military process: "here you were, a meshless, cogless automaton, a body upon which officials had performed clinical autopsy and left all of you that counted back upon the empty seas and strewn over the darkened hills."[43] This is the first alienation effect in the story. The second comes as the force approach Earth when they receive a radio message of welcome from the president of the Association of United American Producers, at which point the story shifts around from an invasion narrative to an ironic account of 1940s American consumerism using the time-honored device of the visitor from another world.

Bradbury creates comedy by bouncing one paranoid perspective off another. The Martians are so dumbfounded by the evident friendliness of Earth that they suspect a plot. Conversely, when Ettil makes contact with a Californian girl, his comments make her suspect that he's a Communist. Writing home about his experiences, Ettil describes the local women as follows:

> There are blonde robots with pink rubber bodies, dead but somehow unreal, alive but somehow automatic in all their responses, living in caves all of their lives. Their derrieres are incredible in girth. Their eyes are fixed and motionless from an endless time of staring at picture screens. The only muscles they have occur in their jaws from their ceaseless chewing of gum.[44]

Probably echoing the "pneumatic" female bodies described in *Brave New World*, this description gives a satirical view of American film culture, which promotes the stereotyped reification of women's bodies and the atrophy of their movement into virtual stasis. It is an ironic conclusion to the description that the organ of speech should only move for consumption. Ettil comically loses his original fears of military confrontation for the more insidious threat of consumerism, which he gradually comes to recognize. Far from being shunned as an alien, the agents of the California film industry try to assimilate him into their productions by asking him to play the role of the Native American! By the end of the story, Ettil yearns to return to Mars to escape from threats on Earth, not from Wellsian bacteria but from a different danger: "A year from now, two years from now, how many Martians dead of cirrhosis of the liver, dead kidneys, high blood pressure, cars, disease. The invasion was indeed lost, the Martians as good as annihilated in a scourge of brutal thoughtless material."[45] Bradbury completely reverses the material benefits of civilization, which were frequently used to justify invasion in order to present them as directly life-threatening.

Mirroring and the gaze more generally make a complex coda to *The Martian Chronicles* in the final story. The title of "The Million-Year Picnic" suggests the extension of a good time into an indefinite future, whereas the narrative is full of references to endings and to seeing as the family attempts to locate itself visually. The son Timothy quite simply can't see Earth; father gazes into the sky to find signs of logic, but they are "not there anymore;" and mother contemplates the Martian landscape as reflected in the eyes of the father. A clear hierarchy emerges where father's viewpoint is dominant. Indeed, he plays the dual role of historical commentator and family destiny, summarizing the developments that have taken place on Earth and destroying the family rocket so that they have no possibility of return. "No more Minneapolis, no more rockets, no more Earth," he declares (218).

For Eric Rabkin this story shows that the "redemption of mythical America can begin."[46] However, the symbolism of endings in the final story is heavily stressed, although it carries an ambiguity that offsets any suggestion of fresh beginnings. The rupture of any contact with Earth isolates the characters; another family is en route. Other than that, we have no information about human settlers. Above all, the final image in the narrative is a deeply ironic one. When asked where the Martians are, father gestures toward the canal:

> The Martians were there—in the canal—reflected in the water. Timothy and Michael and Robert and Mom and Dad.
> The Martians stared back up at them for a long, long silent time from the rippling water. (222)

The freeze-frame ending leaves the image clear, but its significance and duration open. Again and again he has denied the otherness of the Martians and this image acts as an ironic anticlimax to the family's expectation of an exotic revelation. Through this mirror image, Bradbury sheds a somber light over this narrative, where his characters appear to have cut themselves off from their source with only a tenuous hope of a new life. Mars remains essentially a dead landscape.

EXPLORATION ON THE MARTIAN FRONTIER

The solipsistic image closing the final story marks an ironic conclusion to the stories of exploration. Again and again in *The Martian Chronicles* Bradbury implies that the planet is a landscape of desire shaped by the yearnings of the settlers for a promised land, refuge from social abuse, or simply as territory to appropriate. His narrative method strengthens this suggestion by focalizing the stories around central characters in order to dramatize their perceptions. In "The Third Expedition," for example, a rocket crew land on Mars in a place that bizarrely resembles Ohio of the 1920s in the smallest detail:

> Farther up on the green stood a tall brown Victorian house, quiet in the sunlight, all covered with scrolls and rococo, its windows made of blue and pink and yellow and green colored glass. Upon the porch were hairy geraniums and an old swing which was hooked into the porch ceiling and which now swung back and forth, back and forth, in a little breeze. (49–50)

Expecting alien life forms and terrain, to their astonishment they are confronted with a domestic idyll that unnerves them by its sheer familiarity. To the captain it resembles Green Bluff, Illinois, which David Mogen has read as an image of the "vanished American Dream, the small American town lost to history."[47] As the encounters progress, the townsfolk become even more familiar, literally so when one crewman recognizes his grandparents. The astronauts even suspect that instead of flying through space, they have somehow traveled back in time. And yet Bradbury slips in ironic details like the titles of three songs that all suggest an unconscious desire by the crew to return to their small-town childhood.[48]

The irony in such stories lies in the astronauts' expectation of difference, whereas they simply transpose their cultural images onto the new planet. An aside in one of the bridge passages points out that "It was as if . . . a whirlwind twister of Oz-like proportions" had uprooted an Iowa town and planted it on Mars (113). "Fly Away Home" (written ca. 1950, published 2009), repeats the psychological extreme of the astronauts' isolation when they realize the distance they have covered (hence the irony of the nursery rhyme title) and the disappearance of life on that planet. As a compensatory refuge, the men construct a simulation of a main street: "It was a street of no more than six buildings on a side, false fronts, strung with bright red, yellow, green lights."[49] The expense of constructing this displaced film set is noted in the story, which really focuses on ultimate incapacity of the astronauts to deal with the unknown and their blatantly fake construction.

The majority of stories in *The Martian Chronicles* focus on characters' interrogation of their strange new experiences. Their attempts at understanding become a central part of each story's subject. In "The Third Expedition," for instance, the narrative shifts to the captain's thought sequence as he settles down to sleep, a moment signaled by Robert Plank as a transition point for the character's paranoia to start operating.[50] Here, the captain tries to distance himself from the emotionalism of his crew by imagining the paranoid hypothesis of Martians so hostile to Earthmen that they devised an elaborate simulation of home to trap them through telepathy or hypnosis. "Suppose," he thinks, "these houses are really some *other* shape, a Martian shape" (64: emphasis in original). And suppose his brother "will change form, melt, shift, become another thing, a terrible thing, a Martian" (65). "Martian," at this and similar points in the volume, comes to signify the loss of any identifiable shape and therefore identity. The time of sleep as a period of maximum vulnerability was to be used in Jack Finney's 1954 novel *The Body Snatchers*, when pods transform members of a small American town into emotionless replicants. Toward the end of Bradbury's story, the mask of one of the "relatives" seems to slip and there is a hiatus in the narrative, followed by a coda describing the Martians burying the bodies of the astronauts, eerily implicating the reader in the captain's paranoia. The latter's death appears to confirm his worst fears, but typically leaves the reader juggling with uncertainty. This uncertainty recurs throughout the stories, for Jorge Borges in his prologue to *The Martian Chronicles*, evoking a metaphysical horror over identity.[51]

Bradbury had probably already encountered the twin themes of simulation and duplication in John W. Campbell's 1936 story "The Brain Stealers of Mars," which describes a replicant life form that becomes impossible to distinguish from original human subjects. Here, two fugitive atomic scientists land and separate and when they meet again, the one is speaking to his companion with the other's voice. When he is shot the image dissolves:

> The figure of Ted Penton smoked suddenly, and a hole the size of a golf ball drove abruptly through the center of the head, to the accompaniment of a harsh whine of steam and spurts of oily smoke. The figure did not fall. It slumped. It melted rapidly, like a snowman in a furnace, the fingers ran together, the remainder of the face dropped, contracted, and became horrible. It was suddenly the face of a man whose pouched and dulled eyes had witnessed and enjoyed every evil the worlds knew.[52]

The sudden effect of a bullet hole slips into farce as the "creature" comes to sound like a machine. The slow surreal dissolution of the figure restores the eerie dimension to the scene, but then is lost again as Campbell rehumanizes the image, converting it into melodrama.

Bradbury corresponded with Campbell about the publication of his stories in the early 1940s and probably knew "The Brain Stealers" specifically. Bradbury's own approach to Science Fiction subjects has been repeatedly contrasted with the sort of "hard" SF, which Campbell helped to establish. However disturbing his Martians's capacity to produce not just single but multiple simulacra of the Earthmen, Campbell's interest never falls on their psychology, and as a result the uncanny is constantly deflated into essentially practical threats, which can be countered by the Earthmen's weapons. The description of the scene is incoherent in that it keeps slipping between the human and the alien, whereas the whole impact of Bradbury's Martians in "The Third Expedition" and elsewhere lies in the uncertainties they induce. It is never absolutely certain that they exist at all, let alone the question of what shape they might possess.

From an early stage in *The Martian Chronicles*, Bradbury complicates characters' expectations of the alien on Mars, applying black comedy in "The Earth Men," where the arrival of a rocket crew is totally ignored by the local inhabitants. Because the latter fall into recognizable comic stereotypes, we begin to wonder whether the astronauts have been anywhere at all. Indeed, the more strongly they insist on the reality of their voyage, the more convinced a psychologist becomes that they are suffering from a group psychosis. When the astronauts are offered accommodation, the residents' apparent hospitality proves to be in an insane asylum. Bradbury traces out a process of blocked verification where the very grounds for confirming the voyage are denied, hence the appropriate name of the psychologist as Mr. Xxx, suggesting erasure. The story's perspective closes in until the psychologist shoots the captain in a mercy killing and then shoots the survivors to prove his hypothesis. Finally realizing that the material signs of the psychosis persist in the corpses, Mr. Xxx turns his gun on himself.

The story revolves around a bizarre interplay between human perspectives, and the residents are described in an insertion to the original story as "wearing golden masks and blue masks and crimson masks for pleasant variety" (36). "Pleasant" implies that the townsfolk are engaging in a collective masquerade, but one loaded with sinister implications.[53] Eller and Touponce have stressed the importance of masks throughout Bradbury's fiction. Extrapolating from an unfinished novel to be called *The Masks*, started in 1945–1946, they argue that masks are integral to Bradbury's conception of authorship and also to his use of carnival in works like *Something Wicked This Way Comes* (1962). In *The Martian Chronicles* they show how, during his revisions of the stories, Bradbury added a considerable number of references to masks and second, they take masks to indicate the growing sophistication of the Martians themselves: "Unlike the Earthmen who invade the planet, the Martians, although telepathic and prone to mental illness, are psychologically healthy enough to wear masks if they choose to and emotionally balanced enough not to become rigidly identified with them, to wear them as a form of play."[54] The problem with this statement is its naturalization of the Martians as if they existed on the same level of actuality as the human settlers, whereas again and again the stories hint ambiguously at their nature, even suggesting sometimes that they are fantasy figures. In "The Earth Men" masks conceal the features of beings who otherwise resemble Earthlings, bringing their identity into question and strengthening the paranoid possibility that their behavior may be theater.

Masks therefore function as ambiguous objects, multiplying possibilities rather than conferring definite meaning. A story that exemplifies this elusive quality and gives unusually explicit attention to masks is "The Off Season." On one level it seems to show yet another example of a settler trying to create a grotesque simulation of Earth on the new planet. Sam Parkhill's ambition is to create the first hot-dog stand on Mars, but then he is visited by a Martian, figured as a mask floating in midair:

> It was cut from pale blue glass and was fitted above a thin neck, under which were blowing loose robes of thin yellow silk. From the silk two mesh silver hands appeared. The mask mouth was a slot from which musical sounds issued now as the robes, the mask, the hands increased to a height, decreased. (167)

The description implies a human form that would normally wear the mask, just as robes would normally cover a body. Instead, there are gestures toward human limbs and human functions. The Martian does speak, and in a neutral register, as he tries to convey news to Parkhill, but the attempt at communication goes tragically wrong when he shoots at the mask, which collapses "like a small circus tent." From that point on Parkhill refuses to see any positive side to the Martians or their city buildings and blasts away at them with his gun. Bradbury's choice of glass and crystal for Martian masks and buildings constantly implies their fragility. Furthermore, the description quoted implicitly suggests a potential harmony between mask (Martian) and wearer (human), which further implies that, in "killing" it, Parkhill is destroying part of his own humanity. Toward the end of the story, despite his violence, he is given a land grant by a Martian leader on which he can build his restaurant. This development is tied to the hope of thousands of settlers coming to Mars, but shortly before the end Parkhill and his wife see a great eruption of fire on Earth—by implication a nuclear war. This is where the significance of the title emerges, as an understated recognition that no settlers are coming. What starts as a parable of miscommunication ends with an image of futile isolation.

The title of "The Martian" seems to promise description at last, but these expectations are never realized. An elderly couple, newly arrived from Earth, are trying to suppress their grief for their dead son. One night the husband hears a noise at the door and finds a boy standing there who turns out to be Tom—apparently. The couple discovers that others have been having a similar experience. Indeed, "Tom" surrealistically metamorphoses into the dead daughter of another couple. The action of this story takes place almost entirely at night and shows humans constantly running to catch these elusive dreamlike embodiments of the deceased. When pursuers try to seize "Tom," he shifts through a rapid sequence of dissolves and then collapses: "he lay on the stones, melted wax cooling, his face all faces, one eye blue, the other golden" (162). Lacking form or consistency of features, the figure appears to have taken life only from the bereaved settlers. In a separate Mars story, "The Visitor" (1948), a young man is shot when rival settlers fight over possession of his ability to project images of Earth and thus feed their nostalgia.

Isolation and alienation are twin themes, which Bradbury draws on when describing the darker side to the settlers' experience of Mars. When planning *The Martian Chronicles*, he decided: "the essence of my book must be loneliness."[55] In marked contrast with older Mars narratives where space travelers encounter active civilizations, one of the dominant features of Bradbury's landscape is the dead towns, tantalizing images of human absence. By the time that migrants have started returning to Earth, their own settlements come to resemble these deserted towns. In "The Silent Towns," Walter Gripp seems to be living out the predicament of a last man, wandering round his town ritualistically simulating company. And then one day a phone rings and he apparently makes contact with a woman called Genevieve in another town. However, she is no sweet Genevieve and Bradbury denies Gripp a Hollywood ending. Once they meet, in recoil from this overweight glutton, he retires into solitude and the narrative recedes into the never-never time of a folktale.

The telephone is used more extensively to heighten the protagonist's isolation in "Night Call, Collect" (an unchronicled Mars story of 1949), where Sam Barton has been sitting on an empty planet for fifty years—until the phone rings.[56] Instead of communicating with another person, Barton finds himself addressing an earlier self from 30 years ago who prepared multiple relays and recorded messages. The result is a bizarrely introverted simulation of communication where Barton is literally talking to himself. Then what seems to be a call from a newly arrived rocket captain takes him hurrying madly across the landscape, only to discover that even this hope is bogus. In the coda to the story a faulty relay links two electronic voices to each other, closes a circuit and finally displaces the last human voice from Mars.

COLONIZATION AND EMPIRE: THE MARTIAN WEST

There is a constant alternation between presence and absence throughout *The Martian Chronicles*, marking that work's distance from the imperial ideology of earlier SF about space exploration, where appropriation is usually taken for granted. The narrator of John Jacob Astor's *A Journey in Other Worlds* (1894), for instance, sees himself as a latter-day Columbus exploring the Solar System, and the identification of exploration with conquest frequently goes unquestioned, as happens in the climactic end to the 1936 film *Things to Come*. As a spaceship soars into the sky, the commentator John Cabal explains: "for MAN no rest and no ending. He must go on—conquest beyond conquest."[57] The same ideology underpins Willy Ley's popular account of the planets in *The Conquest of Space*, published in 1950, about the same year that *The Martian Chronicles* appeared.

Edmond Hamilton's "A Conquest of Two Worlds" (1932) presents a rare exception to 1930s tales of adventure in interrogating the whole impetus to colonize Mars, whose landscape is naturalized through comparisons with North Africa. Hamilton outlines a series of voyages to Mars that recapitulate the seizure of territory on Earth. The first voyage is an exploratory test of a new atomic means of flight; the second involves more rockets but is patchy since some fail; the third is a much larger undertaking. Hamilton shows how empire is an expansive process and he anticipates Bradbury in setting up Mars as a subject of debate between the astronauts, when one justifies mass killings by insisting: "They had to be conquered. . . . Isn't it worth it? Look at all this planet's resources thrown open to real use now instead of lying unused."[58] The notion of value is primarily an economic one and conquest is rationalized as "correcting" waste and in conveniently erasing the Martians as a factor in events. Bradbury was an avid reader of *Wonder Stories*; he met Hamilton at the Los Angeles Science Fiction Society and the two became close friends, therefore Bradbury very likely knew this story, especially as he would have found its anticolonialism so congenial.[59]

Bradbury repeatedly sets up debates in his Mars stories like "The Strawberry Window" (unchronicled, 1954), which contrasts a settler's belief in a racial mission to spread culture to the stars with his wife's nostalgia for the way of life they have left behind.[60] Debate leads to physical violence and death in "—And the Moon Be Still as Bright," which stands at the conceptual core of *The Martian Chronicles* in addressing so explicitly its concern with colonization. Here, rocket crewmen feel awe at being visitors to Mars, but at the same time uneasily register the fact that theirs is the fourth expedition and that the fate of their predecessors is unknown. The character Spender, though not narrator, is central to this story in drawing the crew's attention to the surprisingly large number of relatively recent deaths in their area, apparently from chicken pox, an important historicizing detail for Bradbury as he revised the story for *The Martian Chronicles*.[61] Here, he draws an implicit analogy with the spread of disease, which has accompanied Western imperial expansion over the centuries, outbreaks of venereal disease in the Pacific or smallpox among the Native Americans (one of the crew members is named Cheroke).[62] As he later explained, "Martians would be first cousins to Indians and I recollected only too well what we had done to the Indians."[63] Spender is a clear surrogate for Bradbury in the range and nature of his comments. He grimly declares that Mars represents the future of Earth and, extrapolating from the traces of culture in the landscape, he claims that the Martians "knew how to live with nature and get along with nature. They didn't try too hard to be all man and no animal" (86).

Spender's commentary includes the method of the story itself when he explains the origin of the title in Byron's "So we'll go no more a-roving" to express the Romantic pathos of the Martians's fate. After his visit to one of the Martian cities, a surge in violence takes place as Spender shoots down members of the crew, probably in a quixotic attempt to stave off migration. His actions force the captain to kill him, thereby enacting his despair at getting his message across and, typically of *The Martian Chronicles*, his fate raises questions for the crew and implicitly for the reader. The tableau image of his burial in a Martian sarcophagus holding his gun in one hand and a Martian silver-leaf book in the other suggests a figure caught between conflicting cultures.

The shoot-out with Spender resembles a displaced Western, an analogy that recurs several times in *The Martian Chronicles*. Bradbury was not alone in conceiving a resemblance between a partly settled Mars and the old American West. This parallel is made explicit in Robert Heinlein's *Red Planet* (1949), where colonization has taken place. An older settler tells the boy protagonist at the end of the novel: "The white man was still studying the American Indian, trying to find out what makes him tick, five hundred years after Columbus— and the Indian and the European are both *men*, like as two peas. *These are Martians*. We'll never understand them."[64] The action of the novel is played out on the by now familiar landscape of ancient cities, canals, and barren terrain. As Robert Crossley has pointed out, this is a frontier society where the settlers are scattered across the landscape, but also where the nascent social forms allow libertarian issues to play themselves out with the simplicity of an adventure.[65] A major difference between Heinlein and Bradbury, however, lies in the physical actuality of the Martians in *Red Planet*, which is never in doubt.

The analogy between exploring space and the American West was used throughout the debates over the U.S. space program, and by Bradbury himself, as we shall see in Chapter 4, to underline that program's continuity with national history. This connection emerges in the separate 1952 story "The Wilderness" (included in some editions of *MC*), where two women are about to fly to Mars to join their husbands. As they are packing, their thoughts constantly drift back to 1849, the year of the Gold Rush and of wagon trains heading west. The analogy is skewed, however, because space travel by 2003, the story's present, has become routine. The two protagonists, Janice and Leonora, personify opposing viewpoints on their journey—Janice registering fear and anxiety, Leonora optimism. It is Janice's perspective that is given priority and through it Bradbury dramatizes perceptions of space. Janice has a nightmare memory of falling down through a pitch-black closet through unknown depths, falling into claustrophobic darkness rather than flying upward into open space. The story thus sets up a charged tension between opposites, between the known and the unknown. The poignancy of leaving behind familiar places is evoked through a fantasy of flight "over schools and avenues over creeks and meadows and farms so familiar that each grain of wheat was a golden coin."[66] The grain of wheat in Whitman regularly symbolizes potential new life, but here focuses on anticipation of loss through a specific object. Space travel to Mars, traditionally described as a forward motion toward the future, for Janice involves the loss of memory itself and, when she receives a transmitted photograph of her new house on Mars, the image is reassuring but ambiguous. At first it resembles her house in America, but then a mismatch between house and context emerges: "the soil was a strange color of violet, and the grass was the faintest bit red, and the sky glowed like a gray diamond."[67] The hallucinatory Martian colors give an effect as if the landscape was being seen through a lens whereby the physical features of Earth are retained but transformed away from the familiar.

Bradbury dramatizes most explicitly the self-deception of settlers expecting a new frontier in "They All Had Grandfathers" (1947), where a newly arrived colonist recalls his grandfather's memories of the old West.[68] Samson Wood is dazzled by the thought of originating new settlements, declaring: "It's like being in on Eden."[69] In the animated dialogue that follows, Mars is hardly described at all, functioning as empty space for the settlers to fill as duplications of the United States: a new Wyoming, a new Texas. As a town is constructed, it becomes evident that the settlers are attempting to actualize images from Western movies rather than any personal memories and Bradbury closes off the narrative with the tombstone of Wood, commemorated as the "First Civilian to Die on Mars." The narrative of beginnings concludes with a somber reminder of mortality. "Payment in Full," another unchonicled story probably from the same period, describes three trigger-happy settlers who shoot down any Martians blocking their conviction that "We're *Earth*! Earthmen! Best in the Universe!"[70] As in the previous story, their aim is to establish a new America, but this purpose is burlesqued as crude and violent nationalism.

It should be clear already that Bradbury does not use the West as a simple analogy to historically underpin travel to Mars, but rather as an intermittent set of reference points for the reader. Gary K. Wolfe has shown how he selected from available paradigms on Mars writing to explore the different impacts of technology on society and, following the Turner Thesis, and the possibility that "the wilderness could transform the colonists."[71] Wolfe alerts us to the cultural symbolism relating to the frontier throughout *The Martian Chronicles* and the attendant shifts of perspective. The thought sequence in "The Taxpayer," for instance, projects Mars as a possible "land of milk and honey" promising release from government control and the threat of war. Ironically, the character is arrested before he can board a rocket and realize his dream. Brief though it is, the bridge passage shows reversal of hopes typical of the larger cycle.

In "—And the Moon Be Still as Bright" Bradbury sets up an explicit dialogue on the ethics of settlement. Here, Spender challenges his crew's assumption of appropriation by presenting Mars as an organic whole threatened by the settlers, who are the spoilers: "We Earth Men have a talent for ruining big, beautiful things . . . this whole thing is ancient and different, and we have to set down somewhere and start fouling it up. We'll call the canal the Rockefeller Canal and the mountain King George Mountain and the sea the Dupont Sea" (73). Spender names three imperial powers—the United States, Great Britain, and France—as the polluters of the planet's ecology. Anticipating by decades figures like the anthropologist Lyubov in Ursula Le Guin's "The Word for World Is Forest" (1977), Spender's voice is that of an elegiac spokesman for a planet about to be ruined.[72] In a later link passage, "The Naming of Names," Bradbury returns to the act of naming as a serial appropriation of the landscape, first of all the names of pioneers and then through the names of local industrial products. The process is described as an act of collective violence: "And the rockets struck at the names like hammers, breaking away the marble into shale, shattering the crockery milestones that named the old towns, in the rubble of which great pylons were plunged with new names: IRON TOWN, STEEL TOWN." (130). The progression here is not toward fresh beginnings but toward death; ironically, the last places to be named are the graveyards.

Bradbury explored the symbolism of names in "Dark They Were and Golden-Eyed" (1949), which he did not include in *The Martian Chronicles*, perhaps because it duplicates a number of major motifs in the cycle.[73] Here, no sooner have the Bittering family arrived on Mars than the father expresses an immediate desire to return, despite the fact that the landscape poses no obvious threat to them except for the wind, which "blew as if to flake away their identities."[74] His fear peaks when the family learns via radio that a nuclear war on Earth has destroyed all the rockets, cutting them off from any return. Of necessity, his thoughts turn to the civilization of the Martians who have "built cities, named cities; climbed mountains, named mountains."[75] Bittering's insight comes implausibly early in the story, given his resistance to any local culture including the food. Then he has a fantasy that his family is "melting" into dark-skinned, golden-eyed figures. The metamorphosis is signaled by a mysterious seepage of Martian words into the family's consciousness, including personal and place names.

The decisive moment comes when another settler tells Bittering to "forget the map" and join them in moving into the Martian villas. The landscape in "Dark They Were" is one of the most humanized in Bradbury's Mars stories, which implicitly motivates the settlers' move. Five years later, a rocket arrives whose crewmen discover the American settlements abandoned and an exceptionally friendly race of "dark people" living in the cities. One of the captain's first jobs is to name the features in the landscape and so the cycle begins afresh. The coda highlights the story's symbolism as a parable of the waves of settlement, each one being signaled by the process of remapping. As Bradbury was to argue in his 1968 discussion of horror movies and fiction that revolved around "naming the unnameable," "the names change from generation to generation, but the need to name goes on."[76] Characteristically of his Mars stories, Bradbury does not resolve the mystery of this change, but instead uses a coda that emphasizes its extremity. After a five-year time gap, another rocket lands on Mars only to find the American settlement deserted. In the hills live what appear to be Martians, who surprise the new crew with their mild manners. So what happened to the settlers? Because the crew can conceive of the races only in separate categories, they have no answer.

Bradbury's evocation of the relation between Martians and Earthmen reflects racial tensions on the home planet. "Way in the Middle of the Air" engages directly with the problem of race in the American South, describing African Americans' desire for emigration to Mars. This time the motivation for space travel is quite simply to escape racism so severe that it is life-threatening. The story is focused through the perspective of southern white males who are astonished and then outraged at the sheer number heading for the rocket terminal, because migration will threaten the stability of the whites' liveli-hood. The sheer scale of the migration is expressed through the metaphor of a river, possibly an echo of Steinbeck, or a flood bursting through the dykes of white suppression. The title of the story is taken from the Woody Guthrie song "Ezekiel saw the wheel / Way up in the middle of the air," which centers on the little wheel of faith running in harmony with the big wheel of God. Although white males supply the perspective, the discourse of the narrative includes allusions to the Bible that link the migration to spiritual salvation. References to a "great wind" (like that which smites unbelievers in the Book of Job) cleansing the landscape and to visionary revelation encode Mars as a promised land of freedom and, by implication, suggest that America is still a land of slavery for the African Americans. The list of their abandoned pos-sessions includes "cartons of Confederate money," a clear signal that they are attempting to flee their collective history.

Bradbury wrote a sequel to this story, "The Other Foot," which he planned to include in *The Martian Chronicles* with a bridge passage showing African Americans on a "spiritual saga in miniature," but he dropped the idea.[77] Here, Mars has been colonized for twenty years by black settlers from the United States fleeing nuclear war. The story describes their excitement at hearing that a rocket is arriving carrying white men. So, to the young the landing will be a spectacle; to older colonists it will offer a chance for racial revenge through reverse segregation. When the rocket lands, an aged white man emerges with "colorless" eyes, as if they had been bleached. When he speaks it is only to recite the cities destroyed in the war and then to ask for help. As the topographical references close in on those areas charged with memories of lynching and other atrocities, the effect again is one of erasure; there is "nothing left of it to hate" (53), and the story closes with the bemused admission by one of the colonists that this was the first time he had ever seen a white man. Although not included in *The Martian Chronicles*, it belongs with those stories describing the red planet as a place of refuge and simply reverses the conventional postwar relation between blacks and whites. Virtually all the action is conveyed through dialogue, thereby erasing appearance and thus one of the causes of racism.

Critics have constantly debated Bradbury's projection of Mars, describing it variously as a "fairyland," a "new frontier," or just "beautifully impossible." There is broad agreement that Bradbury supplies very selective description, but this can help the reader to avoid irrelevant expectations of realism and realize the "only-too-real destructiveness of twentieth-century Earth-culture."[78] As I stress throughout this chapter, however, the descriptions of Mars fluctuate according to the different perceptions of focal characters in each story. Thus, to some the landscape seems featureless; to others the marble buildings of the cities evoke classical grandeur; and to still others the symbolism of crystal suggests fragility and imminent fracture. In the separate story, "The Blue Bottle" (1950), Bradbury concentrates the ambiguous attractions of Mars in an ancient artifact, which one settler finds within a dead city and then another steals. Shortly afterward the latter's corpse is found beside the road and then a surreal transformation takes place:

> The figure of the plump man glowed, began to melt. The eyes took on the aspect of moonstones under a sudden rush of water. The face began to dissolve away into fire. The hair resembled small firecracker strings, lit and sputtering. The body fumed as they watched. The fingers jerked with flame.[79]

Finally the body explodes into mist, disappearing completely. In the context of later Science Fiction films, this kind of process—neither combustion nor quite dissolution—would be the result of some malign agent, but here the event reflects the enigmatic nature of the bottle itself. Bradbury's original title, "Death-Wish," makes the subject explicitly psychological, whereas the narrative suggests an effect rather than an impulse.

THE MARTIAN OIKOS

Throughout *The Martian Chronicles*, Bradbury stresses the importance of dwellings, which raises questions about the settlers' relation to the land. In his notes, he emphasized location on the red planet: "How much nicer if the colonials could look upon space as a Cathedral, with God in His place, and all right with the universe, except that these colonials would be going into space that they had carefully sprayed with equal parts of philosophical cyanide and scientific DDT."[80] Bradbury anticipates by years Rachel Carson's famous critique of pesticides in *Silent Spring* (1962). "—And the Moon" predicts the garbage that settlers will produce, "time for banana peels and picnic papers in the fluted, delicate ruins of the old Martian valley towns" (68). Throughout the series Bradbury uses recurrent details to strengthen his ironies. The passing reference here to picnic papers looks forward to the final story, "The Million-Year Picnic," where an extended family excursion is made into an analogue for the whole enterprise of settling on Mars.

Dwellings imply settlement and the last stories noted imply that settlement carries inevitable negative consequences for the environment. In "The Green Morning" Bradbury makes this issue explicit by describing an attempt to transform the Martian landscape into an area of lush fertility. The adjective "green" in the title is an overdetermined sign throughout Bradbury's works connoting rural fertility, the small town with its communal values, and even youth. Here, the obvious suggestion is of a fresh beginning, where a traveler from Earth named Benjamin Driscoll dreams of how Mars might be:

> And the thing he wanted was Mars grown green and tall with trees and foliage, producing air, more air, growing larger with each season; trees to cool the towns in the boiling summer, trees to hold back the winter winds. There were so many things a tree could do: add color, provide shade, drop fruit, or become a children's playground, a whole sky universe to climb and hang from. (96)

The expansive syntax reflects Driscoll's enthusiasm over the pastoral potential of the red planet. Trees perform the multiple functions of making the "oikos" habitable, protecting human settlers, and offering a playing space for their children. His vision of a "shining orchard" has undertones of Eden but, as usual in Bradbury, carries a problematic ambiguity. It presumes a landscape of loam (the term appears in the story), which fits that of the American Midwest rather than Mars.

Driscoll is explicitly modeled on the nineteenth-century folk hero Johnny Appleseed, who traveled round the Midwest planting apple trees from seed. As early as the 1870s, he was taking on a mythical status as an embodiment of the pioneering spirit of the West, which was giving way to the spread of industrial technology. Thus he came to represent the "romance of frontier life" in the very period when memories of this life were receding rapidly.[81] In the story Driscoll declares a "private horticultural war with Mars" (98), a phrase that Kim Stanley Robinson has explained as implying "the violence of the act to the original Mars, and so it implies also that there will be pacifists in that war, there will be a resistance in that war."[82] Robinson sees Driscoll as attempting an early kind of terraforming, i.e., of planetary engineering, and comments with the hindsight of his own 1990s Mars trilogy that such a project would be socially divisive. It is indeed ironic that a plan to fertilize the planet should be expressed in terms of warfare, the oldest cultural symbolism that Mars has carried. But any account of terraforming Mars, whether by Arthur C. Clarke (*The Sands of Mars*, 1951), Isaac Asimov (*The Martian Way*, 1952), or Robinson himself, depicts that project as a large-scale one requiring massive financial backing for its combination of scientific, technological, and political cooperation.[83] Driscoll's dream may be self-delusion—he faints twice—and a final meaning to "green" could be "naive." Driscoll's pastoral dream contrasts starkly with the following bridge passage, which describes the migrants' rockets as silver locusts (the title of the first U.K. edition of *The Martian Chronicles*).[84] Bradbury compresses the migrants' appropriation of Mars virtually into a single paragraph where the locust analogy suggests a consumptive life and strengthens the major motif of human actions destructively attempting to suppress the unbearable otherness of the new world.

Robinson paid Bradbury the tribute of incorporating his writing into *Red Mars* (1993), the opening volume of his trilogy. Here, the landscape carries the traces of earlier writings in place names like Burroughs and Bradbury Point, the latter being an important mineral outcrop. Early references in the novel to masks and passing mention of Johnny Appleseed further strengthen Bradbury's presence in Robinson's narrative. In the preamble to *Red Mars*, Robinson notes how, after the *Mariner* and *Viking* space probes, "everything changed," but that did not imply the dismissal of earlier Mars writing. In his preface to the 2001 edition of *The Martian Chronicles* Robinson strikes a careful balance between recognizing the imaginative spread of fiction by Burroughs and Wells, and the dependence of this fiction on the writings of Percival Lowell. For Robinson, Bradbury was a transitional figure moving out of the older phase of Mars writing: "He understood that because Lowell's romantic vision of an inhabited planet had been wrong, all the Martian fiction of the first decade of the century had also been wrong, that that whole world was lost; but he also understood that we had populated Mars with very powerful figments of our imagination, [which] were there for good, and would live on."[85]

Whatever promise Mars might hold for the settlers from Earth, Bradbury never allows us to forget death, whether from disease, from conflict between settlers, or from the extinction of an ancient species. Around the midpoint of the story cycle, warnings of impending war increase. "The Luggage Store" bridge passage now evokes a collective return to Earth despite its dangers. Mars modulates into a place of hostility with the description in "The Off Season" of massed "natives" attacking settlers with their sandships. Then one of the many reversals takes place in the series. In "The Watchers" flashes from Earth are described as "Morse-code flashes" (180), partly a glance at Mars folklore since from 1919 to 1922 Marconi was convinced that he was receiving radio messages from that planet and partly a sign of reversal in that Earth has now become the dead planet. Morse implies a message, here decoded to mean "COME HOME." The settlers project new life into an abandoned Earth just as war breaks out, and they start a reverse migration.

AFTERMATH: "THERE WILL COME SOFT RAINS"

The transition into the third aftermath section of *The Martian Chronicles* occurs in "The Long Years," which describes how an archaeologist named Hathaway (also the ship's physician in "—And the Moon Be Still as Bright") has been stranded with his family for decades on Mars. Then unexpectedly a rocket from Earth lands, carrying the crewmen of Captain Wilder from the expedition. The arrival promises rescue until the crew notice discrepancies between their memory and the age Hathaway is claiming for his wife and daughters. When an astronaut discovers the latter's graves, the captain realizes that Hathaway has constructed lifelike replicants of his family. Hathaway himself suffers a fatal heart attack from the discovery and the robots are left behind, engaging in an extended semblance of family life. The fact that Mars has become a "tomb planet" is demonstrated in the daily action of the "wife," who emerges from her house "for a long moment, looking at the green burning of Earth, not knowing why she looks" (204). Unconsciously simulating the migrants' yearning gaze at the home planet, the figure actually confirms human absence.

This forms the context of one of Bradbury's most anthologized stories, "There Will Come Soft Rains," which opens with a house coming alive with the dawn of a new day, except that there is no living human presence at all. Talking alarm clocks and labor-saving machines act out a simulation of family life, which reminds us on every line that the family is absent. The house is typical, likewise the evoked lifestyle, and even Bradbury's choice of location, Allendale, adds to its typicality.[86] As the sun rises, the story's focus shifts to the outside of the house and the single most potent image:

> The entire west face of the house was black, save for five places. Here the silhouette in paint of a man mowing a lawn. Here, as in a photograph, a woman bent to pick flowers. Still farther over, their images burned on wood in one titanic instant, a small boy, hands flung into the air; higher up, the image of a thrown ball, and opposite him a girl, hands raised to catch a ball which never came down.[87] (206)

The wall has become the screen for negative photographic images, which both resemble a family photograph (which no one will see) and also recall one of the iconic images of Hiroshima—"nuclear shadows" as they became known—where the bomb blast imprinted a human shadow of a ladder on the wall of a house. In the story, Bradbury positions the reader problematically as an observer where no observers appear to exist.

Bradbury's title is taken from a 1920 poem by Sara Teasdale apparently celebrating the order of Nature, but which actually draws a grim message of Nature's indifference to human disaster:

Robins will wear their feathery fire,
Whistling their whims on a low fence-wire;
And not one will know of the war, not one
Will care at last when it is done.

Unusually, Bradbury includes the full text of the poem, selected "at random" by the circuitry of the house, as if human choice has become irrelevant. Where Teasdale uses natural creatures to comment on the human lot, Bradbury incorporates animals into the domestic scene as robots or VR simulations in the nursery walls like those occurring in "The Veldt."[88] Through his impassive chronicling voice he implies that the technologies of the house and of nuclear bombs are two parts of the same complex, displacing and then erasing human presence. The story presents a serial narrative of death—of the family, then the family dog, and finally of the house itself bursting into flames, "its bared skeleton cringing from the heat" (210). The final irony of the story lies in the machine repeating the date, which implies that the house has stood as an empty memorial to the war for twenty years. With its collapse into ash, this ends and the story's predictive title is contradicted entropically as the last mechanical voice runs down. We shall see in the following chapter that a nuclear strike marks the climax to *Fahrenheit 451*, and that a number of related stories dramatize local aspects of a resulting war: the announcement of a new role for garbage collectors to gather corpses, characters in flight from the blasts, an old man's memories of prewar, and so on.[89]

The Martian Chronicles marked a breakthrough in Bradbury's career, thanks in no small part to Christopher Isherwood's review praising its originality and situating it within a new wave of SF offering "adult speculation about the dangers of galactic imperialism and the future of technocratic man." Anticipating later critics, Isherwood wondered whether Bradbury was writing SF in any conventional sense because "his interest in machines seems to be limited to their symbolic and aesthetic aspects."[90]

As soon as *The Martian Chronicles* was published, Bradbury began investigating the possibility of a film adaptation. John Huston expressed interest in the project, and others even considered making it into a musical.[91] Bradbury himself claimed to have written "four or five scripts" over the years, but it was not until 1980 that the series was adapted for an NBC miniseries directed by Michael Anderson with three episodes: "The Expedition," "The Settlers," and "The Martians." Bradbury collaborated with his old friend Richard Matheson on the scripts and later recalled: "I did over . . . most of the stories there, because the original was a bore."[92] Neither Matheson nor Bradbury was happy with the result.

LATER MARS PUBLICATIONS

Bradbury continued to publish Mars stories intermittently, virtually all dating from the late 1940s. One exception, "The Lost City of Mars" (1967), has a visionary dimension rare in *The Martian Chronicles*, from its opening ("the great eye floated in space") to the ambitions of the rocket captain Wilder who gazes down at the "frontier cities" of Mars: "We'll light those worlds a billion years off, and the children of the people living under those lights this instant, we'll make them immortal" (265).[93] What complicates this ambition is the fact that Mars has already been subjected to extensive human settlement and the variety of Bradbury's characters precludes reading the story as a simple exploration narrative. Thus we have a rich yacht-owner, a pair of actors, a big-game hunter, and an alcoholic poet, all joining Captain Wilder in his search for a fabled lost city, which feeds their different desires. It becomes an enormous theater within which the actor Beaumont can perform; a highway where the poet can drive to his "death"; a "museum of weapons" for the hunter; or a place where Captain Wilder can act out his messianic dreams: "He walked on a water of space. He stood upon a transparent flex of great eye" (290).[94] The climax comes when the city's mechanism closes down the entrance, trapping most visitors inside. The story describes the projections by different members of the culture, unrelated to a larger history, as in *The Martian Chronicles*.

In 2004 Bradbury discounted commercial reasons for Mars settlement, arguing that "the final reward on Mars might well be not spices or gold, but the squashing of egos and a promise of immortality. . . . The footprint on the moon is being filled with eternal dust and Mars still waits to have its canals filled with our dreams."[95] As testimony to the force of his fictional evocation of Mars, Bradbury was invited to contribute a foreword to a special space issue of the *National Geographic* magazine for October 2008. In his memoir-essay "My

Mars" Bradbury returns to a theme he has repeated many times, namely that his is a Mars of the imagination. He recalls an interview from 1976 when he witnessed the landing of the Viking 1 space probe and was questioned about the absence of cities and inhabitants. His answer was categorical: "Don"t be a fool. . . . WE are the Martians! We're going to be here for the next million years. At long last, WE ARE MARTIANS!"[96]

We have seen how Mars is used by Bradbury as a site to consider alternatives to the culture of Earth, and two stories include the censorship of books within their subjects, which was to become a major concern of *Fahrenheit 451*. "The Exiles" (1949) counterpoints a rocket's approach to Mars with the actions of "Martians" who are in fact the avatars of authors like Poe and Ambrose Bierce, whose fiction has been banned. Bradbury sets up a hybrid narrative combining space travel with a pastiche Gothic landscape in order to satirize the cliches of technological progress. Without understanding his own motivation, the captain has brought along a stock of the banned books, and as he emerges from the rocket announces that they are entering a "new world," an assertion totally at odds with his cargo and the very landscape of Mars.

TRANSITIONAL CODA: "USHER II"

Of the Mars stories, "Usher II" engages most directly with the enforcement of literary censorship. Despite Bradbury's attempts to link it with the story cycle in *Chronicles* through a bridge on creeping red tape, it was dropped from the British edition, and Bradbury subsequently recognized that it did not fit in with the overall sequence.[97] The protagonist William Stendhal has fled Earth and constructed a simulation of Poe's House of Usher in a gesture of opposition to the reality enforcers who operate even on Mars. As in *Fahrenheit 451*, Bradbury blurs any distinction between humans and books; both alike are "executed." The story traces out the conflict between Stendhal and the local authorities who are determined to stamp out fantasy. Thus he is visited by an "Investigator of Moral Climates" who tells him that his building has to come down. After being taken on a brief tour, a robot ape kills this man, being replaced by a robot instructed to give a favorable report to the organization. With the help of a horror-film specialist whose films have been confiscated back on Earth, Stendhal organizes a grand reception for a group of would-be censors and the tale runs through a series of pastiche scenes from Poe's tales (including "The Masque of the Red Death" and "The Cask of Amontillado) where each guest is killed. The story could thus be seen as taking a fantasy revenge on the censors. It is framed by readings from "The Fall of the House of Usher" and ends with Stendhal and his companion watching the collapse of their house from their departing helicopter. He is the main survivor in this parable of triumphant fantasy.

"Usher II" is a thematic hybrid in combining Mars as refuge with the institutional attempts to control literature and therefore, Bradbury implies, human thought. It functions partly as a polemic for Gothic fantasy as well as literature generally and dramatizes the position that Bradbury adopted frequently in his nonfictional prose that literature could, indeed *should*, give expression to suppressed fears of death. In its political dimension, however, it points toward Bradbury's dystopias of this period and particularly to his famous classic, *Fahrenheit 451*.

CHAPTER 3

FAHRENHEIT 451 IN CONTEXTS

Fahrenheit 451 has achieved widespread recognition as a classic among postwar American dystopias. Thanks to the publication of a number of uncollected stories and of drafts, we are now in a good position to identify the different elements that went into the composition of the novel. Around 1947 Bradbury began a work to be called, after Matthew Arnold's "Dover Beach," *Where Ignorant Armies Clash by Night.*[1] Drafted first as a stage play and then as a prose narrative, this work takes place some two hundred years into the future against a background "land of fused ruins and broken vehicles."[2] Framed against the aftermath of the Fourth World War is a society that ritualizes killing and the destruction of books. Bradbury's protagonist is sometimes named Muerte, i.e., "Death," and the action focuses on his crisis of conscience when he refuses to destroy the last copy of Shakespeare. His resistance to the regime anticipates a central theme in the final novel, as does Bradbury's animation of the books to be burned. Thus in one fragment we are told: "The book turned and fought, like some small white animal caught within the fire. It seemed to want very much to live, it writhed and sparkled and a small gust of gaseous vapor blew up from it."[3] Bradbury hasn't yet managed the clarity of metaphor that was to relate books to birds in *Fahrenheit 451*. These surviving fragments give hints of what Bradbury described to a member of the *Harper's Weekly* staff as a comment on contemporary society: "I believe that by a complete reversal I have made the values of our time stand forth in relief. The story is one of anarchy and disillusion, of death and destruction and the art and value in a world set to valuing it."[4]

PEDESTRIAN AND FIREMAN

Bradbury's *Where Ignorant Armies* project shows the dystopian direction his writing took in the late 1940s, when he repeatedly evoked negative or destructive social norms in his speculative futures. Among Bradbury's early stories, one became incorporated into the novel as part of its backstory and has repeatedly been anthologized as a satire on the TV generation. By Bradbury's own account, "The Pedestrian" (1951) constituted one early stage in the composition of *Fahrenheit 451*, one loosely based on his experience when he and a friend were stopped by members of the Los Angeles police for walking. It was originally planned as "sort of a monologue" and when Bradbury wrote his theater adaptation he introduced a second character to set up a dialogue on the issues raised.[5] The story's generic title implies that the protagonist is the last of his kind. The opening establishes a spatial contrast, which is to become central: "To enter out into that silence that was the city at eight o'clock of a misty evening in November, to put your feet upon that buckling concrete walk, to step over grassy seams and make your way, hands in pockets, through the silences, that was what Mr. Leonard Mead most dearly loved to do."[6] The paradoxical combination of prepositions invites the reader to focus on outside as a virtually dead space. Although the story is situated in an unnamed suburbia of the future (2053 A.D.), the sidewalk has already become a ruin, a visual sign of disuse and therefore of social change. Every descriptive detail in the opening suggests imminent or actual endings: of the day, the year, and ultimately of social communication. The most basic symbolism of a road is to evoke purpose, the means of getting from place to place, but in Mead's case the streets have lapsed into sheer expanse, spatial markers for social purposes that no longer exist. Bradbury's use of the second person in his opening has a particular poignancy in a story about endings, because it suggests repeatability while evoking a society where the very desire to walk has lapsed.

The story anticipates *Fahrenheit 451* in its evocation of domestic interiors peopled by "grey phantoms," whose activities are determined by television programs. As Mead passes the houses, he sees the flickering of the TV screens and engages in fantasy greetings: "'Hello, in there,' he whispered to every house on every side as he moved. 'What's up tonight on Channel 4, Channel 7, Channel 9? Where are the cowboys rushing, and do I see the United States Cavalry over the next hill to the rescue?'"[7] Every house and every inhabitant has become as interchangeable as the TV channels and the programs themselves. TV voices have replaced living dialogue. The only exchange takes place between Mead and a robotized police car, not with its officers. In effect, Mead is interrogated over the orthodoxy of his actions. His claim to be a writer is ignored; he has no wife, and therefore by implication deviates from a statistical norm. The outcome is that Mead is arrested and taken away to the Psychiatric Center for Research on Retrogressive Tendencies. As a walking anachronism, he has to be removed from the scene.

For this story and for the novel, Bradbury was drawing on David H. Keller's 1928 story "The Revolt of the Pedestrians," which describes how the automobile achieves such dominance that pedestrians are gradually forbidden from most roads and transformed into an alien species that it is fair game to run down. This future world runs on crude Darwinian lines where the "world was crazed by a desire for speed."[8] As Montag discovers in *Fahrenheit 451*, hidden away from the cities are secret colonies of pedestrians planning resistance to the state.

"The Fireman" was the novella that Bradbury published in February 1951 as a first version of the novel to come. Eller and Touponce have shown that differences from the novel include an increase in cultural criticism, but also note the absence from the final novel of any explanation of the paradox that books are being both produced and attacked.[9] There are other differences of varying importance. The novella starts with the card game at the fire station, thereby lacking the gradual lead-in offered in the novel by Montag's encounter with his young neighbor Clarisse. As we shall see, the novel develops the drama of his growing dissatisfaction, whereas in "The Fireman" his restiveness is given right from the start. In the novella Clarisse's fate is attributed to a reckless joyrider; she is killed "for no purpose at all."[10] In the novel, by contrast, her mysterious disappearance raises the paranoid possibility of removal by the authorities. The multiple literary allusions, the final references to apocalypse, and the complex symbolism of fire are yet to come in "The Fireman," whose very title, like "The Pedestrian," locks Montag into a social category. In contrast, Bradbury's title for the novel evokes a process charged with symbolic potential.

As early as the novella, Bradbury had decided on a clear structure. He later explained: "I constructed 'The Fireman' in three acts with a sort of general overall pattern of beginning, middle, and end, and this helped me later on when I began to build on that frame and began to turn it into *Fahrenheit 451*." At the end of each section in "The Fireman" and the novel alike, there was a strong "curtain line" to maximize the unfolding drama.[11]

The novella was published in H. L. Gold's *Galaxy* magazine, which attracted Bradbury because of that editor's avoidance of the prescription he found in other Science Fiction journals. In the same issue where "The Fireman" appeared, Gold wrote that he was encouraging new writers to "discard the shabby wrappings in which Science Fiction has been embalmed; mummified, almost."[12] Apart from this editorial openness, another contributor to *Galaxy* was to become a close friend of Bradbury's. In December 1950, Richard Matheson published one of his most famous stories, "When the Waker Sleeps," which ironically inverts the title of H. G. Wells's dystopian novel *The Sleeper Awakes*. Set in the far future, Matheson's story describes a streamlined urban society from the perspective of a captain in the state militia. Within this militaristic society, "the people were the machines, more than the machines themselves. A slave race, a despicable residue, hopeless, without hope."[13]

Matheson's dystopia broadly resembles Bradbury's and in 1951, shortly after reading "The Fireman," Matheson began a correspondence triggered by their shared social concerns. Bradbury stressed his desire to expand his coverage of instant media gratification. As he explained, "the great centrifuge of radio, television, pre–thought-out movies, and so forth. Gives us no time to 'stop and stare.' Our lives are getting more scheduled all the time." Matheson agreed wholeheartedly and commented on their shared purpose of "tearing shreds out of television and movies and Joe McCarthy and the insidious rise of a materialism in this country almost as bad as that in Russia."[14]

Bradbury was completing *Fahrenheit 451* against the background of the 1952 presidential election, when his own favored candidate Adlai Stevenson lost to Eisenhower. Bradbury attributed this in part to Stevenson's failure to speak out against McCarthyism, which he himself did that same year in the Hollywood *Daily Variety*, declaring: "let us send McCarthy and his friends back to Salem and the 17th century."[15] Bradbury has repeatedly made the purpose of his novel clear, considering it a "direct attack against the sort of thing he stood for," and in a 1976 interview he expanded on this: "Well, that all came about during the Joseph McCarthy era. . . . Everybody sort of sat around and let McCarthy throw his weight around and nobody was brave. So I got angry at the whole thing and said to myself that I didn't approve of book burning; I didn't approve of it when Hitler did it, so why should I be threatened about it by McCarthy?"[16] What Bradbury did not know was that when he spoke to a group in Malibu in 1959 about "The Fireman" and other writings, the event was monitored and reported to the FBI by an informant. A former member of the Communist Party paid Bradbury the indirect compliment of having reached a "large audience" and declared that the "general aim of these Science Fiction writers is to frighten the people into a state of paralysis or psychological incompetence bordering on hysteria."[17]

READING AND FREEDOM

This assertion from an unexpected quarter raises one of the central issues of *Fahrenheit 451*: the accessibility and impact of books. "The Library" (written 1947) is the first sketch in a series of writings by Bradbury on the library as a cultural space. Its opening establishes its central situation in no uncertain fashion:

> The people poured into the room. Health officials reeking of disinfectants, sprin-
> klers in their hands. Police officials, fierce with blazing badges. Men with metal
> torches and roach exterminators, piling one on another, murmuring, shouting,
> bending, pointing. The books came down in avalanche thunders. The books
> were torn and rent and splintered like beams. Whole towns and towers of books
> collapsed and shattered. Axes beat at the windows, drapes fell in black sooty
> clouds of dust.[18]

Here, the emphasis is clearly on assault as the space is invaded by anonymous officials whose actions associate books with criminality and risks to health.

Bradbury uses an expansive rhetoric where the books become indistinguishable from the building and from society in general. The only counter-voice is anonymous, simply named as "A," but he articulates a collective consciousness of readers whose voice pulls against the official ideology of book burning as cleansing or disinfecting. The officials in the sketch are indistinguishable not only from each other but also from their implements.

"Bright Phoenix" (1947–1948) elaborates on the nature of libraries and gives a more substantial account of book seizures. Here, the book-burners themselves are members of a fascistic militia called the United Legion. Now the narrator is the librarian of long standing who figures his workplace in pastoral terms: "I considered my library as a cool cavern or fresh, ever-growing forest into which men passed from the heat of the day and the fever of motion to refresh their limbs and bathe their minds an hour in the grass-shade illumination."[19] Green could literally denote the color of the reading lamps, but throughout Bradbury's works it suggests broader connotations of civic and psychological harmony. Unlike "The Library," where endings are presented as inevitable, the very title of "Bright Phoenix" hints at regeneration. The librarian evokes a place of timeless peace rudely disrupted by the incursion of a single official, closely followed by his fellow legionnaires, who come to seize many of the books. Their key piece of equipment consists of a "Baal incinerator," a large black oven where the impounded books are burned. The latter's uniforms suggest a quasi-military role, which is bewilderingly blocked by the librarian's pretense of not understanding their purpose. In that sense it is a tale of passive resistance, extended to the staff of the nearby café, who throw quotations at the officer to his increasing embarrassment. This anticipation of the quotation duel in *Fahrenheit 451*, reducing the officer to near-breakdown and, temporarily at least, defeats him. The ending of the story leaves it quite ambiguous whether or when the officials will return. The detail that the library has been selected in a "test town" implies a larger national plan, which might or might not be put into action.

The last rehearsal for *Fahrenheit 451*, "Pillar of Fire "(1948), extends even further Bradbury's social satire and use of fire symbolism, while examining the relation between past and present. The story is set in 2349, by which time all graveyards are being emptied. The protagonist William Lantry is a man out of time, the last corpse to escape the destruction of his grave, and one who lived during the first years of the twentieth century. Bradbury combines the Gothic theme of the living dead with the futuristic world of space travel in order to set up an actively hostile perspective on signs of "progress." The focal location in Lantry's town is the Incinerator:

> It never closed. . . .
>
> William Lantry entered the wide, well-lighted door. It was an entrance, really; there were no doors to open and shut. People could go in and out, summer or winter, the inside was always warm. Warm from the fires that rushed whispering up the high round flue to where the whirlers, the propellers, the air-jets pushed the leafy grey ashes on away for a ten mile ride down the sky.
>
> There was the warmth of the bakery here.[20]

Bradbury here sets up an ironic disparity between the incinerator as a place to visit and the incongruous analogy with a bakery. Published only three years after the end of the Second World War, this description clearly invites comparison with the concentration camps. The story's title evokes a visible sign of God, which through the incinerators has become secularized and commodified. Fire has become a symbol of life itself, officially pagan in tracing fire's origin from the Sun and burning as a symbolic return. Thus the heart of the incinerator resembles a "golden river" flowing up into the sky, death being refigured paradoxically as a bright, spectacular source of life.

The symbolic polarity of the story revolves around an opposition between light and dark, one which Eller and Touponce have explained as follows: "the Apollonian sun of rationality and the Dionysian dark side of the mind encounter one another."[21] This commentary risks taking the story as a kind of psychic drama, whereas the narrative uses Lantry's growing estrangement to question the norms of the society, in particular its flight from death. Without conscious planning, Lantry turns into a rebel who sabotages his home incinerator, causing a massive explosion. At the same time he visits a library, always symbolic for Bradbury of the lost archive of the past, and requests Poe, Lovecraft, and other writers, whose works have been destroyed in the "Great Burning." Again paradoxically, Lantry can rebel against the regime only by imitating its own activities. He plans to go "from town to town, from country to country, destroying the Burners, the Pillars of Fire, until the whole clean magnificent framework of flame and cauterization was tumbled.[22]

Unlike Montag, who simply withdraws from burning, Lantry plans to turn the regime's practice against itself, blithely ignoring the fact that each explosion kills hundreds of people. Inevitably he is arrested and questioned about his actions. Although his original purpose was to reinstate the carnivalesque side to horror, Lantry's interrogator McClure insists that he would simply be placing himself in ultimate isolation. As they prepare Lantry for incineration, he recites a mantra of the literary tradition the regime is attempting to wipe out: "I am Dunsany and Machen and I am the legend of Sleepy Hollow."[23] As in *Fahrenheit 451*, he draws no distinction between works and authors, and at the moment that he is being thrust into the incinerator, he shrieks a line from Poe's tale of immurement, "The Cask of Amontillado." The would-be liberator has become Gothic victim.

Looking back from the 1970s, Bradbury explained "Pillar of Fire" as being "caused by the quasi-intellectuals who mob through our society bullying us about our tastes, telling us that comic-strip cartoon books are bad for our digestion, worse for our imagination, and so should be burned."[24] Bradbury here clearly alludes to the 1948 burnings of comic books in Binghamton, New York, later endorsed by the psychologist Fredric Wertham, whose 1954 study *The Seduction of the Innocent* attacked the supposedly corrupting effects of comic books. Wertham later became included in Bradbury's list of reality instructors to be attacked in the cause of imaginative freedom.[25] "Pillar of Fire" pits Lantry against a rationalistic, utilitarian and supposedly progressive society where space travel has become a norm. In that sense, as Bradbury recognized retrospectively, "Pillar of Fire" was a trial run for *Fahrenheit 451*. Fire is promoted by the state as a cleansing force bringing peace and security. A character in the dramatization makes explicit the utopian ideal of janitorship that would be pursued further in the novel: "We've finally done it," he exclaims. "Cleaned the earth, tidied up the soil, cleansed mankind of flesh and bones, of ribs and skulls." Lantry counters this attack on the imagination with a little help from Aldous Huxley by retorting: "Oh, unbrave new world that has such cowards in it."[26]

BRADBURY AND THE DYSTOPIAS

This allusion to one of the most influential dystopian novels signals an important link between the two writers. Bradbury had been reading Huxley since high school and finally read *Brave New World* at the end of 1944.[27] By 1950 he claimed to "have admired Huxley for years" and later described Huxley as his "literary hero" since reading that novel.[28] Bradbury finally met his hero in 1950 while he was working on the novella version of *Fahrenheit 451* and subsequently praised Huxley's capacity to mediate between different cultural areas.[29]

Bradbury drew on a number of key features of *Brave New World* for his own novel. Huxley describes an economic utopia based on efficiency where the state slogan of "social stability" rationalizes an institutional suppression of history. Essentially, it is a present-tense culture where books have virtually disappeared. As in *Fahrenheit 451*, the disappearance of books has not only happened by government fiat, but mainly from a collective lack of interest in them, although Chapter 12 opens with Controller Mustapha Mond blocking publication of a scientific work that might be "potentially subversive." Citizens instead can enjoy the "benefits" of organized games, "feely" cinema (Huxley's extension of the "talkies"), synthetic music, and clothes of simulated material. Technological progress has culminated in a culture of immediate gratification through soma, the state drug, the "feelies," and "solidarity Services." Huxley later explained such episodes as state-directed: "In *Brave New World* non-stop distractions of the most fascinating nature (the feelies, orgy-porgy, centrifugal bumblepuppy) are deliberately used as instruments of policy, for the purpose of preventing people from paying too much attention to the realities of the social and political situation."[30] By the 1950s, Huxley saw this fantasy being realized in contemporary America.

In *Brave New World*, happiness is achieved through gratification. When Bernard Marx questions Lenina about freedom, she retorts: "I am free. Free to have the most wonderful time. Everybody's happy nowadays."[31] The concept of freedom is offset by characters' fears of being stigmatized as different and therefore abnormal. Again in anticipation of Bradbury's novel, one of the two protagonists of *Brave New World* (Bernard) is a misfit going against the system and is advised by the Director that he is simply going through a phase that will pass. The Controller Mustapha Mond, like Bradbury's Beatty, functions as a spokesman for the system. Indeed, the dialogue between Mond and John Savage in Chapter 16—the conceptual core of the novel—anticipates the ex-change of quotations between Montag and Beatty, with the same weighting of the argument toward stability and general happiness. Where Montag is supposedly shot down toward the end of Bradbury's novel, Bernard's dissatisfactions with the regime become converted into a feely on flagellation and he becomes such a media celebrity that he finally commits suicide. Despite other similarities, the endings of *Brave New World* and *Fahrenheit 451* contrast starkly in that Huxley gives the reader an image of despair whereas Bradbury opens up the possibility of change, however symbolic.

Huxley draws our attention to the political malleability of words themselves. Helmholtz Watson remains one of the few characters still interested in books, but he views language behavioristically as a technician of effects, devoting his inventiveness to slogans and lecturing on the "use of rhymes in moral propaganda and advertising."[32] Bradbury's 1948 story "Referent" describes an institutionalized training facility that draws on Huxley and possibly on Korzybski's General Semantics movement, which was influencing SF writers like A. E. Van Vogt, Robert Heinlein, and John W. Campbell. The year is 1997. A boy called Roby is having his spell on Orthopaedic (literally "corrective educational") Island, a kind of dystopian summer camp with a regime of Semantics and other subjects. As one of the officials tells him, "everything controlled, dear boy!" One day a mysterious spacecraft lands and disgorges a tall pale man, who bewilderingly changes shape constantly, claiming to be a *"pure* referent" outside any sign system.[33] "Referent" deals with one of Bradbury's most abstract themes, the referentiality of nouns, but the issue of institutional control links it with Huxley's regime and the exploitation of "semantic cue words" by the advertising company in Pohl and Kornbluth's *The Space Merchants* (1953).

Bradbury was clearly more influenced by Huxley than Orwell, but also by a third work, acknowledged in an essay of 1953: "Consider the similarity," he states, "between two books—Koestler's *Darkness at Noon*, laid in our recent past, and George Orwell's *1984*, set in a future now behind us. Once we were poised between the two, between a dreadful reality and an unformed terror."[34] We shall see shortly what Koestler suggested to Bradbury. With Orwell, looking back on his own novel, he has stated: "I deliberately did not read 1984 because I knew I would be working on a similar novel and did not want to be influenced."[35] While Huxley suggested a satirical method and an ideal breadth of mind, Orwell's novel came to suggest an expectation of disaster, which Bradbury wrote against in two essays called "Beyond 1984."

In 1979 he predicted that that the year would not be a "Kremlin gargoyle or an Orwellian beast," arguing that the future lay with the development of the U.S. space program.[36]

Fahrenheit 451 belongs in that body of SF published just after the Second World War, which gradually took over the function of social criticism previously performed by realist fiction. In one of the first pieces of criticism on these works, Kingsley Amis described Science Fiction of that period as an "instrument of social diagnosis and warning." He gives pride of place in his discussion to writers ranging from Philip Wylie to Alfred Bester and Bradbury himself. Indeed, he praises *Fahrenheit 451* as the "most skillfully drawn of all Science Fiction's conformist hells."[37] The novel shares an overall pattern common to two of the most famous dystopias of the period. Frederik Pohl and Cyril Kornbluth's *The Space Merchants* ran originally as a serial, "Gravy Planet," in *Galaxy* magazine during 1952, the year after "The Fireman" had appeared in that same journal. Bradbury had known Pohl since 1939 and read Kurt Vonnegut's *Player Piano* (1952) soon after publication, starting a friendship with that writer.[38]

All three novels focus on a protagonist working within an organization with which he becomes increasingly dissatisfied. Under the impact of a catalytic character or event, these dissatisfactions gradually come to a head and result in final separation from that organization. In *Player Piano*, Paul Proteus is working within an industrial complex loosely modeled on General Electric, and Vonnegut explores the latter's human cost for the protagonist's lifestyle: "It was an appalling thought, to be so well-integrated into the machinery of society and history as to be able to move in only one plane and in one direction."[39] As in *Fahrenheit 451*, the narrative voice shadows Paul's consciousness, making dissatisfactions come to the fore as the novel progresses. The difference lies in the subtlety of this process. Where Bradbury expresses the growth of Montag's awareness through metaphor and gesture, Vonnegut loses the psychological dimension to the drama through explicit statement. Mitchell Courtney in *The Space Merchants* is a "copysmith" within an advertising agency, a title which ironically straddles "wordsmith" and repetition. Since all three novels project their respective organizations as models of government, dialogue becomes ritualized from the pressure toward conformist "normality," and as a result any kind of unorthodox behavior is officially interpreted as pathological.

Courtney's latest project in *The Space Merchants* is to persuade customers to invest in migration to Venus, despite the detail that the planet is not life-supporting. Like the TV shows in *Fahrenheit 451*, the promotional video projects a stylized version of domestic life, showing a "spacious suburban roomette in the early morning." The scene of a nuclear family having breakfast dissolves into a "highly imaginative series of shots of Venus as it would be when the child grows up—verdant valleys, crystal lakes, brilliant mountain vistas."[40] Tom Moylan's comment on this novel applies equally well to Vonnegut and Bradbury when he argues that *The Space Merchants* was "written at a time when the twin disciplinary apparatuses of consumerism (which commanded obedience to a new culture of immediate gratification) and anticommunism (which commanded loyalty by way of the imposition of fear."[41] Oppositional groups are evoked throughout *Player Piano* and *The Space Merchants* as shadowy subversives, only emerging as a present actuality late in *Fahrenheit 451*. These novels trace their protagonist's movement to locations symbolically outside their regimes while at the same time questioning the very possibility of such a separate existence.

In all three dystopias the protagonist is initially defined through his position within an organization. Paul Proteus is an expert on managerial orthodoxy; Mitchell Courtney is a specialist in designing adverts and in the manipulative use of words; and, of course, Guy Montag's own specialism is the detection and destruction of illegal books. Like the FBI of the time, Bradbury's firemen respond to anonymous messages tipping them off about neighbors. Whatever the positions held by these protagonists, their duties carry political implications in that they are well placed within the local regime to close off dissent. They are, in short, organization men. In his classic 1956 study, which popularized this phrase, William H. Whyte identified a new ethic of corporate pressures working against the individual, where the organization became a utopian model of government.[42] Bradbury's choice of Montag's surname may refer to the first working day of the week, and the first visual detail given of his appearance is his helmet, the institutional sign of his role.

THE POLITICS OF *FAHRENHEIT 451* AND SYMBOLISM OF FIRE

Fahrenheit 451 narrates the growing tension between Montag's initial loyalty to his organization and the regime on the one hand, and his mounting dissatisfaction with his occupation on the other. These conflicted loyalties for Kevin

Hoskinson make the novel characteristic of the Cold War period, although Bradbury carefully avoids including historical details that would date quickly.[43] Also evocative of the early 1950s is the Orwellian practice of anonymously reporting neighbors to the authorities; it is one of Bradbury's many ironies that Montag is betrayed by his wife. The novel's topography includes place names that evoke the United States but otherwise distinguishes only symbolically between the generic locations of city and countryside. Similarly, descriptive specifics do not suggest a specific period. In a 1953 essay Bradbury identifies the action as taking place in 1999, a date suggesting maximum imminence.[44]

By linking the firemen with Ben Franklin, cofounder of the first fire service in 1736, Bradbury ties them into American national history, but then of course inverts their function. By so doing he conflates two civic functions—the police and fire service—and associates Montag's work with the detection of social nonconformity. As the novel progresses, explicit allusions broaden the narrative's historical resonance, but this time to burning as a means of control. In one of his prefaces to the novel, Bradbury discusses its gestation through the draft stories discussed earlier, referring to the "Chief Censor" in "Bright Phoenix" and elsewhere he recalls seeing newsreels of the 1930s: "when Hitler burned a book I felt it as keenly . . . as his killing a human, for in the long sum of history they are one and the same flesh."[45] The links are clear, strengthened in the novel by an allusion to Nicholas Ridley who was burned at the stake in 1555. Censorship, book-burning, and execution for heresy are all part of the same process for Bradbury, one with both a long history and a certain topicality in the United States. In a 1953 speech, President Eisenhower told students at Dartmouth College: "Don't join the book burners. . . . Don't be afraid to go into your library and read every book."[46] And in the same year the poet Richard Armour offered practical advice on "How to Burn a Book," stating that "an increasingly popular place for book burning is the middle of a street or, even better, a town square. This makes possible the burning of a larger number of books at one time. . . . Another advantage is that this type of burning can be watched by a large number of townspeople and can become something of a social event."[47] Armour's facetious suggestions are repeated by Faber in *Fahrenheit 451* as an ironic comment on crowds gathering "for the pretty blaze."[48]

In centering his narrative on firemen, Bradbury skillfully exploits a disparity between the familiarity of the term and their actual function. This estrangement effect was strategic. As he later explained, he was attempting to engage with a subject that would not date quickly. Thus, *"Fahrenheit 451* has social commentary in it," but "it has Science Fictional tricks to keep your interest. . . . From the very start of the novel, everything is fantastic, everything is futuristic," including the work of the fire department.[49]

To readers in the early 1950s the image of an official carrying a fire hose and containers of kerosene would recall the flame throwers from the Second World War, in other words a soldier rather than a policeman. This effect is even more pointed in Truffaut's film adaptation where the hand-piece resembles a machine gun. The famous opening of *Fahrenheit 451* is a rhetorical set piece, which introduces a whole range of fire symbolism, not least its associations with power:

> It was a pleasure to burn.
>
> It was a special pleasure to see things eaten, to see things blackened and *changed*. With the brass nozzle in his fists, with this great python spitting out its venomous kerosene upon the world, the blood pounded in his head, and his hands were the hands of some amazing conductor playing all the symphonies of blazing and burning to bring down the tatters and charcoal ruins of history (1).

The typographic separation of the first sentence from the following paragraph increases the ambiguity of "burn," which, if transitive, looks forward to the objects enumerated here; if intransitive, it suggests fever, even of a sexual kind.[50] The main paragraph evokes the power of burning, evoking its results as spectacle. Then through the snake analogy, Bradbury conflates the orgasmic pleasure of consumption and pollution in a generalized and internal description, but an anonymous one. It is only after this paragraph concludes that Montag is named. In other words, his identity emerges from his generic institutional actions. The "he" of this paragraph could be any fireman.

The primary connotation of fire is with change, which Bradbury makes a condition of his rhetoric. The mobility of symbolic associations implies an obsession with power by the operative, as if he could control history itself. As python, he momentarily adopts the role of the earth dragon in mythology; as director, he appears to act on behalf of a larger collective (the state), although his manual actions are basically limited to pointing the hose in a certain direction. For all its emphasis on destruction, the opening reference to "pigeon-winged books" introduces a major motif linking books with birds, traditional embodiments of free life. As Donald Watt has shown, the complex shifting symbolism of fire underpins the action of the novel at every turn, between the broad poles of "burning as constructive energy, and burning as apocalyptic catastrophe."[51] Just as fire changes significance from scene to scene, so there is an interplay throughout the novel between light and darkness. One of the first signs of the latter comes in the opening scene when Montag sees his own mirror reflection as a "minstrel man." The introspection implied by mirrors can develop only after the stimulus of Montag's meeting with Clarisse, but already blackness is carrying associations of conformity (the uniform) and the performance of a public role distorting his inner self. Ultimately the regime's institutional color links its actions with death.

Through the catalyst of Clarisse, burning shifts from an institutional activity to an internal fever, a dissatisfaction growing below the level of his consciousness. The "infection" starts with Montag's hands, the limbs of action, and gradually extends throughout his body and mind. The ideological justification of the book-burning is through an appeal to health. Control is thus encoded as welfare. If the environment is kept clean and tidy, everyone will live better as a result. Writing on the film adaptation of *Fahrenheit 451*, though his comments apply equally well to the novel, George Bluestone argues that "collective pyromania does not treat its objects of destruction as enemies to be fought but as infections to be cauterized."[52] Throughout the novel, dissent is presented pathologically as a disease to be cured. Bradbury ingeniously weaves this ideological motif into the most sinister "creature" in the novel, the mechanical hound. The hound can kill, but by injecting substances that are benign in a medical context, namely morphine and procaine. Both are anesthetics and in that respect link in with Bradbury's depiction of the regime as supporting and extending tranquilizer use, his own version of Huxley's soma.

The opening paragraph of the novel establishes Montag's function as focalizer but not narrator, a crucial distinction that right from the start indicates the importance of the novel's subtext. What Montag witnesses sets the conditions for events, but the rhetorical third person hints constantly at a space for inferences, which initially can be drawn only through the regime's ideological projection of dissent as illness. Clarisse begins the process of exposing Montag's dissatisfaction by asking disturbingly simple questions like

"Have you *read* any of the books you burn?" (5). She describes herself as "seventeen and I'm crazy" (5), as if an official label supplied a convenient mask for her eccentricity. Symbolically, she is associated with candlelight rather than harsher electric light and also performs the function of weaving Bradbury's "The Pedestrian" into the backstory of the novel, recasting the pedestrian as her uncle. For all her quiet, childlike style, Clarisse encourages Montag to start asking questions of his fellow firemen, a risky thing to do at best, but something that immediately arouses the suspicion of Montag's superior Beatty.

If Montag is the focal figure to which all characters are referred, Beatty performs the roles of supervisor, tutor, and therapist when Montag claims to be ill. Eller and Touponce read him as a Nietzschean nihilist who relishes but discards contradictions, but Beatty represents a figure who appears in a number of dystopias—Mustapha Mond, O'Brien in *Nineteen Eighty-Four*—namely the official who is never completely defined by the regime despite his high position within its hierarchy.[53] Beatty was also suggested by Arthur Koestler's *Darkness at Noon*, which Bradbury read in 1944 and which was a formative influence on his novel. The Soviet dissident is interrogated at length by Ivanov, who combines historical instruction with psychoanalysis, and Bradbury later acknowledged that "the relationship of the fire chief and Montag, in many ways, is reflected in the communist leader and dissident."[54]

The dialogue with Beatty at Montag's home when the latter calls in ill constitutes the ideological core of the novel, the scene where the guiding principles of the state culture are revealed. Bradbury skilfully sets up a misleadingly benign situation where Beatty is puffing thoughtfully on his pipe, but as the scene progresses the smoke becomes so dense that it hides Beatty, who remains as a disembodied but authoritative voice. His habit of addressing Montag in the third person can also be read ambiguously either as infantilizing or as a strategy for denying Montag's individuality and referring to him as a typical case. Without ever quite accusing him of reading books, Beatty neutralizes such an act as a phase every fireman passes though. He also explains cultural history, despite the regime's line that things have always been like this, as an acceleration out of the nineteenth century: "Then, in the twentieth century, speed up your camera. Books cut shorter. Condensations. Digests.

Tabloids. Everything boils down to the gag, the snap ending" (52). Beatty defines the present age through its new medium and mimes out the very process he is describing through truncated sentences. The transformation is explained as a triumph of the media: "thanks to them you can stay happy all the time"; but also as a perverse form of democracy, "each man the image of the other; then all are happy" (55). What Beatty minimizes in his account is agency, as if the changes he describes simply happened as spontaneous processes. But, as Rafeeq McGiveron has argued, "mass exploitation in the novel begins long before the minority pressure" and has its roots in the possibilities of manipulation embedded in the media themselves.[55]

There is an ironic twist to Beatty's exposition; despite Montag's claim that the two men are "talking," the scene has virtually become an extended monologue, a "lecture," as Beatty himself admits. Montag's silence throws his superior's words into prominence as if through him Bradbury was mounting an ironic challenge to the reader to refute or accept his words. There is a paradox in Beatty's account, however. By definition, he is articulating the very awareness that these cultural changes are encouraged to exclude. Is he a unique case or are there other Beattys? And secondly, despite the fact that he is speaking as the apologue of a system that is being satirized, his explanation coincides closely with Bradbury's own. Casting himself as a representative of the "custodians of our peace of mind" (56), Beatty explains de facto censorship as a removal of disturbing elements. If a book "upsets" people, remove it. The incinerator, which in Bradbury's early library stories performs a sinister destructive function, here functions as a means of cleansing. Beatty slides easily from books to people in his recommendation of cremation in the "Big Flue" by the same logic of removing any source of disturbance from the culture.

The counter-role to Beatty's is played by Faber, the retired English professor who engages in a real dialogue with Montag rather than merely expounding ideology. His introduction enables Bradbury to bring out the political issues and he supplies an external critical view of the regime that questions Beatty's near monologue. The meetings with Faber are synchronized with Montag's growing awareness of a clash of voices like that between the Bible and the electronic advert in the subway. Thanks to Faber, Montag's external perspective on the media is sharpened through his ironic dialogues with Mildred and her friends, a process that culminates when he watches a look-alike of himself being hunted down and shot on the TV. By this point Montag has developed a capacity to see through the cinematic tricks (soft focus, long shots), which are exploited to supply viewers with a fiction of closure.

Montag's second confrontation with Beatty comes when he exchanges quotations with Montag in a latter-day battle of the books, which Beatty clearly wins. This episode underlines a metafictional irony that has hardly been commented on. Because books are banned in this future world, the reader is from the very beginning implicated in illegality by simply taking up the novel to read. Furthermore, the novel never allows us to forget the status of books as objects or as texts, and deploys allusions and quotations toward this end. Peter Sisario has commented rightly that Bradbury is ironically "using books to underscore his ideas about a world in which great books themselves have been banned."[56] As Montag relearns the skill of reading, he quotes from Swift, Boswell, and finally Arnold's "Dover Beach" to articulate the impoverished lifestyle of Mildred and her friends. The latter poem references the tension between scientific evolutionism and religion, focusing on the loss of faith, and its quotation thematically introduces the biblical passages that occur in the conclusion.

These passages form part of Montag's attempts to make fresh sense of his situation, whereas the "quotation duel" is framed, or rather controlled, entirely by Beatty as a dream in which he ridicules Montag by drawing on a greater range of texts. The "exchange" is essentially a piece of power play on Beatty's part, just as he uses the card game with the firemen as an implicit test of orthodoxy. Beatty's speed of quotation assaults Montag like a physical attack, and his passages repeatedly subvert category distinctions between animal and human, folly and reason. In short, Beatty's quotations become, to use one of his own appropriated phrases, a "torrent of verbiage" that Montag is unable to resist, all the more threatening because mounted with the secret knowledge that Montag has been betrayed to the authorities (103). The only way that Montag can silence Beatty is by burning him, turning the state's weapon against its own enforcer.

The end of Part Two thus marks a turning point in that Montag now becomes situated as a murderer as well as dissident, a change symbolized by his destruction of his home. Bradbury has directed his satire of postwar American society against the very sign of prosperity in that period. Montag's generic neighborhood is described by William H. Whyte as being part of the "packaged villages that have become the dormitory of the new generation of organization men."[57] This world of identical houses, lived in by identical residents, is satirized in Pohl and Kornbluth's *Gladiator-at-Law* (1955) where a suburban housing development ("Belle Reve") has degenerated into a slum ("Belly Rave"). Whyte reported on Park Forest, a commuter suburb near Chicago, which started selling homes in 1951. A marketing brochure declared: More home for a woman to enjoy / And more for a man to come home to.[58] The gendering of activity couldn't be clearer. The man goes to work; the woman is the "homemaker," as Montag's wife Mildred proudly declares.

This suburban lifestyle was satirized in Shepherd Mead's *Big Ball of Wax* (1955), which describes an America as it might become by 1992. As in *Fahrenheit 451*, the home is dominated by television. Whole walls are convertible into TV screens and programs flattened out into a show. Even the weather forecast becomes a performance: "The master of ceremonies changed hats—of which he had at least two dozen—told a joke, and then switched to cameras in Manhattan, White Plains, and Garden City. It was raining in all three places. A pretty girl dressed in pink and blue Momsday colors brought out big cards with the temperature, barometric pressure, wind velocity" (8).[59] *Big Ball of Wax* brings together a number of themes dealt with in Bradbury's own depiction of suburbia: the new dominance of the media, the use of synthetic materials and labor-saving gadgetry, the standardization of "custom-built" housing, the reduction of reading matter to comic strips, and the promotion of consumables like "Joylies," a nicotine substitute.

In his description of television programs in "The Fireman," Bradbury presents a similar stream of spectacles: "there on the screen was a man selling orange soda pop and a woman drinking it with a smile; how could she drink and smile simultaneously? A real stunt! Following this, a demonstration of how to bake a certain new cake, followed by a rather dreary domestic comedy, a news analysis that did not analyze anything . . . and an intolerable quiz show naming state capitals."[60] The speed of this sequence is subsequently explained by Beatty in the novel as an acceleration away from thought. Thus the news program is negated and the quiz show described as projecting an early form of what Bradbury later called "factoids," contextless snippets of information.

In *Fahrenheit 451*, Bradbury focuses specifically on the TV show as a simulation of family life. Mildred's routine combination of tranquilizers and TV viewing anticipates Marshall McLuhan's argument in *Understanding Media* (1964), i.e., that the contemporary media induce a state of narcosis in the consumer. Television thus becomes an electronic tranquilizer. For Mildred, pills and television reinforce each other and for this reason Mildred has been described as embodying "just about every form of self-narcotization available in this society."[61] Her addiction to the family sitcom functions as a substitute for actual family life and her dream of a fourth-wall television screen is a fantasy of total enclosure. As in Vonnegut's *Player Piano*, her speech has atrophied to brief cues and responses, and the "interactive" TV program presents only a simulation of participation. In another, the effect is of speeding in a fast car, whose noise makes conversation virtually impossible.

Although Bradbury foregrounds the media, he situates them within a larger process of consumption that reduces Mildred's body to disparate features: "her eyes with a kind of cataract unseen but suspected far behind the pupils, the reddened pouting lips, the body as thin as a praying mantis from dieting, her flesh like white bacon" (45–46). Consumption is evoked as an atrophy of the body and a disease of vision, a key sense throughout the novel. In the aftermath of Mildred's overdose, Montag imagines walls between himself and his wife. In the draft of this episode as preserved in *Long after Midnight*, the symbolism of barriers has not yet emerged. In its early form, the passage conveys separation in terms of explicit attention to the media: "They were never together. There was always something between. A radio, a television set, a car, a plane, nervous exhaustion, a mad rushing, or, simply, a little phenol-barbitol."[62] The prose here mimes out a hectic tempo to daily life. This proliferation of technology implies a mechanistic view of the body, which becomes evident when medical technicians "service" Mildred after her overdose. The very fact that such visits are routine raises questions about the happiness that Beatty claims is universal and at the same time introduces

Bradbury's second subject. The citizens of this brave new society are reduced to the single function of consumption, and television with the other technological features of the society have become "instruments of state control."[63]

NUCLEAR WAR

Bradbury's ironic evocation of suburban material comfort is set against a widespread fear of the period, which SF addressed more directly than any other genre, namely the fear of war. He suggests the effect of, and perhaps the intention behind, television is to distract society from politics in general and specifically from signs of war. If Lewis Mumford was right that suburbia offered the possibility of a retreat into a private world, the resulting dissociation of personal life from the political is shown though the characters' lack of reaction to the jets that repeatedly roar overhead. The first description is the loudest: "the sky over the house screamed. There was a tremendous ripping sound as if two giant hands had torn ten thousand miles of black linen down the seam. Montag was cut in half. He felt his chest chopped down and split apart. The jet-bombs going over, going over, going over, one two, one two, one two" (11). Mildred is literally unconscious at this point, but metaphorically she and her friends fail to register the sound of the bombers.

We saw in *The Martian Chronicles* how nuclear war was evoked as a fear motivating the flight from Earth or blocking settlers' return from Mars. With the exception of "There Will Come Soft Rains" it was a distant issue, referred to but never described, whereas in "The Fireman" war is established right from the start as imminent. Within the first few lines of a voice-over the radio announces: "War may be declared."[64] In that respect the novella takes the reader straight into one of the dominant fears of the period. By the late 1940s this had become one of the dominant subjects in SF stories, and in 1947 *The Bulletin of the Atomic Scientists* introduced its famous cover icon of the Doomsday Clock set initially at seven minutes to midnight. Its 1950 articles included a hypothetical description of the bombing of Washington and a whole issue on civil defense against atomic attack. Bradbury's grim sketch of a postnuclear automated household, "There Will Come Soft Rains," inspired by one of the photographs of Hiroshima, first appeared in *Collier's* magazine in 1950. In October the following year the magazine devoted a whole issue to future reportage called "Preview of the War We Do Not Want," which included contributions by Arthur Koestler and the novelist Philip Wylie, together with graphic descriptions of the bombing of New York and Detroit. Also in 1951, the U.S. authorities first showed the *Duck and Cover* civil defense film for schools. In these ways the expectation of war became institutionalized as an imminent threat where time itself took on a critical significance as a countdown to zero hour.

In *Fahrenheit 451*, as Montag's promotion of reading becomes more explicit, so does the revelation of the international context to the action. In Part Two of the novel, he attempts to force a consciousness on Mildred of America's place in the world by contrasting its triumph in a series of atomic wars with poverty elsewhere in the world, an indirect allusion to the Marshall Aid scheme. Bradbury's novel was published against the immediate background of the Korean War, and at one point Montag disrupts Mildred's gathering with her friends by questioning them about the war currently being waged. When asked why their husbands are missing, Mrs. Phelps's answer is typical: "Oh, they come and go, come and go . . . the Army called Pete yesterday. He'll be back next week. The army said so. Quick war" (90). The staccato phrases exemplify the culture of sound bites identified by Beatty elsewhere, here functioning like a reassuring mantra of official statements, which might or might not be true.

War is presented as serial in the novel. There have already been two nuclear wars (three in "The Fireman"), but the assumption in the scene just discussed is that it will happen elsewhere. The climax comes with a local nuclear strike. Montag imagines Mildred in her hotel room watching the TV screen; then "in the millionth part of time left, she saw her own face reflected there, in a mirror instead of a crystal ball, and it was such a wildly empty face . . . that at last she recognized it as her own" (152). Bradbury here faces a problem confronting any writer trying to describe a nuclear strike. A detonation would last only a fraction of a second but Bradbury awkwardly tries to draw out the duration of the event to moralize it as a last moment of self-realization. Also Mildred has already receded into the past of a consumer culture that Montag has abandoned.

When Bradbury turns his attention to the fate of the city, the rhetoric works more powerfully as a quasicinematic sequence:

For another of those impossible instants the city stood, rebuilt and unrecogniz-
able . . . erected at last in gouts of shattered concrete and sparkles of torn metal
into a mural hung like a reversed avalanche, a million colors, a million oddities,
a door where a window should be, a top for a bottom, a side for a back, and then
the city rolled over and fell down dead. (153)

In a freeze-frame effect, Bradbury retains the scale of the city, but gives it a
surreal transformation into suspended fragments and displaced parts of a
whole that no longer exists. The bomb blast, in other words, marks a rupture
not only to the culture but to Bradbury's mode of narration, as we shall see.

In his writings from around 1950, Bradbury uses the short story form to
give us partial glimpses of the larger narrative of nuclear war. In common
with other writers of the period, he evokes different phases of expectation
and aftermath in his treatment of the bomb. "The Last Night of the World"
(1951), occasioned by Bradbury's anxieties over the Eniwetok H-bomb test,
presents a let's-pretend dialogue between a man and a woman about how they
would deal with the end of the world from a nuclear war. With a light irony
Bradbury replaces apocalypse with a comic realism. The detailed practicali-
ties of the speakers' lives prevent them from imagining an ultimate end, and
the title remains what it was at the beginning—a hypothesis. "The Garbage
Collector" (1953) is a similar dialogue narrative raising questions about the
announcement that Los Angeles garbage collectors will be expected to collect
corpses after a nuclear strike. This last was written out of Bradbury's indignation over the "terrible irony" of reducing the human body to garbage.[65]

In these stories and "The Highway," where a Mexican peasant hears from
fleeing travelers that "it" (i.e., nuclear war) has finally broken out, Bradbury
approaches the subject of war through realism but using an ironic disparity
between the potential scale of the event and the small situations where it is
registered. "And the Rock Cried Out" (1953) uses an even more oblique perspective by describing the increasing crisis experienced by a young American couple
traveling in Latin America while nuclear war in 1963 has destroyed the United
States and much of Europe. A newspaper headline announces that "the day
of the white people of the earth is over and finished" and the story dramatizes
the Webbses' painful discovery of this change through the erosion of every
security they had taken for granted.[66] The story traces a process of loss where

the travelers are blocked from crossing the border, forced to leave their car, and take refuge in a hotel during celebrations of "victory." Webb himself points out the historical irony of their situation, which is heightened by nuclear war. Bradbury's near-future extrapolation typically presents a remote perspective on this cataclysm to dramatize racial tensions. The other SF element of the story is introduced by an elderly local man who tells the Webbs that he has always been a keen reader of Jules Verne and used to speculate over a machine "that would help every man, for an hour, to be like any other man" (231). This kind of empathy machine, however, remains purely speculative, and the story reminds the reader throughout of the unbridgeable distance between the travelers and the locals. During the summer of 1957, Bradbury worked on a screenplay from this story, which was never filmed, Bradbury later reflected, because the racial subject was "considered politically dangerous."[67]

Paul Brians has shown that, from the very nature of this new form of warfare, in its potential scale and brevity, nuclear war fiction has much more in common with descriptions of apocalyptic disasters than other wars.[68] Bradbury's 1950 sketch "Bonfire" demonstrates this tendency by linking the destruction of artifacts like books and paintings with the killing of humans and ultimately with nuclear Armageddon. The focal character draws historical analogies with 1939, but ultimately his efforts at understanding fail before the sheer scale of the process. Bradbury concludes on an apocalyptic note, taking his narrative into a posthuman future: "The earth blew up and burned steadily for a thousand million centuries."[69] "To the Chicago Abyss" (1963), in contrast, explores survival in a nuclear aftermath where a totalitarian regime has outlawed any mention of the prenuclear past. The setting near a crater that used to be the location of Chicago contrasts with the bomb blast in *Fahrenheit 451*, which knocks flat the urban structure of that culture by suggesting a void and therefore a lack. The story traces out a dialogue between past and present as an old man wanders the area trying to fill the void by reciting the names of consumer items lost in the war. It is as if he has become a compulsive archive of lost products, whose recitation becomes an act of dissidence against the totalitarian regime attempting to suppress such memories. He sees the absurdity in his actions, declaring to one of his few listeners: "All I am, really, is a trash-heap of the mediocre, the third-best hand-me-down useless and chromed-over slush and junk of a racetrack civilization that ran "last" over a precipice."[70] The old man thus acts as the elegiac spokesman of a forbidden past.[71]

One of Bradbury's most ingenious treatments of nuclear war came in the story "To the Future," which first appeared in *Collier's* magazine in 1950. A young couple have used a time travel company to escape from a war in 2155 and from their work in producing nuclear ("hydrogen-plus") bombs and biological weapons. Bradbury uses a staple Wellsian theme of Science Fiction but reverses the direction of the travel, which is here an attempt at flight from an unbearable future back to Mexico in 1938. The future has become internalized by Susan as nightmare. She sees the "fifty thousand rows of disease cultures in their aseptic glass tubes, her hand reaching out to them at her work in that huge factory in the Future; the tubes of leprosy, bubonic, typhoid, tuberculosis, and then the great explosion. She saw her hand burned to a wrinkled plum."[72] The future is briefly evoked as a time of self-destructive militarism where the regime's technology has been directed entirely into the arms business.

A header in *Collier's* announces of the couple: "they are being searched out by men from another world."[73] However, Bradbury's aliens prove to be agents pursuing through time from a quasi-FBI agency called the Searchers. His revised title of "The Fox and the Forest" foregrounds this theme of pursuit, but rather at the expense of the ironies of time. The reader, like the protagonists, is positioned between a remote threatening future and a vulnerable past. When one agent is killed by them in a traffic "accident," the couple fall in with an American film crew and are offered the possibility of going to Hollywood. Until, that is, the director starts outlining a scenario that exactly matches their own situation. In a grim metafictional twist, Bradbury closes down the narrative after the director's camera projects a blue light that makes them disappear—presumably back to 2155. The presence of the film crew raises a sinister suggestion of how elaborately the couple's situation is being scripted. The detail of the blue light resembles a criticality accident from a nuclear device, implying that the couple haven't simply been removed but also fatally injured. Ironically, the same issue of *Collier's* where this story appeared carried an article about the commander of the task force testing H-bombs in Eniwetok Atoll; in other words, documenting the development of the very future that Bradbury's story was protesting against.

Science is central to nuclear war narratives. Bradbury's friend Henry Kuttner wrote a series of stories in the 1940s about the telepathic mutants (the "Baldies") produced by the radiation from a massive war, the "Blow-Up." And in his novel *Fury* (partly written by his wife C. L. Moore; serial 1947, book 1950), Earth has become a wasteland from uncontrolled atomic energy with a human remnant establishing itself in subterranean settlements on Venus. At the other extreme of technophobia, *The Long Tomorrow* (1955) by another of Bradbury's mentors, Leigh Brackett, describes two young boys' resistance to a postnuclear rural fundamentalism that attempts to suppress science. When they finally reach the legendary Bartorstown, the archive of this suppressed past, their guide tells them: "The bomb is a fact. Atomic power is a fact. . . . You can't deny it, you can't destroy it."[74] Bradbury's treatment of science tends to be more implicit than either of these writers, though he constantly suggests that the bomb and media emerge from a common pool of technology.

PASTORAL APOCALYPSE

In *Fahrenheit 451*, Bradbury removes Montag from the city, which is emblematic of the regime, to an alternative rural landscape. Indeed, the last phase of the novel replaces quasirealist narration with a symbolic sequence of scenes suggesting rebirth. Montag crosses a river into a new life; after his "execution" on TV, he is welcomed "back from the dead" by the Book People. The significance of the phoenix's regenerative life cycle is now made explicit.[75] Throughout *Fahrenheit 451*, Bradbury has insistently linked books, birds, and people. It is therefore consistent with this symbolism that in the last section of the novel people should *become* books. Collectively, the Book People represent a metaphor made flesh. As Eller and Touponce have rightly pointed out, the Book People imply a notion of textual production, which continues from authors to readers in an open-ended continuum.[76] Even more importantly, they enact the reappropriation of language and the reconstitution of memory common to dystopian misfits and rebels.[77] Geoffrey Hartman has argued cogently that the exclusion of authors' and readers' names alike "shows what ideally happens in the act of reading: if there is a sacrifice to the exemplary, it involves the aggrandizement neither of author nor of reader but leads into the recognition that something worthy of perpetuation has occurred."[78]

It is an important detail that Montag should be welcomed into the group by Granger, whose name recalls the populist movement of the 1860s and 1870s, dedicated to improving the lot of U.S. farmers. Like them, the Book People are rural, anticentralist, and loosely communitarian. Montag's first encounter around a campfire recalls the imagery of one of Bradbury's favorite novels—*The Grapes of Wrath*—and suggests that the movement reflects a populist response to hardship. As Granger explains to Montag, the movement took place spontaneously: "thousands on the roads, the abandoned railtracks, tonight, bums on the outside, libraries inside . . . over a period of twenty years or so, we met each other, traveling, and got the loose network together and set out a plan" (146). The evocation of hobo camps carries historical resonances with the 1930s and through a "metaphoric time-travel," while Montag recaptures lost childhood memories like the scent of leaves.[79] Though referenced through the past, these fireside discussions represent an unmediated communication lost in the dystopian world of the novel. Despite the consistency of this fire motif, John Huntington has argued that Bradbury ignores the implications of his "idealized hobo mystique," never considering the hardship that could lie behind the Book People's lives or the possibility that books themselves may have contributed to the novel's dystopian present.[80] In that respect Bradbury's allusions to history are selective in being heavily determined by the needs of his symbolic polarities.

The multiple meanings of fire, so central to *Fahrenheit 451*, are also exploited, more austerely, in Walter M. Miller's 1959 novel *A Canticle for Leibowitz*. Here, a massive nuclear war, mythologized as the "Flame Deluge," brings about a rupture in Western culture, and the novel retraces history as a rediscovery of technology, which ultimately leads to yet another nuclear war. As a commentator reflects toward the end of the novel, "have we no choice but to play the Phoenix in an unending sequence of rise and fall?" (280–281).[81] Miller is clearly drawing on the same pool of symbolism as Bradbury in having fire at different points signify rebirth, the growth of knowledge, communal action around a hearth, and even destruction.

It is in his description of the preservation of history that Miller's account approaches Bradbury's. In *A Canticle* the postnuclear Dark Age threatens the very existence of culture, a threat focused on the fate of books. A popular, neomonastic movement gets under way:

Its earliest habit was burlap rags and bindlestiffs—the uniform of the simpleton mob. Its members were either "bookleggers" or "memorizers," according to the tasks assigned. The bookleggers smuggled books to the south-west desert and buried them there in kegs. The memorizers committed to rote memory entire volumes of history, sacred writings, literature, and science, in case some unfortunate book smuggler was caught, tortured, and forced to reveal the location of the kegs. [The founder of the movement is strangled and burned alive.] Some of the book kegs were found and burned, as well as several other bookleggers.[82]

Miller puns on "bootleg" to draw an implicit analogy between rum-running during Prohibition (usually in kegs) and the covert preservation of books. As in Bradbury, the members of the movement are associated with hoboes, separated from any identifiable political cause, and basically identified as the opponents of a widespread assault on any traces of culture. Miller's novel describes the broader process of regaining cultural memory and expands very little on the quoted passage, which probably pays homage to Bradbury. The political undertones of the movement to preserve texts initially lead nowhere because, as Susan Spencer has pointed out, "by not giving privilege to any particular genre or subject, the monks have effectively depoliticized the medium."[83] Apart from the contrast between Bradbury's emphasis on literature and philosophy and Miller's "memorabilia," which includes all texts, a very striking difference between the novels emerges here. In *Fahrenheit 451*, we have seen how Montag's emerging consciousness sets a limit to the narration. The novel's perspective sticks rigorously to what Montag hears and sees, whereas Miller's narrator articulates an awareness of history much broader than any character within the novel. Miller adopts a prophetic narrative voice beyond the limits of any historical moment and repeatedly invites the reader to cross-relate figures and images from different periods. In the passage quoted earlier, for instance, criminal activity is revised into the promotion of cultural survival.

The sheer density of Miller's historical echoes implies that history is a script that humanity is fated to repeat again and again. The structure of *A Canticle* is cyclical in that it extrapolates an imminent point of nuclear war from which to construct a recapitulation of western history culminating in the same cataclysm that started the sequence. The only part of its conclusion that does not completely close the loop is the launch of a spaceship toward other worlds, carrying a saving remnant of humanity. In the introduction to his collection of stories about nuclear war (*Beyond Armageddon*), which includes Bradbury's "There Will Come Soft Rains" and "To the Chicago Abyss," Miller locates a common "nostalgia for things past," but also, more somberly, signs of an ambivalence toward science. "We worship reason in the West," he declares, but "the development of the Bomb was a triumph of intellect."[84] For him, therefore, reason itself becomes deeply suspect because of its destructive results.

In making his grim observations in 1985, during the last superpower confrontations of the Cold War, Miller attempts to estrange us from cultural values we have been taking for granted. Bradbury, in contrast, embeds the reader within an apocalyptic sequence so that we, like Montag, turn our eyes forward toward a posttext. It is important that his choice of text should be Ecclesiastes, which he cites for moral support on the last page of the novel: "A time to break down, and a time to build up" (3:iii). The passage underpins the destruction-reconstruction sequence just noted and the quotation from *Revelation* that follows further strengthens Bradbury's symbolism of living objects: "*And on either side of the river was there a tree of life, which bare twelve manner of fruits, and yielded her fruit every month; And the leaves of the tree were for the healing of nations* (158: italics in original).[85] Leaves introduced Clarisse in the opening and are associated throughout with sensual contact with Earth, which Montag regains only once he has crossed the river. The river in the quotation is shown as a divine revelation but coincides with the river followed by the Book People as a direction finder. Within the narrative and the quotation alike, it offers an image of promise, surcharging the last line of Bradbury's text—"when we reach the city"—with collective hope beyond its ending. The simple fact that the last scene takes place in a morning carries connotations of hope although it has been criticized for expressing only a "vague optimism."[86]

The use of the countryside as a location symbolically external to the novel's urban culture enables Bradbury to avoid the claustrophobia of Koestler and Orwell, where state enforcement carries execution as the ultimate end. In "The Jail," an austere story adapted from a teleplay in the 1960s, Bradbury explores punishment for speaking out against the government as a process of erasure where the culprit is filmed by cameras "printing his life on their inner eyes."[87] The montage narrative traces out an imposed dissociation of the character from his body and an elaborate application of technology that masks the humanity of his guards and reshapes the protagonist's identity. The fact that all this is filmed—presumably in secrecy—positions the reader uncomfortably as the passive subject of a state-promoted object lesson: "all the nation must watch and learn what it meant to speak out against its beautiful and kind government."[88]

FAHRENHEIT 451 AND CINEMA

This explicitly authoritarian control of vision does not occur in *Fahrenheit 451*, but because Bradbury uses Montag as the perspective character, the novel already possesses strong visual elements in its narrative even before we consider its adaptation. Montag's first encounter with Clarisse, for instance, is described in cinematic terms as if the girl is moving along a "sliding walk" (3). Once they start talking, the perspective closes up on Clarisse's eyes reflecting images of Montag. And when he reaches his house he mentally projects onto the wall a memory image of the girl. The meeting radically affects Montag's conditions of seeing. The morning after Mildred's overdose the world seems to have sunk into a monochrome "dark gray" and when Montag goes to the firehouse he is unnerved to realize that the firemen are "all mirror-images of himself" (30). Mirroring recurs throughout the novel, reflecting Montag's evolving capacity to discover versions of himself in others.[89] His progression therefore combines a visual recognition of similarities and differences, but also a growing intelligence in his visual scrutiny of scenes.

That initial encounter with Clarisse heightens and estranges Montag's sense of vision so that even without opening his eyes he can see a defect in his wife's eyes. He develops a sharper sensitivity to the welter of synthetic color and sound, which bombards his senses from the television: "Behind her the walls of the room were flooded with green and yellow and orange fireworks sizzling and bursting" (56). The sensory overload here of color without image and therefore without meaning connects implicitly with the "smoke pattern" of Beatty's pipe as he expounds the regime's media practice. The fact that during the latter, Beatty's features become invisible suggests the confusion, visual and conceptual, which he is creating in Montag. The culmination to this process comes when Montag no longer recognizes his own home as he burns it down and when he is repositioned as a spectator of himself refracted through thousands of TV screens and finally simulated in his own screen "death." When he finally joins the Book People, one sign is their capacity to "look at the world and turn it over with their eyes" (139). Thus, even before any screen adaptations were planned for *Fahrenheit 451*, Bradbury had written a cinematic dimension into the narrative handling of scene, perspective, and image.

Truffaut's 1966 film engages in a complex dialogue with the novel, bringing out important issues implicit in Bradbury's narrative. When working on the script in 1962, Truffaut aimed at a screenplay that would be "quite faithful to the book, but much more realistic and closer to home." Originally he had conceived of an "SF film, set in the future and backed by inventions and gadgetry and so on."[90] But then along came the first Bond films, Pop Art, and other developments, which necessitated a major rethink, involving far fewer futuristic elements. Later, in 1965, he elaborated on this position by stating that the "visual principle of the film will be contemporary life with just a slight twist."[91] An early scene that embodies this estrangement effect occurs during the first raid. Montag's acolytes help him into the fireproof suit as if he were a cleric donning his robes, an action that captures the ritualistic aspect of the book burning.

Truffaut sent Bradbury his screenplay and also invited him to come and watch the filming, but Bradbury declined, preferring instead to give Truffaut a free hand. Accordingly, Bradbury played no part in the making of the film other than to recommend Bernard Herrmann to compose the score. After seeing the movie, Bradbury sent Truffaut a telegram congratulating him on its effects, though later added the proviso that he thought Montag escaped from the city too easily: "I feel we need a longer period of tension in the running chase before the lovely quiet period at the very end."[92] In his review of the film, Bradbury recognized the major decision that had been taken by the director: "Truffaut rejected certain technological and/or science-fictional (for they are the same) devices. Gone are the jets from my future sky, the Mechanical Hound from my street, the wall-to-wall TV from my parlor."[93] The removal of the jets in effect removes the nuclear theme; with the Mechanical Hound goes a sinister application of law-enforcement technology; and the reduction of television sets to 1960s proportions removes the crowding out of domestic and psychological space by the media. In a 2002 interview, Bradbury recalled that he advised Truffaut to drop the novel's second subject, to "eliminate the atomic bomb thing. You don't need it. It's an extra threat. But the real threat is ignorance—and the lack of education."[94]

The resulting imagery of the film is difficult to identify in terms of period consistency. There are, for instance, traces in many scenes of obsolete objects, like a rocking chair, whose function is explained by Clarisse; but in fact the film repeatedly juxtaposes old and new for surreal effect. The telephones in use throughout tend to be old-fashioned models. His wife Linda proudly shows him a cutthroat razor as the "latest thing." And Montag watches his own execution on a television screen inside a disused railway carriage. Partly, such scenes reflected Truffaut's desire to avoid 1960s gadgetry; more importantly, they foreground the ambiguous nature of the technology of everyday life. Tom Whalen rightly declares that "visually the film never lets us forget the past, especially with its many incongruous images from earlier times," as a result complicating the viewer's sense of time throughout.[95]

Truffaut's adaptation transposes the action into Europe, not only through settings but also through acting styles. Oskar Werner, who plays Montag although he was originally brought in for the role of Beatty, speaks a heavily accented English and in 1965 had appeared as an East German intelligence officer in *The Spy Who Came in from the Cold*. Anton Diffring (taking the part of Fabian, Montag's suspicious colleague) had played Nazi officers in a number of films including *The Heroes of Telemark* (1965). The role echoes the black uniforms, the sound of their jackboots when we see the firemen marching in formation—all suggest analogies with the Second World War, which Truffaut recognized in his *Fahrenheit 451* diary. When Montag starts reading books and carrying out his duties, "he's in the uncomfortable position of the character in the gestapo who would like to get interested in the Resistance without it really upsetting his life."[96] Where Bradbury leaves it strategically vague how many people oppose the regime, Truffaut evokes a whole network of resistance from the very first raid when an anonymous telephone call warns the resident to get out.

Truffaut's decision to have Julie Christie play both Clarisse and Mildred, in order to show the two sides to the same woman was problematic because Bradbury clearly set them up for contrast in terms of age and mentality.[97] He later complained that "you couldn't tell the difference," perhaps referring to the visual trick of distinct hair styles.[98] In the novel, Clarisse is an ethereal character who seems to drift into Montag's consciousness and then finally drops out of the action after having served her purpose, while in the film she is both older and a teacher. The novel contrasts her with Mildred in terms of verbal responsiveness, sensitivity to external Nature, and a cheerful indifference to social categories, whereas in the film their similarity is made explicit when Montag tells Clarisse that Linda, as his wife is renamed, is "rather like" herself and when Clarisse acts out the role of Montag's wife when she telephones the fire station to report that he is sick. In their different responses to books, the two women act out rival voices in the morality play of Montag's consciousness. Clarisse asks him why books are burned, to which he gives the bland reply that it's just a job; Linda cannot even bring herself to use the word, exclaiming with disgust: "I found these things in the house." Clarisse thus plays the questioner and historical commentator, explaining what a rocking chair was to the bemused Montag.[99]

Linda, like her counterpart in the novel, is a prime example of a consumer, living a vicarious family life through television. The "family" show is introduced by a brief, ostensibly factual, report on the latest quantity of books to be burned and the number of "antisocial elements" detained. In other words the soap opera is framed by a report on political control, which clearly signals the former's function as a distraction from any serious thought. Truffaut cleverly exploits the projected space of the screen when the host invites the viewers to "come in" to the program. Two men are seen discussing an abstract issue of dinner-table spaces in a room without any features at all. As their discussion proceeds, they walk toward the camera, taking up new positions on either side of a window division; in order to make the program "interactive," one asks: "what do *you* think Linda?" The dialogue is constructed so as to avoid specifying any subject and leaves intervals where virtually any response could be incorporated. Nevertheless, when the actors turn to the camera at the end of the program and declare "Linda, you're absolutely fantastic," they are feeding her narcissism, a theme that Truffaut introduced to counterbalance the element of militarism in the film.

This sequence is one of the most important in the movie because its use of shot/reverse shots constantly reminds us of the act of viewing. Truffaut's audience becomes the observers of the viewers, who themselves become part of the television spectacle, an effect indicated in Linda's unconsciously metareferential remark, "I could have been an actress." For Mark Bould, the critics took a hostile position toward the film because of its "failure to be like a conventional action-adventure movie" in its ambiguities and suggestiveness. He argues that Truffaut attempted to realize Clarisse's criticism of her society imagistically through constant estrangement effects. Thus "he 'textures' the visual image" through jump cuts, slow motion, wipes, and a whole range of cinematic devices that remind the viewer of issues of representation.[100]

The television sequence also draws our attention to a central feature of dialogue in Montag's culture, namely its reduction to banality or covert catechism. Later Beatty tells him: "Montag has one quality I appreciate greatly. He says very little." The issue, however, is not that he is laconic, but rather that every dialogue with Beatty enacts a covert test of Montag's orthodoxy. When, at the end of the television program, Linda declares with satisfaction that she gave all the "right answers," she is, of course, fooling herself with an illusion of choice but also unconsciously participating in a broader rhetoric of repetitive orthodoxy articulated more threateningly by Beatty.

The film significantly extends the social complexity of the regime in *Fahrenheit 451* by depicting its educational and therefore self-perpetuating dimension. Apart from other facilities, the fire station contains classrooms and, as already noted, Clarisse is a teacher. In the former, Montag starts a class to blue-shirted cadets with instructions on how to hide books, applying the principle that "to learn how to find we must first learn how to hide." In other words, they are instructed to imitate the very actions they are training to eradicate. When Montag accompanies Clarisse to her school we are given shots of corridors where identical jackets hang along the walls and where classes can be heard reciting multiplication tables. This learning by rote makes an obvious satirical comment on that society, but also has an ironic relation to the rediscovery of reading in the film. When Montag first starts *David Copperfield*, he demonstrates ignorance of textual conventions by laboriously reading out every detail of the title page, tracing every word with his finger just as a young child might do. The uncertainty and monotony of his reading here fits appropriately into Montag's learning curve, but by the time we encounter the Book People at the end of the film, their reading styles do not mark a significant advance in expression. For George Bluestone, the problem lies in Truffaut's attempts to depict a rebirth of oral literature in the natural surroundings of woodland. The scenes open up no promise because the Book People "recite by rote, as mechanical as computers."[101] Bradbury avoids this awkwardness through the typographical conventions of representing oral delivery within the printed text, without indications of intonation.

Books in the film at different times are treated visually, thematically, and orally, and their prominence bears directly on Truffaut's handling of authority. In his *Fahrenheit 451* diary, he noted: "I hope no one will read any deliberate meaning into the choice of books. . . . Quite deliberately, personal choice had little to do with it. The point was to film the books as *objects*. . . . Some books were chosen for their sentimental value, because their covers recalled certain epochs."[102] These statements can only be taken as disingenuous because, in fact, books have a predictably central role to play throughout the film. As Laura Carroll has rightly argued, "books are hidden, revealed, furtively or openly handled, pocketed, fingered, wetted, rifled, torn, read and burned."[103] There is scarcely a single scene where books do not figure, explicitly or implicitly. The opening raid, for example, visually encapsulates the regime's ideology as a bag of books falls in slow motion to the ground from a high-level apartment balcony. In his first conversation with Clarisse, Montag declares: "books are just too much rubbish"; the bag scene appears to confirm his assertion. However, when the books fall out of the bag, the viewer's immediate reaction is to try to scan them. This proves to be difficult because Truffaut moves forward scenes containing books so rapidly that reading the images appears to give place to spectacle, flattening out of the differences between books associated with controversy and others "with an affectless impartiality that makes full use of the uncomprehending mechanical gaze of the camera."[104]

It seems at first then that Truffaut is cinematically enacting the regime's reductive attitude toward books, but in fact the sheer scenic variety of how they are viewed induces a complex attentiveness that runs more and more against the official line. As the action progresses, the camera comes increasingly to convey Montag's perspective. The first burning tantalizes viewers with more titles than we can comfortably register. Then his contacts with Clarisse begin to sensitize Montag to the historical and cultural issues implicit in the book burnings. Next, he witnesses a woman's deliberate choice of martyrdom as she burns herself with the books. In this scene, the firemen discover a secret library, a covert archive of books from all periods. As Beatty instructs Montag on their worthlessness, he insists that there is only one way to ensure equality: "so we must burn the books, Montag," adding with emphasis *"all the books."* At this point, the camera reveals the book he is holding—none other than *Mein Kampf.* The brief imagistic allusion to Hitler reinforces implicit analogies that have already been emerging with Nazi Germany and more generally strengthens the political dimension to the book burnings. Thus the selective close-ups on titles by antiestablishment figures like Henry Miller and Jean Genet, or banned works like the Olympia Press edition of *Lolita,* associate the books with differenct forms of dissidence within a broader context of reading signaled by popular paperback series like Penguin Books. In the library burning, the camera follows Montag's perspective when it lingers over a book of paintings by Salvador Dali, blown open page by page in the heat of the fire. Brief close-ups on the texts further reflect Montag's growing fascination with books before the fire produced fades to black.

Color symbolism is paramount throughout the film and blackness in such scenes denotes erasure—of texts and of the past alike. Once he admits his new interest in reading to Linda and her friends, Montag declares in a throwaway pun: "you're just killing time." In contrast, an earlier scene shows Montag struggling through *David Copperfield* in a white bathrobe evocative of a monk's habit. Montag's reading of Dickens takes on the quasicinematic quality of a voice-over, as if he is enacting an alternative story of his life. In short, despite his diary notes to the contrary, book titles play an important part in Truffaut's film, predictably so because film and novel trace out a common trajectory from treating books as featureless objects to discovering their variety and vitality.

If Montag resorts to Dickens through a kind of self-reinvention, the film carries far less hope than the novel in its conclusion. Truffaut admitted: "There are, in fact, two endings—the time where Montag burns up the Captain. Then a vague manhunt begins, vague because it isn't menacing enough, and tacked on after this phony chase is the sequence with the book people."[105] If Beatty is taken as an establishment anti-self to Montag, the moment when the latter turns the fire hose, not just on his house but on his superior, marks a clear break with his own past and his passage from law enforcement to criminality. As in the novel, the official news service demands the closure of Montag's ultimate "death," but the pursuit is shown primarily through long shots, including an incongruous sequence of flying firemen (despite Truffaut's decision to avoid Science Fiction effects), which never generate the urgency of the novel. Montag reaches the Book People thanks to a disused railway line, which ends in a buffer; in the final scenes of the film, Truffaut uses a fixed camera and shows the Book People walking to and fro across the frame. Coincidentally, it was snowing during the shooting, which further helped to strengthen the impression of bleak stasis. For the reviewer in the *New York Times*, the effect was uninspiring but typical of the whole film: "What a dismal image," he exclaimed, "we have here of the deathless eloquence of literature."[106] For him, the main problem was dullness, but there is also the issue of narrative direction. Bradbury's novel gestures beyond the end of the text toward a culminating point of arrival in a new and better place, whereas the film's ending minimizes movement and therefore progression.

FURTHER ADAPTATIONS

Despite reservations, Bradbury's enthusiasm for the 1966 film remained undiminished. Indeed, he received so many comments about Truffaut's decision to allow Clarisse to survive into the coda with the Book People that he wrote the change into his own adaptation of *Fahrenheit 451* for the stage and for the music-theater in 1993.[107] In his play script, Bradbury carefully delays revealing her face. Recognition is signaled by Montag, who repeats her own original question: "Are you happy?"[108]

When Bradbury met the art historian Bernard Berenson in the 1950s, the latter suggested a sequel to *Fahrenheit 451*, set in a postburning future where the Book People become the target of his satire. "You could do a chapter on each book," Bradbury recalled, "and how it was boned, marrowed, broken, collapsed in ruins and put back together by morons or well-meaning pedants who remember their own interpretation of the soaring lines."[109] Despite his enthusiasm for the suggestion at the time, Bradbury never acted on it.

As early as 1955, Bradbury had been approached by Charles Laughton and a Broadway producer about writing a stage script for his novel. This he did, only to have it rejected.[110] Later, when writing a fresh script for a 1979 stage production in Los Angeles, Bradbury claimed that the characters wrote themselves: "I asked. *They* answered." One of his key changes was to fill out Beatty's paradoxical character by having Montag visit his home, only to discover huge packed bookcases. Beatty explains that he used to be an enthusiastic reader but that his dissatisfactions with the books grew with age:

> "Why, life happened to me." The Fire Chief shuts his eyes to remember. "Life. The usual. The same. The love that wasn't quite right, the dream that went sour, the sex that fell apart, the deaths that came swiftly to friends not deserving, the murder of someone or another, the insanity of someone close, the slow death of a mother, the abrupt suicide of a father—a stampede of elephants, an onslaught of disease.[111]

Beatty is here given a more complex personal life and history. Faber's role was similarly developed for the stage script and, on the return of Clarisse, Bradbury explained: "I felt the same need to save her, for after all, she, verging on silly star-struck chatter, was in many ways responsible for Montag's beginning to wonder about books and what was in them."[112]

Plans for a remake of the film of *Fahrenheit 451* have progressed in fits and starts. In 1994 Bradbury himself was working on a new screenplay to star Tom Cruise but the project was shelved in 2000 because Cruise was tied up in the filming of Kubrick's *Eyes Wide Shut*. Soon after that, Frank Darabont took over the project and wrote a script that was to have starred Tom Hanks until he withdrew. As of 1983, there were reportedly ten scripts in existence, including at least one by Bradbury himself, who exclaimed with frustration that "all you have to do is open the book and shoot the pages."[113]

In 1951, while working *on Fahrenheit 451*, Bradbury complained to Richard Matheson about the "great centrifuge of radio, television [and] pre–thought-out movies" that was undermining public capacity for attentive thought, and over the years since publication, Bradbury has commented repeatedly on this subject.[114] A 1979 coda, written partly in response to a request to include more female characters in the novel, simultaneously addresses censoring, the pursuit of political correctness, and easy-to-read digests by ironically echoing the cadences of Beatty: "simplicity itself. Skin, debone, demarrow, scarify, melt, render down and destroy. Every adjective that counted, every verb that moved, every metaphor that weighed more than a mosquito—out! Every simile that would have made a sub-moron's mouth twitch—gone!" And, in case any reader hasn't grasped his argument, Bradbury declares: "The point is obvious. There is more than one way to burn a book" (209).

Bradbury's intermittent commentary on his novel has consistently stressed the continuing relevance of its critical engagement with the media long after the specific paranoia of the McCarthy era had passed. In a 1998 interview, he stated that "almost everything in *Fahrenheit 451* has come about, one way or the other—the influence of television, the rise of local TV news, the neglect of education."[115] And in 2007, on the occasion of receiving a Pulitzer Prize, he denied that it was about government censorship so much as "how television destroys interest in reading literature." This happens through the transmission of "factoids," gobbets of useless information without context.[116]

Given the subject of *Fahrenheit 451*, it is a supreme irony that in 1967, unbeknown to Bradbury, the editors at Ballantine bowdlerized the novel for a high-school edition, removing references to nudity and drinking, and also expletives.[117] Although the original text was restored in 1980, the novel's acceptability in the classroom continues to be widely debated on U.S. high school boards. Bradbury viewed his novel as a work in progress, not only from his dystopian sketches in the late 1940s, but also through his stage and film adaptations. Right up to his death, he was planning screenplays, so far unpublished. *Fahrenheit 451* was the most famous work to emerge from Bradbury's lifelong preoccupation with literacy. We turn now to another central interest that ran throughout his career—space.

CHapTeR 4

BRADBURY ON SPACE

Throughout his career, Bradbury expressed his sense of writing in the Space Age, a time which he felt was characterized by the visual sublime, and from his earliest writings space was an important concern. In the first number of *Futuria Fantasia* for Summer 1939 Bradbury included his poem "Thought and Space," which opens: "Space—thy boundaries are / Time and time alone. / No earth-born rocket, / seedling skyward sown, / Will ever reach your cold, / infinite end." He is already imagining space as an expanse to be filled by the imagination. Conversely, his biographer Sam Weller has recalled: "In his last years, Bradbury told me he intended to write a new Science-Fiction novel. He'd started on an idea about a group of Catholic cardinals who travel into the deeps of space to prove the existence of God."[1] For Bradbury, space was the big subject, constantly drawing him to explore its potential in his fiction, essays, films, and other projects. In the mid-1960s Bradbury told the Italian journalist Oriana Fallaci:

Let us become Martians on Mars, Venusians on Venus, and when Mars and Venus die, let us go to the other solar systems, to Alpha Centauri, to wherever we
manage to go, and let us forget the Earth. Let us forget our solar system and our
body, the form it used to have, let us become no matter what, lichens, insects, balls
of fire, no matter what, all that matters is that somehow life should continue.[2]

Bradbury not only saw flight into space as the ultimate physical and speculative act. Here, he figures it as a willed realization of an evolutionary destiny
somehow independent of physical form. As early as 1953, he was speculating
"why build rockets at all?"; space retained a speculative and spiritual fascination
for Bradbury throughout his career, whether expressed through the media
of fiction, film, and prose.[3]

THINGS TO COME AND THE EARLY STORIES

A formative film in shaping the imagination of the young Bradbury was Alexander Korda's *Things to Come* (1936), a film, he later recalled, "which grew a
wild flock of children to become astronauts and land on the Moon and Mars."[4]
In 1967, during a visit to Houston to report on the Apollo program, he met
the astronauts, Bradbury remembered the line from the film: "Which shall it
be, the stars or the graves?" In his response to the 1971 Mars orbiter, he again
recalled the ending to the film, writing: "the journey is long, the end uncertain, and there is more dark along the way than light, but you can whistle."[5]

In the climactic conclusion to Korda's film, the "space gun" is launched
partly to save a human remnant from the anarchy of the mob attacking the
spaceship. It falls to Cabal—pilot, leader, and commentator—to point out the
grand destiny that the flight is enacting. For mankind, there is "no rest and no
ending. He must go on—conquest beyond conquest. This little planet and its
winds and ways, and all the laws of mind and matter that restrain him. Then
the planets about him, and at last out across immensity to the stars. And when
he has conquered all the deeps of space and all the mysteries of time—still
he will be beginning."[6] Cabal is given the last line of the film—"Which shall
it be?"—articulating a choice for humanity between accepting physical limits
and risking an attempt to break through these limits. Bradbury was to recall
this line on a number of occasions and clearly found the scene inspirational,
despite its dated articulation of exploration as serial conquest. For Cabal, and

later for Bradbury, space offered a metaphysical expanse to voyagers of the imagination.

One of Bradbury's earliest treatments of this subject was "King of the Grey Spaces" (1943, revised in 1962 as the title story of Bradbury's "book for boys," *R Is for Rocket*).[7] The title of the volume (and its companion *S Is for Space*, 1966) suggests a school primer, possibly glancing at the extended crisis in science education that followed the Soviet launch of the Sputnik satellite in 1957. Indeed, Bradbury later recalled that "people, especially kids, went crazy over Science Fiction after Sputnik lit the sky."[8] In the story, Bradbury's narrator is a boy named Chris (Columbus?) living near a rocket launch site. In its account, of Chris's gang the first pages of the story recall Mark Twain, an acknowledged influence on Bradbury. The original version conveys the boys' excitement at the base, but by 1962 Bradbury had focused this excitement visually, as in the following description:

> The big rocket came out of its plastic work canopy like a great interstellar circus tent and moved along its gleaming track towards the fire point, accompanied by a giant gantry like a gathering of prehistoric reptile birds which kept and preened and fed this one big fire monster and led it towards its seizure and birth into a sudden blast-furnace sky.[9]

The slow pacing of the description enables a string of metaphors to emerge like the rocket itself—circus show, primeval monster, creature giving birth—and this is surely the main point of Bradbury's narrative here. The rocket suggests far more than mere technology; it triggers the imagination of its observers. Stretching the credibility of his boy-narrator's perspective, Bradbury uses the latter to suggest how the rocket marks the culmination of a "hundred years of dreaming" in an America of the near future where flights to the Moon are relatively commonplace. The central part of the story focuses on Chris's desperate efforts to get the school grades necessary for selection by the Astronaut Board. Of course he succeeds, partly by sheer will, and the narrative thus describes a rite of passage. At the beginning of the story, Chris is peering at the launch site through a fence; in the last line, he passes "beyond the fence" in a rite of passage toward his first flight and toward a manhood that will recapitulate the grand national narrative of exploration and discovery.

This story gives only a partial view of Bradbury's treatment of space, which from the very beginning had its darker sides. In his early stories, space travel is variously imagined as inducing psychosis, as a transposed version of world war, and in one case as a reversal of the perspective we were just considering. "I, Rocket" (1944) is narrated by an immobilized war rocket, "who" describes coming alive through the launch ceremony and the allocation of a captain. Bradbury uses the sentient rocket as an unobserved witness to the psychological and physical dangers of space travel.

The opening stories in *R Is for Rocket* elaborate and expand on the symbolism of its central icon. The original title of the second story, "Next Stop the Stars" (1956), carries far more upbeat implications than Bradbury's substitute, "The End of the Beginning," echoing Churchill's announcement of the Battle of Egypt in 1942, which explicitly complicates narrative sequence. It describes parents in their garden gazing up into the night sky to see their son flying in his rocket. The couple's thought sequence, which expands outward like their field of vision, but their sense of being at the end of an age is more than countered by the father's thoughts, which shift into a private celebration of the future by negating this "end": "Man will be endless and infinite, even as space is endless and infinite. . . . Individuals will die as always, but our history will reach as far as we'll ever need to see into the future."[10] Through his pride in his son's achievement the father becomes in his own way a commentator on history and is used by Bradbury to set up a technological link between the father's lawnmower (which makes a "racket") and rocket, and—via the song "A wheel within a wheel. Way in the middle of the air" (used as a title in *The Martian Chronicles*)—to relate both through a biblical image of visionary revelation. However, because the father frames these associative links, they remain merely speculative and the story ends on the mundane note of him mowing the lawn.

It should already be evident that, despite the unqualified assertions Bradbury was to make about space travel during the 1960s and beyond, his stories show real ambivalence over this subject. "The Rocket Man" (1951) is a clear case in point. It returns to the hopes of a young boy to become an astronaut, which are played off against the perspective of his parents. The son's ambition to repeat his father's career is blocked by his mother's secrecy over his job. As usual, Bradbury focuses the narrative on a symbolic object, in this case the dust which the son shakes out of his father's uniform. He is so fascinated that he puts the dust under a microscope and stares "down upon brilliant motes of meteor dust, comet tail, and loam from far Jupiter glistening like worlds themselves that drew me down the tube a billion miles into space, at terrific acceleration."[11] It is a measure of the boy's naïveté that he is simply drawn to the exotic and distant, without thinking of its possible consequences.

If the boy has hopes for his future, his father embodies experience and even when he warns Doug, "Don't ever be a Rocket Man," his son's fascination with the glamour of space travel persists. One of the strongest associations of dust is with death, little more than a word in the boy's consciousness, and the traces he finds in his father's space suit actually predict his fate. One day he does not return and the report states baldly: "His ship had fallen into the sun."[12] Does that imply an Icaruslike parable against space flight? Bradbury leaves no explicit conclusion, only a summary of how the mother and son continue to live their lives according to the timetable of the now dead father. In "The Gift" (1952), which describes a boy's first voyage in a spaceship, a nuclear family travels together on an excursion. The time is Christmas Eve, though the rocket is taking them to a "place where there was no time at all." When the boy pleads for his present, he is led to a porthole and gazes out "at the burning and the burning of ten billion billion white and lovely candles . . ."[13] The image straddles echoes of a traditional Christmas with hints of a new scale of perception as the sentence trails into ellipsis. Bradbury mimics the enthusiastic rhetoric of a child while setting up a basic contradiction between timelessness and the seasonal measure that would give meaning to the boy's experience.

Bradbury constructs *R Is for Rocket* around a central set of themes and symbols. "The Golden Apples of the Sun," originally the title story of a 1953 collection, contains numerous hints to the reader of how to read the whole volume. The story describes a space mission on its way to the sun in a vessel with the multiple names of *Copa de Oro* (cup of gold), *Prometheus*, and *Icarus*. The crewmen speculate on the varying symbolism of its name, but without mentioning the title's possible source in W. B. Yeats's poem, "The Song of Wandering Aengus," where the speaker—"old with wandering"—yearns for an ultimate union with his loved one in the sun. The vessel's names link its enterprise with imperial plunder (the buccaneering of Henry Morgan), the theft of fire from the gods, and the mythological victim of his father's design of wings to escape from the labyrinth.[14] These multiple allusions initially overload the story's symbolism, but they also contextualize the action within some of the main cultural narratives of Western culture. The function of these allusions is not unique in Bradbury's stories, as we shall see.

In "The Golden Apples," because of the enormous temperatures encountered by the spaceship, its refrigeration system is crucial for the crew's survival, and their possible collective fate is suggested when the first mate perishes from a leak in his protection suit. When the cooling system malfunctions, the captain remembers an image from his childhood of the early spring thaws. Already the main symbolic oppositions are emerging, which bind the whole volume together: age against youth, frost against fire, and, most crucially, life against death. In his 1962 volume on the Space Age, Arthur C. Clarke explains how the first time he read this story he decided that it was a "charming fantasy" but was then beginning to consider a mission to the sun as a viable possibility.[15] However, Clarke misses the main point about the story, namely its symbolism. A voyage to the sun is potentially suicidal, as the captain fears if the technology of the spaceship fails: "He saw the skin peel from the rocket beehive, men thus revealed, running, running, mouths shrieking, soundless. Space was a black mossed well where life drowned its roars and terrors."[16] As the vulnerability of the rocket is revealed, a second metaphor emerges, that of the cup, which could be taken as a life-enhancing container or tool. Indeed, it forms part of the repaired cooling pump that saves the lives of the crew, thus resolving the tension throughout the story between the sun as life source and destroyer.

THE GRAND NARRATIVES OF SPACE EXPLORATION

Bradbury's stories of space travel constantly allude to a grand cultural narrative of the dream and realization of flight. Thus "The Flying Machine" (1953) has been described by Bradbury as "Science Fiction in reverse" because it extends this ambition back into Chinese antiquity.[17] The 1956 story "Icarus Montgolfier Wright" (collected in S Is for Space) most explicitly demonstrates this expansive process by conflating three famous accounts of flight by constructed wings, balloon, and plane. Each of the three narratives dissolves into the next through montage within the consciousness of a young astronaut about to fly to the Moon:

> Dreaming he smiled.
>
> He saw the clouds rush down the Aegean sky.
>
> He felt the balloon sway drunkenly, its great bulk ready for the clear running wind.
>
> He felt the sand hiss up the Atlantic shelves from the soft dunes that might save him if he, a fledgling bird, should fall. The framework struts hummed and chorded like a harp, and himself caught up in its music.
>
> Beyond this room he felt the primed rocket glide on the desert field, its fire wings folded, its fire breath kept, held ready to speak for three billion men.[18]

The protagonist's consciousness becomes a composite field of "remembered" experiences of flight, which expands toward the narrative present. The story consciously directs the reader beyond its ending, halting on the verge of rocket flight—in other words on the eve of a new age—hence, Bradbury's strategic decision to place the story last in the collection *S Is for Space*. Characteristically, the story revolves around the twin metaphors of bird-flight and fire.

Bradbury's stories frequently use their narratives to set up dialogues on the ethics and purpose of space travel. In "The Man" (1949), where a rocket captain describes space travel as an endless searching since Darwin shattered religious belief. When a rocket lands on a distant unnamed planet, the locals greet it with indifference, to the indignation of the crew: "Don't they realize how big this is?" one exclaims.[19] The emphasis in this story falls squarely on the desires of the explorers, especially when triggered by the report of a man with quasimessianic powers of healing. Even though he realizes that it is probably a futile quest, the captain decides to continue his voyage in pursuit of this figure in order to destroy him. As his rocket flies into space, a spectator on the ground reflects wryly in words that recall Cabal's in *Things to Come*: "And he'll go on, planet after planet, seeking and seeking, and always and always he will be an hour late. . . . And he will go on and on, thinking to find the very thing which he left behind here, on this planet."[20]

Where exploration is figured as compulsive in "The Man," Bradbury gives one of his most austere accounts of an accident in space in "Asleep in Armageddon" (1948, later title "Perchance to Dream"), where a lone astronaut,

Leonard Sale, by sheer luck survives a collision between his rocket and a planetoid. He is told over the radio that a rescue ship will be with him in six days. The terms of the narrative are thus set as ultimate solitude and disorientation in space and time. Sale's consciousness becomes a field of voices and machine sounds that generate intermittent coherence and then lapse. These voices might be hallucinatory, or might really emanate from the spirits of dead warriors from a long-destroyed planet in the asteroid belt. Through most of the story, he holds a running dialogue with himself where he tries to will himself into retaining sanity. Despite these efforts, Sale slides into nervous exhaustion and imagines his consciousness as a field of battle between two warriors. An attempt at suicide fails and he makes several futile efforts to shoot himself. Then liberation comes. Another spaceship docks to rescue him but Sale's ego collapses completely: "His face was riven with emotion. It was the face of a saint, a sinner, a fiend, a monster, a darkness, a light, one, many, an army, a vacuum, all all!"[21] The rescue comes too late and Sale dies. In "Icarus Montgolfier Wright" the protagonist's consciousness is expansive as if he is including all other accounts of flight within his own desire. "Perchance to Dream," however, destabilizes the field of consciousness into a shifting babble of voices, many of which might be hallucinatory.

THE SHAW CONNECTION

The scenario of a spaceship being struck by a meteor is also used in a tribute to Bernard Shaw, whose play *Back to Methuselah* was an important influence on Bradbury. In "G.B.S.—Mark V" (1976), a member of a spaceship crew begins a dialogue with the "cuneiform-tablet robot of George Bernard Shaw" instead of indulging in the sexual toys used by the rest of the crew. The description is misleading because, despite his age, Shaw is primarily dramatized as a voice. The two share the awe-inspiring spectacle from the spaceship: "All of space was around them, all of the Universe, and all of the night of the celestial Being, all the stars and all the places between the stars, and the ship moving on its silent course."[22]

The Shaw character expounds a vision of the cosmos as a field of forces where shapes are formed and reformed: "Where *are* we?. . . . Why, we are the miracle of force and matter making itself over into imagination and will. Incredible. The Life Force experimenting with forms. You for one. Me for another." No sooner has Willis the protagonist registered this transcendental vision than a crew member "kills" Shaw by turning off the machine. This reminds us of the materiality of the robot and also of the spaceship, which explodes in a meteor shower "like a shredded balloon."[23] Willis survives in a space suit and so does Shaw (whose circuitry has reconnected in the explosion), but the story pays no attention to the issue of physical survival. Its fade-out ending shows the young man and the old man indefinitely continuing their dialogue into another time. Bradbury is clearly using the Space-Age narrative as a parable of learning from a member of the older generation of writers.

Bradbury's interest in Shaw was long-standing, and he gives that writer a whole scene in his novel on the filming of Moby-Dick, Green Shadows, White Whale (1992) where the Shaw character describes Back to Methuselah as his "contribution to the modern Bible."[24] The play was regularly printed with an extended preface and postscript where Shaw elaborated on evolution and the life force: "You are alive; and you want to be more alive. You want an extension of consciousness and of power. You want, consequently, additional organs."[25] Shaw turns here to Lamarck, who saw a recapitulation of evolution in each individual birth and who uses the example of the giraffe desiring to crop leaves from high trees and as a result developing a long neck from sheer will power. Apart from mounting a protest against the "hideous fatalism" of Darwin, Shaw also opens up an inspirational role for writers as contributing to a new secular scripture. Shaw's play and his self-commentary address Science Fiction by referencing the stories of H. G. Wells and Samuel Butler, and he anticipates the Space Age by declaring that "men gaped foolishly at the million billion miles of space and worshipped the astronomer as infallible and omniscient."[26] So, whatever promise the telescope and microscope might bring is outweighed for Shaw by the danger of an emerging "priesthood" of scientific experts.

Bradbury's debt to Shaw is evident generally in his subsequent public statements on the space program, where he constantly asserts his belief in hope, sometimes with crude stridency. There are more specific signs of influence, however. In 1978 Bradbury traveled with Carl Sagan on an Atlantic liner, and he later recalled a dispute over the theories of evolution held by Darwin and Lamarck. Where Sagan was insisting on the survival of the fittest largely by chance, Bradbury was far more inclined to Lamarck's theory of wished survival, declaring: "especially in this year, this Age, we more than survive through accidental fitness. What do we do? We tell our neck to stretch tall. And, by God, the neck stretches!"[27] His example is taken straight out of *Back to Methuselah* and his assertion is based, not on scientific fact, but on Shaw's imperative of the need to believe. Ultimately, the latter's life force replaces the traditional deity with a willed drive "towards a goal of all-knowingness and almighty power over nature."[28] We shall see how this article of faith finds expression in Bradbury's commentary on the Space Age. In 1980, when commenting on the space shuttle, Bradbury drew again on Shaw's beliefs when he asserted that "machines, if properly built, can carry our most fragile dreams through a million light-years of travel without breakage. Such machines, and the Shuttle with them, are the armor of our Life Force."[29]

When contributing to a 1997 symposium on Shaw and Science Fiction, Bradbury reminisced about his meeting in 1954 with Bertrand Russell soon after completing his script for the film of *Moby-Dick*, where he enlisted Russell's support for Science Fiction as a fellow "idea visionary."[30] Bradbury uses Shaw's initials as part of the title for his 1997 essay, "GBS: Refurbishing the Tin Woodman," paying tribute to Frank L. Baum's *The Wonderful Wizard of Oz* and thereby identifying one of his main themes in the essay: the importance of technology in SF. As he puts it, "much of Science Fiction, of course, has collapsed in a tangle of robot legs."[31] The Tin Woodman properly speaking is closer to a cyborg than a robot since he has been replacing his organic limbs with prosthetic substitutes, but without ever losing sentience or even emotion.

Bradbury's essay makes an extended plea for the larger vision he dramatizes in "G.B.S.—Mark V." Indeed, he directly extrapolates his discussion with Russell into an imagined exchange with Shaw, where the latter joins in a chorus of voices articulating the perspective that Bradbury summarizes in relation to time: "the entirety of our past, everything to do with mankind, has been Science Fiction," admitting "not much science, of course, and one helluva lot of fiction. But nevertheless, the art of imagining this afternoon, this midnight, tomorrow at dawn." By the time of writing (1997) Bradbury no longer needed to argue the case for the importance of SF. Nevertheless, the essay recapitulates his debate with Sagan, asserting: "it is tempting to theorize that since we humans are cognizant of our cognizance, we have begun to teach our genes and chromosomes behavior. We dream a long neck, build it, and reach up to the Moon, then Mars, then the Universe."[32] Bradbury also pits Shaw against the late pessimism expressed in Wells's *Mind at the End of Its Tether* (1945), where he turned against the hopes of *Things to Come* and gloomily declared that "events now follow one another in an entirely untrustworthy sequence."[33] By this point in his career, Wells had lost faith not just in the "Becoming Factor," but in narrative itself. If nothing is connected, the very possibility of story collapses and this is where Bradbury's optimism finds expression. Adopting the persona of Shaw, he declares a dramatic message of hope: "There *is* no end, but only an eternal Beginning. . . . I write me a *new* text, H. G., not from tomb to tomb, death to death, but launch pad to launch pad, rockets shouting fire, men shouting a joyful rage against unknowingness. Come, H. G., shed that despair, Canaveral is the kindergarten of Time, Evolution, and Immortality."[34] Bradbury's adopted voice derives not only from Shaw, but also from Melville's Ahab, Shakespeare, and even Wells's Cabal. The last quotation suggests that Bradbury used Shaw and others to set up his own contemporary palimpsests written over earlier texts to promote the cause of space exploration.

IT CAME FROM OUTER SPACE

Space was central to Bradbury's fascination with film. Thanks to the publication of some screenplays, it is only now becoming evident how active Bradbury was in SF cinema. In 1952 he was invited by Universal Pictures to write a script for a monster movie. This marked his earliest substantial involvement in the Hollywood system. The working titles for the film included *Ground Zero* and *The Atomic Monster*, which link the subject to the nuclear fears of the period, but the final title clearly shifted the genre toward Science Fiction: *It Came from Outer Space*. Bradbury played a major part in producing the script, and the movie could be seen in his career as transitional between his complex treatment of the alien in *The Martian Chronicles* and his subsequent writings on the Space Age. A blazing object crashes in the hills near the town of Sand Rock, Arizona. It is taken to be a meteor by John Putnam, a local writer and amateur astronomer, until he visits the crater and discovers a spacecraft in the depths. From that point on townsfolk either disappear or become transformed into zombielike figures. As the takeovers multiply, even Putnam's fiancée Ellen succumbs and he manages to save the community by interceding on its behalf with the aliens.

The film's setting, a small town within the Arizona desert, alerts the viewer to the precarious relation of civilization to Nature, and also confirms Vivian Sobchack's description of 1950s monster movies: "Watching these films with their abundance of long shots in which human figures move like insects, their insistence on a fathomless landscape, we are forced to a pessimistic view of the worth of technological progress and of man's ability to control his destiny."[35] When Putnam gazes out into the desert and declares "it's alive and waiting for you," his warning is completely ambiguous. Is the threat from the desert itself or from the alien creatures? The early parts of the film establish the desert as potentially disturbing to human perception in inducing hallucinations and mirages, hence the suggestion throughout the film that the perceptions and reactions of the townsfolk is a central issue.

By 1953 alien invasion had become an established subject in film and fiction alike. Robert Heinlein's *The Puppet Masters* (1951), which Bradbury would certainly have known, describes the attempted takeover of the United States by sluglike creatures that fasten onto their human hosts. Similar potential threats are posed in the films *Flying Disc Man from Mars* (1950), *The Thing from Another World* (1951), and most famously *Invaders from Mars* (1953). Mars had been well established as a source of alien threat in H. G. Wells's *The War of the Worlds* as novel, radio adaptation, and then, also in 1953, through George Pal's film transposition of the action into California.[36] Works like these helped to create the cultural milieu of *It Came from Outer Space*, which simultaneously exploits the alien invasion genre and references the latter's clichés. When Putnam finds a spacecraft, the helicopter pilot who has taken him to the crash site exclaims in disbelief: "You're not going to tell them you saw Martians down there"; as the news story breaks, a radio announcer declares that "no-one has yet turned up any bug-eyed monsters threatening Earth." The local newspaper reports Putnam's story under the headline "Star Gazer Sees Martians." Through these details, the film ingeniously thematizes the issue of credibility, made more explicit in the draft screen treatments, while presenting an alien arrival.

The film exploits perspective and image throughout in order to avoid the very clichés mentioned in the local news reports. As Putnam descends into the crash site he sees at its heart a spherical construct with hexagonal sides—an image evocative of a honeycomb. As he approaches this, a door slides open and he sees what seems to be a huge pulsing eye. However, before we can properly register the image, the shot reverses on to Putnam, as if through a bubble, and this becomes a hallmark of the aliens' intelligent but different gaze being directed against the humans. The film was promoted through its use of 3-D to give a new effect of immediacy, which draws the viewer into the perspectives shared by Putnam and the others.

From the beginning of his career, Bradbury had tended to avoid alien invasion stories. A rare exception is "And Then—The Silence" (1942), but this reverses perspective to present the Earthmen in their "silver ships" as the true aliens coming to an inhabited planet. Similarly in 1952, just as he was a about to start work on *It Came*, Bradbury wrote a story called "A Matter of Taste," where a spaceship from Earth lands on a planet inhabited by rational spiderlike creatures who make tortuous attempts at communication with the humans. This time they are the real aliens when measured against quite different norms. The first astronaut is a "pale-colored creature, almost hairless."[37] Indeed, the whole notion of the alien emerges as a question of habits of perception. Body shape is separated from mind and remains the insuperable obstacle to sustained contact between the two groups; the human captain can communicate only with his hosts if he keeps his eyes shut. Bradbury ducks the physiological complication of speech by having this communication take place through telepathy, and in effect the narrator enacts an ideally rational human perspective far superior to that of the astronauts. For *It Came*, by analogy with *The Day the Earth Stood Still*, Bradbury "wanted to treat the invaders as beings who were not dangerous, and that was very unusual."[38]

Bradbury had to compromise over this issue, and in the film the more threatening aspect of the aliens emerges as they begin to take over different humans, creating identical simulacra in a series of transformations that anticipate *Invasion of the Body Snatchers* (1956). As happens in other "takeover" films, the signs of the change are negative: a loss of facial expression so that appearance becomes a mask, a toneless voice, and a tendency to walk mechanically. In some of Bradbury's drafts, Putnam walks by wax dummies in shop windows, graphic images of alienated humanity. One of the most surreal moments in Bradbury's "film story" comes when Putnam shoots the replicant of his fiancée:

> CLOSEUP of Ellen's face. Her mouth begins to scream. The scream changes terribly, from high to a choking, low sound. The face almost splinters. It looks like a smashed windshield, a spider-web of cracks and shards. It sparkles like luminescent fire. The eyes glow red-hot. The face begins to melt. Her voice *melts*. "Ah . . . ah . ." she moans, the voice moans.[39]

Bradbury has taken a cliché of 1950s horror movies and transformed it into an image of fracture, then of radiance (difficult in a black-and-white movie), and finally of liquescence. In the print version of the story, which appeared in the *Super Cinema Annual* for 1955, the aliens are explicitly described as amoebalike creatures that ooze everywhere, anticipating the red jelly of *The Blob* (1958), which absorbs everything in its path. Bradbury avoids such crudity by having the fiancée's face undergo rapid visual shifts away from the human form. There is no comparable moment of visual melodrama in the film, but rather a general tension between the aliens' threat to the community (and, by implication, to the nation at large) and their message to Putnam that their destination was another world and that they only need to repair their craft. In short, they are only passing through.

The film straddles benign and malevolent versions of the alien, which culminate in a dialogue between Putnam and his simulacrum. This scene is clearly designed to present mirror images of humanity where "Putnam" addresses his human counterpart as the other raises his gun. The twin explains the ideal behind their voyage: "What dreams we had. How wonderful it was going to be, to see other planets and peoples. The brotherhood of God, we said."[40] The aliens' departure thus represents a breakdown of communication as much as a failed power play. Glossing the film's political implications, J. Hoberman argues that the "battle in the liberal invasion vision does not pit earthlings against extraterrestrials but a rational liberal worldview against reflexively hysterical, ignorant paranoia."[41] Putnam is predictably ignored by the journalists who pursue the more sensational account of the landing. He is given the role of commentator, drawing historical analogies like those we saw in *The Martian Chronicles*, by asking: "How did we treat the American

Indian? We killed them, or put them on reservations. How have we treated the Africans? Exploited and used them."[42]

It Came from Outer Space was a box-office success, seen several times by a young Steven Spielberg, (of whom, more later). After their successful collaboration over the screenplay, Bradbury and Harry Essex got back together in 1976 to work on another Science-Fiction movie. Essex's idea was to be based on Dr. Jekyll and Mr. Hyde, involving a scientist presiding over a case of evolutionary recession. One idea he considered was having the creature grow from a spore brought back to Earth in an experimental rocket, but finally both agreed to base the film on Bradbury's 1946 story, "Chrysalis" (the lead story of S Is for Space), which describes how a scientist has fallen into a coma and developed a green carapace after absorbing "radiations." The story centers on a debate over whether he is unnatural, diseased, or the embodiment of a new phase in the life cycle. The last possibility, expressed by a physician, seems to be confirmed in the story's conclusion, where the protagonist walks into the desert and takes flight: "He soared up quickly, quietly—and very soon he was lost among the stars as Smith headed for outer space . . ."[43] The ellipses here not only avoid narrative closure, but also open up an indefinite narrative potential reflecting Bradbury's optimistic sense of how the space program could develop. The chrysalis phase of evolution implicitly identifies flight with full humanity. In a 1980 interview, Bradbury recalls achieving physical maturity in his teens: "I was ready to fly, the real self was coming out."[44] A surviving section of the screenplay opens with a pre-title sequence describing the semiconscious state of the human subject, but the project was never realized. Essex admitted to Bradbury that the screenplay should have focused on the feelings of the human subject under transformation so as to avoid the clichés of earlier monster movies.[45]

SPACE-AGE CINEMA: 2001 AND CLOSE ENCOUNTERS

As we shall see, Bradbury's statements on the space program repeatedly stressed the sheer scale of the project, and in 1967 he told the American Society of Cinematographers: "the trouble with the Space Age is that we have yet to catch it on our screens."[46] The following year, a film was released which finally seemed to match up to his expectations. Arthur C. Clarke's famous collaboration with Stanley Kubrick in the making of 2001: A Space Odyssey (1968) realized their common dream of giving epic expression to space exploration. One of the working titles, *How the Solar System Was Won*, draws the Western parallel explicitly, whereas the final title conflates Homeric exploration with the Space Age. As Clarke explained in the film *The Making of 2001*, Kubrick and he wanted to "relate to the public the wonder and beauty and promise of the new age of exploration which [was] opening up before the human race."[47]

The film presents a narrative in four phases linked by desire focusing on the skies. Evolution is figured in the film as extended outward movement from Earth, introduced through the famous slow-motion segue from the primitive bone tool to a space satellite. Kubrick alternates the action between the sublime spectacle of the planets and different constructed interiors, using wide-angle and other devices to avoid the latter seeming constrictive. The action moves slowly forward in a series of surges from Earth to the sky, to the Moon, to Jupiter, culminating in the transcendence of body limits by "creatures of radiation." As Bowman passes through the Star Gate, the religious imagery becomes more and more evident. The pod passes over a sea of fire in a scene-challenging description: "The idea was almost beyond fantasy, but perhaps he was watching nothing less than a migration from star to star, across a bridge of fire."[48] The bridge shifts into a "pillar of fire," recalling the image of divine guidance from Exodus.[49] The suggestion, clearer in Clarke's novel than the film, seems to be that Bowman is entering a new dimension, a conception scarcely imaginable in film terms because Clarke seems to envisage disembodied minds roaming the universe at will. Such a culmination implies that Clarke shared Bradbury's perception of flight into space as a potentially transcendental experience.

The reception of the film was mixed.[50] Bradbury attended the Warner Brothers premiere with Arthur C. Clarke, when the film was some four hours long. However, Bradbury's review of *2001* did not focus on the issue of length, but framed its trenchant criticisms with praise for Clarke as "one of the finest writers in science-fiction literature," supplying the guiding idea of the project. Bradbury expressed unreserved enthusiasm for its spectacle: "Technically and photographically it is probably the most stunning film ever put on the screen. The special effects machineries that were built are truly beyond belief. One has a total feeling of being in another century." He focuses his praise on the opening and the ending for placing the viewers in the "fantastic cycle" of evolution stretching from age to age. However, in the central sections of the film the astronauts are played by "two Antonioni people," who betray the grandeur of the subject who, as "living zombies, walk careless through the void of their own lives in space." No one cares whether they live or die because "there are no human beings in the film." Bradbury found a total absence of human drama: "the tragedy is that no people are allowed to inhabit Outer Space. There is no hearth, no fire, no focus about which to gather us poor ape-people who extend our hands toward light and warmth asking to make tribes against the night."[51] In a 1969 interview, Bradbury repeated his praise and criticism by declaring that "it's a gorgeous film. One of the most beautifully photographed pictures in the history of motion pictures. Unfortunately, there are no well-directed scenes, and the dialogue is banal to the point of extinction."[52] Later he was to tie his criticisms to the film's length and also to his perception that "the actors talked forever about nothing!"[53]

Where Bradbury found a mismatch between visual spectacle and the depiction of astronauts in *2001*, he had no reservations at all about Steven Spielberg's *Close Encounters of the Third Kind* (1977). Bradbury contributed an introduction to a tie-in volume with fulsome praise for the film's spiritual dimension. He declared:

> We have needed to be bound together to the Universe, to the Cosmos. We have needed to collect our souls, our thoughts, our flesh, all in one packet, to feel a compound of the earth we live on, the sun we circle, the nebula we inhabit, and the stars beyond the stars. We are, after all, the Star Children.[54]

For Bradbury, Spielberg's film crossed barriers and genres, was "apolitical," and religious in a nondenominational sense. His extraterrestrial visitors "chart out the most titanic territorial imperative," inviting the viewer on a journey. Bradbury found a greater self-awareness in this film than in *2001* and explained that it demonstrated knowledge of the cosmic center: "and the center is that moment in Time when two fleshes reach across a billion year experiment in birthing and look at each other." Bradbury locates a symbolism of connectedness, which he summarized in 2008 on the occasion of Spielberg receiving a Lifetime Achievement Award, by stating that in the film "we are in touch with another part of the universe, and the two halves of the universe are connected."[55] In 1978 he summarized the impact of the film as dramatizing an apotheosis of humanity: "The great truth it teaches is that human beings, no matter what their shape, size or color or far star-country of origins, are on their way to Becoming."[56] Bradbury didn't waver in his estimate of *Close Encounters* as the "greatest film of Science Fiction ever made" and the unique case of a "religious film" made by a "Science Fiction director." Soon after seeing the film, he contacted Spielberg, who told him that he could never have made it if he hadn't seen *It Came from Outer Space* as a young boy.[57]

Bradbury praises *Close Encounters* because he sees it as celebrating humanity by transcending cultural boundaries, but makes little comment on its method. However, contributing to Thomas Durwood's same 1978 volume quoted earlier, Carl Sagan gave an altogether more cautious and skeptical view. He felt that the film based itself on an uncritical view of UFO sightings, though he did admit that it went counter to the Hollywood tradition in presenting extraterrestrial contact as a peaceful event. He drew a passive reactive message from its suggestion that humanity should await a visitation (which Bradbury himself contradicts in his accounts of human searching) and—Bradbury notwithstanding—found the physical similarity between ETs and humans quite implausible.

The same year that *Close Encounters* was released, Bradbury published an essay that made a position statement on the religious dimension to his own fiction. "The God in Science Fiction" opens by asserting a continuity between space flight and mythology, classical and Christian: "so old myth and new circumnavigate the stars, rebuild old dreams, repromise better destinies on far worlds we cannot now imagine."[58] Tracing out religious motifs in his fiction, Bradbury attributes his reconversion, after lapsing from the baptism of his childhood, to working on the film adaptation of *Moby-Dick*, reinforced by Bernard Shaw.[59] The most cogent aspect of the essay lies in Bradbury's self-evident need to believe in a transcendent purpose, which also informs his grandiose claims for Spielberg's film.

Bradbury's mythic reading of *Close Encounters* tends to ignore the cultural implications of its specific imagery. Despite his universalizing of the subject, the film remains rooted in postwar American depictions of UFOs and invading aliens. The early sequences in the Gobi Desert and India gesture toward a global scale to the action, but the investigators are all western; and the film follows the pattern of earlier alien landings, while revising them toward a positive spiritual encounter. When a small boy smiles with pleasure at the approach of the UFOs, his mother tries to close down her house in panic, and the two responses embody Spielberg's attempt to replace older perceptions of alien hostility with benign welcoming. The fact that the first beings to emerge from the flying saucer are Americans returning home and that the aliens physically resemble children are further signs of Spielberg's reversals. The famous five-note sequence, which triggers a musical dialogue with the aliens, is based on a western musical intervals and the emergency measures of the army, the camp constructed near the focal mountain of the visitation (named, ironically, Devil's Tower) both recall earlier American films. The action ultimately celebrates a national tradition of spiritual responsiveness as figured by the increasing use of the flying saucer as a source of radiance.[60]

Bradbury's interest in SF film continued throughout his career. He described *The Day the Earth Stood Still* as a "fine attempt to speak to mankind today about its problems on Earth" and in 1981 he was approached by Fox to write a script for a sequel.[61] In the original movie the extraterrestrial Klaatu breaks through the cliché of the hostile monstrous alien by bringing a message of peace. Personifying the logic felt to be missing from the world of 1951, his final address to political leaders carries a threat that aggression will carry automatic consequences.

Bradbury's sequel, subtitled *The Evening of the Second Day*, extends the Christian implications of the original by having its action on Christmas Eve and by conflating its setting—the Vehicle Assembly Building at Cape Canaveral—with a church. In 1951 the flying saucer lands near Washington, D.C. Bradbury's relocation of the landing suggests that the space program is central to humanity—a position he repeated constantly in his prose. Klaatu is now replaced by his daughter, a beautiful commentator on progress over the last thirty years. Recognition of the latter is offset by Klaatu's threat to neutralize technology unless, as she states: "if you have done as you say you will do, grown to fit your promise, given yourselves back to yourselves as a gift."[62] The original film's warning against aggression has been dissipated into a general plea for humanity.

MOBY-DICK IN SPACE

Bradbury's earlier collaboration with John Huston on the film of *Moby-Dick* (1956) was a major event in his career, though seemingly outside the area of Science Fiction. In fact, SF remained a major reference point during that project and evolved into *Leviathan '99* (2007), where Bradbury moved "the Moby Dick mythology beyond the stars" and some 200 years into the future.[63] A breakthrough came when he conceived of the climactic ending to the script: "My inspiration was to have Moby Dick take Ahab down and wind him in the coiled ropes and bring him up among the harpoons on this great white bier, this great cortege, this funeral at sea."[64] In his 1992 memoir-novel, *Green Shadows, White Whale*, Bradbury describes this scene as a part-resurrection, crucial to the narrative that was to evolve from his screenplay. While working on the film, in 1954 Bradbury received the news that he had been given an award by the National Institute of Arts and Letters in recognition of his contribution to American Literature. This carried an important symbolism for Bradbury, which countered Huston's ironic addressing as "H. G." as if he were a Wells clone. Hence his exclamation: "At last! God! For years people have called me Buck Rogers or Flash Gordon."[65]

With Norman Corwin's help, around 1960 Bradbury converted his screenplay for *Moby-Dick* into a Space-Age radio drama called *Leviathan '99* and completed the script in 1966. It was submitted to NBC but later broadcast by BBC Radio Three in May 1968.[66] This was subsequently reworked as a play script in 1972 and then expanded into a novella, published in 2007 with *Somewhere a Band Is Playing* in a volume entitled *Now and Forever*.[67]

An important intermediary text by Bradbury stands between the film of *Moby-Dick* and *Leviathan '99*, namely a 1962 "declamatory essay" (his own description) called "The Ardent Blasphemers," written as an introduction to *20,000 Leagues Under the Sea*. Here, he treats Verne as a courtesy American writer and draws an extended comparison between him and Melville in their descriptions of technological attacks on the universe. In that sense, both Ahab and Nemo are blasphemers, with the difference that while Ahab rages against Nature, Nemo accepts the natural world. Bradbury posits a negative, destructive mentality in America contrasted with a different tradition by the heirs of Verne and thereby ties both authors to the period of the Cold War, declaring: "we in America are just emerging from a period inclining toward the Melvillean. We are tempted to hurl our sick heart into God's face." Bradbury extrapolates Ahab into the atomic age:

> Ahab might explode a hydrogen bomb to shake the foundations of God. But in the fright-flash of illumination, at some distance. We would see Nemo reperusing

notes made in mathematical symbols to use such energy to send men to the stars rather than scatter them in green milk glass and radioactive chaff along the shore.[68]

In a 1980 interview, Bradbury explained the relation between the two protagonists: "The mad captains are identical, one is totally insane, and strikes God, the other plugs into the scientific method and solves the problems of the universe by using the energy of God creatively."[69] Although he focuses in the essay on two figures from fiction, in an interview of 1967 he generalizes blasphemy into a characteristic of America, which is constantly challenging social patterns with new inventions. In that sense, he admits, "we are an exceptionally blasphemous people."[70] There is thus a latent national theme embedded in his use of Melville and Verne.

Leviathan '99 is based primarily on a strategy of transposition, where seagoing vessels have become spaceships and the sea open space. His narrator is born in space from parents returning to Earth from Mars. Ishmael undergoes training as an astronaut for a mission he has yet to learn and this is one of the points where the analogy with Melville's novel becomes less direct. The orthodox purpose of a space flight would be "charting stars and exploring worlds," a purpose with no direct commercial aim.[71] The equivalent to Queequeg is a humanoid called Quell (from the German *Quelle* or "source"?), a tall green telepath from the Andromeda Nebula. Because Bradbury's narrative started out as a radio script, the visual dimension is minimized. Characters are primarily perceived through their voices, a fact that minimizes Quell's alien dimension and which situates him more easily within the crew of the spaceship *Cetos 7* (in Greek "whale"). The object corresponding to the white whale is a massive comet named Leviathan, described by the captain as the "brute chemistry of the universe thrown forth in light and trailing nightmare."[72] This transposition loses one of Melville's main ironies by excluding sentience from the captain's demonic Other, although Bradbury was clearly drawing on the mystery and superstitions associated with comets.[73]

So far Bradbury follows the trajectory of Melville's novel. One of the most striking innovations, however, is his complex treatment of space and space-related technology. Ishmael, for instance, reveals himself from the beginning as a rhapsodist of space whose narrative links the animate and inanimate. As he flies toward the rocket launch site, he reflects: "I was warmed by the real fire of great birds of steel, and felt the floodgates of the vast and waiting universe swing open my soul."[74] The metaphorical sequence here progresses from metal to body and then spirit, a progression that recurs throughout *Leviathan '99* and which constantly returns to the sublimity of space; space is never empty in Bradbury's narrative. As the spaceship flies further outward, it passes through "electric clouds," areas where the crew can tap into radio signals broadcast in the past.[75] Not only does space thus emerge as a kind of archive; the technology of the future gives characters access to a collective past, which is positively inspiring in its "clouds of old radio times that spoke in tongues."[76]

Space has a spiritual dimension here and a mystery debated by the characters. In the episode corresponding to Father Mapple's sermon, Bradbury's character commemorates those lost in space but also predicts a merging of self with Other in the crew's voyage: "On far worlds you will meet your own flesh, terrifying and strange, but still your own. Treat it well. Beneath the shape, you share the Godhead."[77] As we would expect, the dominant figure on the *Cetos 7* is the captain, scarred as in Melville, but "burned blind in space some years ago" by Leviathan. Whiteness has become transposed in Bradbury's narrative onto the captain's hair and dress, a visual sign that retains Melville's ambiguity: does it signify blankness or purity? The captain himself forces together spiritual opposites in his perspective on Leviathan, declaring that he touched the hem of its garment (as if it were messianic), "and then that virgin whiteness, jealous of my loving glance, rubbed out my sight."[78] His white uniform completes the impression of Moby Dick's mysterious appearance being moved on to the captain himself, who claims to see with an inner sense.

In transforming Melville's narrative for the Space Age, Bradbury introduced a latent analogy with radioactivity, which is left implicit for the most part. When whipping up his crew's enthusiasm for pursuing and in some unstated way "catching" the comet, the captain promotes radioactivity as the "largest treasure of all time." In the climax of *Leviathan '99* the captain articulates the comet's approach as a force, a "great white holy terror" filling all space and exclaims: "Oh God, that fire, brighter than ten million suns," part-echoing the words of Robert Oppenheimer at the Trinity atomic test.[79] Bradbury's captain describes how the radiance of the comet allows him to see the bones of his crew members, as if they have been exposed to X-rays or some other form of radiation, and the explosion which destroys the *Cetos 7* appears in Ishmael's account to rupture the very order of the universe. Listeners to Bradbury's radio drama would almost certainly have picked up this allusion and with it the recontextualizing of Ahab's death wish within the Cold War.

COMMENTARY ON THE SPACE AGE

The evolution of *Leviathan '99* through the different media is symptomatic of Bradbury's practice of adaptation throughout his career, and the fact that an essay played an important role in this process takes us to the last aspect of Bradbury's writing on space. From the 1950s on, he adopted the role of public commentator on the U.S. space program and his articles on that project make up a serial extension to his own fiction. During a 1975 seminar, he declared: "that's my business—to find the metaphor that explains the Space Age, and along the way write stories."[80] Bradbury saw the Space Age as a realization of a dream of flight, which had a history as long as humanity itself and one with a religious dimension. In 1960 he called on the readers of the *Los Angeles Times* to rise to the challenge of space not because of competition with the Russians, but because it can be a unifying national purpose. The latter could be fulfilled through a reinvigoration of Science Fiction, which for too long has been a term of disapprobation. "We must broaden the field," he insists, "by bringing into it the best from many areas of thinking and creativity."[81] Bradbury's emerging missionary zeal is clearer than what he expects from his readers, but his consistent enthusiasm for the space program sets him apart from other SF writers like James Blish or Cyril Kornbluth who, as Albert I. Berger has shown, tended to be wary of the institutional organization of science and the security apparatus that accompanied it.[82]

Two exceptions to Berger's account would be Bradbury and Arthur C. Clarke, though for different reasons. Bradbury was partly inspired to take long view of space and evolution by his reading of the anthropologist Loren Eiseley. He first encountered the latter's essay "The Fire Apes" in 1949, which attacked humanity's species arrogance, and from then on Bradbury followed Eiseley's writings closely, enthusiastically reviewing three of his books.[83] In *The Invisible Pyramid* (1971) Eiseley defines humanity through desire: "man would not be man if his dreams did not exceed his grasp"; he extrapolates from a fungus that fires a seed capsule into the air as an analogy for humanity's outward reach into space, describing humans as the "spore bearers."[84] The pyramid of Eiseley's title is the accretional construction of knowledge over the ages and, in the 1976 NASA symposium *Why Man Explores*, Bradbury recommended making a short film using the pyramid as a metaphor of rocket building. He was drawn to the sheer reach of Eiseley's writings and to his capacity to find large evolutionary implications in small objects and situations.[85]

Bradbury's vision of space flight as common dream was shared by his contemporary Arthur C. Clarke. In the preamble to *The Exploration of Space* (1951), Clarke discusses the symbiosis between Science Fiction narratives and scientific research, asserting that "the conquest of space must obviously have a fundamental appeal to human emotions for it to be so persistent a theme over such a span of time."[86] Clarke's enthusiasm for developments in rocket technology is offset by his underplaying of the fact that only superpowers would have the funds for the massive investment necessary to support such projects, and, because of the imperatives of the Cold war in the 1950s, that investment would be given a military direction. Soon after the publication of *The Exploration of Space*, Bradbury met Clarke on a visit to Los Angeles and was photographed holding a copy of the book.[87] There is little doubt that Bradbury was familiar with its argument and their meeting marked the start of a long-standing friendship.

By 1962, Clarke saw fresh literary potential in the development of this program, commenting that "surely the discoveries and adventures, the triumphs and inevitable tragedies that must accompany man's drive toward the stars will one day inspire a new heroic literature."[88] Clarke was responding enthusiastically to the emerging promise of the Space Age as an opening up of an infinite field of endeavor. Contrasting his view of human potential with the routinely triumphalist rhetoric of earlier books like Willy Ley's *The Conquest of Space* (1950), he insists: "space can be mapped and crossed and occupied without definable limit; but it can never be conquered." And then, drawing an analogy with the dispersal of ants around the surface of the Earth, he warns: "so it will be with us as we spread out from the Earth, loosening the bonds of kinship and understanding, hearing faint and belated rumors at second—or third—or thousandth hand of an ever-dwindling fraction of the entire human race."[89] In a similar spirit, in 1960 Bradbury hoped that the challenge of space could transcend Cold War politics: "I think Space can be our purpose," he declared, "can rally our directionless teen-agers, can open new fields of creativity for the short-story writer, the novelist, the composer of operas, and the dramatist. . . . We are going to the stars. We cannot turn back."[90] Where Clarke attempts to divorce space technology from military purposes, Bradbury would even separate space travel from technology itself as a leap of the imagination. Both writers, however, were united in their fervent promotion of space as the ultimate reach outward of the imagination.

Bradbury's writings on the U.S. space program constantly engage in a dialogue with SF concepts and tropes. In 1960 he wrote a report for *Life* magazine, "A Serious Search for Weird Worlds," on the enormous Green Bank radio telescope erected in West Virginia under Project Ozma (named after one of Frank L. Baum's principal Oz characters) which began operating in 1959. The purpose of this radio telescope was to search for evidence of life on other planets, which, if discovered, the scientists hoped would lead to an exchange of information. Bradbury glances briefly at the controversial reports from 1899 onward from Nikola Tesla that he had detected radio signals from Mars, summarized in a 1901 essay, "Talking with the Planets." The controversy entered SF folklore and was subsequently used in some of Bradbury's Mars stories, even though he seems to have been aware of a kind of mirror logic operating in Tesla's claims: we have the technology, therefore some extraterrestrial race must also possess it.

Bradbury predicts the first Mars lander, declaring: "there, under automatic TV and camera equipment, a historical event will occur: mankind, by remote control, will meet his first Martian—a bacterium jittering under a microscope." And then the novelist's imagination clearly takes over for a moment: "a half million years ago, when Earth's half-apes gamboled in an eternal nightmare spring, did civilizations rear temples, forums and ocean cities across Mars? Have the people gone to dust, or perhaps burrowed underground to escape the bitter weather?" Bradbury's clear allusion to the long-held conviction that Mars was an ancient world is only one of the many points where the essay connects with *The Martian Chronicles* specifically and with SF more generally. He admits what a staple subject of the genre invasion from Mars had become and speculates on the ironic possibility that invasion could occur through astronauts unwittingly carrying organisms back to Earth. The subject of biological invasion would be famously explored at the end of the decade in Michael Crichton's *The Andromeda Strain* (1969). Bradbury is clearly fascinated by the increasing overlap in projects like Ozma between SF and scientific speculation. However fantastic it sounds, "the thought that spores, drifting down the star winds, may have carried life from other nebulae to ours" was regarded by the scientists as possible.[91] The scenario envisaged in the opening of *Invasion of the Body Snatchers* may not be pure fantasy after all.

The second major theme which Bradbury discusses in "A Serious Search" is yet another central issue in SF. Suppose we have successfully constructed a rocket and somehow negotiated the distance from Earth, and we meet a Martian—what will it look like? His answer stays initially close to the human form: "The alien creature at our rocket door might have eyes, ears, nose and mouth, might even have a skeleton on top of which would sit the appendage called 'head' in which it would locate, through successive biological experiments, its main seeing organisms." Bradbury imagines the history of extraterrestrial species in Darwinian terms as a "competition between life forms" but then seems to revive the SF cliché of the bug-eyed monster by speculating that this creature might have a third eye or a different body temperature, or even resemble insects. In case the reader imagines that he is indulging in fantasy, Bradbury brings the reader back to Earth and back to America: "We have our own history of Indian-white relations to look back on with dismay. But these were, though savages, men. Confronted with beings resembling cockroaches, will we pause to consider whether their I.Q. is 50 or 250? Or will we simply build the grandest shoe in history and step on them?"[92] We have already seen how Bradbury draws this analogy in *The Martian Chronicles*. Here, he is simply making explicit an issue that was to be explored later by SF writers like Judith Moffett, Ursula Le Guin, and Orson Scott Card, namely the cultural coding of appearance.

THE FLIGHT OF THE SPIRIT

In his 1962 essay "Cry the Cosmos," Bradbury defines the present as the "Age of the Chrysalis," an age coming into being through flight, as he had suggested in his 1946 story with that title. The whole essay is constructed around opposites: Earth and space, life and death. Bradbury uses SF imagery here to open up large perspectives on human action and to embody opposite consequences. Thus "the rocket that can lift us to the greatest freedom since Creation can also blow us to kingdom come."[93] Like Bradbury's other essays on space, this piece works through shifts of metaphor rather than discursive argument so that the rocket can appear as a phallic image of creation or an object of technology. In a transcendental move, he dematerializes a human being into an "idea, a concept, a way of doing, a motion toward light or dark." Like a latter-day evangelist, Bradbury attacks the American preoccupation with gadgetry and narrow religious sectarianism, proposing Science Fiction as an ideal cultural means "with shorthand to educate ourselves to our central scientific and moral problems."[94]

Bradbury's writings on space during the 1960s took on an increasingly religious tone, and his 1962 story "The Machineries of Joy" gives us an indication of this emerging emphasis. Here, a group of Catholic priests are debating the ethics of space exploration against the background of experimental launches from Cape Canaveral. President Kennedy had announced the Moon program in May 1961, and the resulting flurry of publicity gives a topicality to the priest's discussion. Bradbury introduces a historical element when one priest reminds the others that Pope Pius XII had given his blessing for space travel in his address to the seventh Congress of the International Astronautical Federation, and the debate that follows sets SF clichés of bug-eyed monsters against the sobering fact of an impending launch. Thus, the story ends with a prayer by the older priest for the astronaut: "let the thing go well, going up and coming down, and think of the man in that contraption, Jesus, *think* of and be with him."[95] Essentially, the story sets up a debate about the issue Bradbury was addressing in his essays: how to think of space travel.

In 1967 *Life* magazine commissioned Bradbury to write an article on the Manned Spacecraft Center in Houston. In this piece, "An Impatient Gulliver above Our Roofs," which won two awards, Bradbury stresses a general continuity between SF and the development of the space program and at the same time finds in his visit to Houston the realization of a childhood fascination with space that began as early as 1929. In that year, as he explains, "I lay abed and lit my ceiling with night visions—bright films produced, developed and sprocketed through my head—of impossible futures. These endless entertainments I flashed up, blinking, to fill my walls. There I saw myself running down vast gantry wharves where rockets hung like a harvest of whales. There I lofted toward Alpha Centauri, wandered the dead seas of Barsoom [Edgar Rice Burroughs's Mars], and drowned in Venusian rains."[96] Bradbury describes these memories as a sort of mind cinema, one of countless signs of his fascination since childhood with film.

Bradbury's encounter with Project Apollo appeared to realize these childhood dreams. One of the first images he records is a quasicinematic perception of futuristic technology: "I stood agape amidst giant electric eyes and ears. I watched ruby-red laser beams flash down black tunnels like the trapped glance of a salamander freshly furnace to life. I saw whistling centrifuges that could throw my wits against the back side of my skull." Bradbury powerfully evokes an all-encompassing visual field where the barrage of perceptions allows him no vantage point of detachment. Here, sheer scale is everything and the image becomes a springboard for a vigorous attack on down-scaling in American culture, especially through the medium of television, which reduces size and thereby fails to do justice to the grandeur of its images. He waxes indignant over the diminution of a Saturn rocket and of *King Kong* because the first is "redesigning mankind" and the second is "one of the greatest adventure movies ever made." Thus he declares: "we misproportion any art if we make a lapdog of it." "We Americans," he continues, "because of our reverse-telescope vision given us by TV, are still Singer's-midget oriented, myopic. We have grown too casual about the Saturn-Apollo rocket simply because we can reach out and cover it with one hand palmed on the picture tube."[97]

Singer's Midgets played the Munchkins in *The Wizard of Oz* and the allusion nudges us toward an analogy, which Bradbury pursues throughout the essay between the Houston center and a Hollywood film studio. As he later recalled, a key moment in writing the essay came when he realized that he was "looking at a theater."[98] Thus the astronauts are described as stars before the fact: "We are training and retraining, rehearsing and re-rehearsing flesh-and-blood actors who are to perform in the Olympean drama of the Star Wilderness." Center and studio both have their directors, costumes, and props, but above all both have size and it is through size that the sublime grandeur of the concept and the physical scale of the space program can be perceived. Apart from the latter's future promise, Bradbury records his visit as a return: "In going to Houston I not only went back to a country learnt from science-stories and comic strips as a boy, but to movies seen and loved when I was 10, 11 and 12." The continuity between these works and the Apollo program is given a clear nationalistic dimension when Bradbury draws parallels between the astronauts, Columbus, and pioneer explorers. He also takes evident satisfaction in the parallels between the Houston simulation modules and his story "The Rocket" (from *The Illustrated Man*), where a father builds his family an "illusion-camera-obscura box" fitted out with a film projector and technical props in order to give them the illusion of rocket travel. In Houston he finds the same principle being applied since "each module was clustered over with motion-picture television equipment, screens and all the dream paraphernalia."[99]

Bradbury celebrates the space program as the realization of a primal impulse to travel. In brief, he declares, "we go to Space because we must. We are anthill men upon an anthill world. Time, in its great blind soldiering from one end of the universe to the other, might tread us down. We would avoid the dumb brute's careless walk. So the ant dares name himself king of some yet further hill." By the end of his essay Bradbury has moved into the realm of the mythic where the problematic size of humanity is compensated for by the grandeur of their actions. He looks forward to a notional future point where the last rocket has departed from Earth and the last man is looking back on the sequence of human achievement. Once again this was not a new perception for Bradbury. To conclude his reflections he quotes from a much earlier last man fragment, which reaches its apotheosis in space flight:

> And the rocket goes to space.
>
> And the empty Earth is left behind as the children of Adam and Ahab and Nemo and Moses bid the Black Sea of Space to move aside so they might pass.[100]

Bradbury had earlier celebrated this subject in one of his best-known poems, "Christus Apollo," which he published as a coda to *I Sing the Body Electric!* (1969). Here, he combines the story of Christmas, the national narrative and a declaration of human potential to evoke the working of the life force as motion into outer space "to birth ourselves anew."[101] Unlike the situational limits of Bradbury's stories, his voice here is expansive and speaks collectively for the nation and all of humanity. Bradbury had earlier taken the name of Project

Apollo as defining a new age and in a 1971 review foresaw the emergence of a "great new chronicle" on the Space Age.[102]

In "The Ardent Blasphemers," Bradbury links Verne with Melville as setting a trend for later SF writers through their protagonists' restless inability to accept the material universe as it is. In "An Impatient Gulliver," Bradbury conflates the Eden and Exodus stories with these writers in a composite grand narrative where humanity is always moving on to its next phase, hence his indignation during a televised panel in 1972 on the Moon landing. When the latter's value was questioned, Bradbury retorted: "This is the result of six billion years of evolution. Tonight, we have given the lie to gravity. We have reached for the stars . . . And you refuse [to] celebrate? To hell with you!" (ellipses Bradbury's).[103]

In November 1971, the Mariner 9 space probe reached Mars and went into orbit. To signal the importance of the event a panel discussion was arranged at the California Institute of Technology with Bradbury, Arthur C. Clarke, Carl Sagan, and others. Bradbury used the occasion to restate his enthusiasm for Edgar Rice Burroughs and to gloss his 1949 story, "Dark They Were, and Golden-Eyed," which describes the experiences of a family of settlers on Mars, as follows: "the day finally comes when they find that the odd weathers and peculiar temperatures of the Red Planet have melted their flesh into new shapes, tinted their skin, and put flecks of gold into their now most fantastic eyes."[104] In short, he explains, they have become Martians. Bradbury cites Hazlitt's essay "On Going a Journey" ("the soul of a journey is liberty, perfect liberty") and launches into a Whitmanesque celebration of his own fictional subjects:

> I sing paradoxical man.
>> I accept not only his flesh but the bones within his flesh and the sin marrowing those bones.
> I sing the entire man, then, going into Space.[105]

For him the Mars probe forms part of an extended reach outward charged with symbolism, and in that sense Bradbury sees the event as a continuation of his own imaginative enterprise in *The Martian Chronicles* and related fiction.

For his part, Clarke endorsed Bradbury's enthusiasm for Burroughs and also paid tribute to Stanley Weinbaum's *Martian Odyssey* as formative in shaping our image of Mars, though he clearly found the continuing influence of Percival Lowell oppressive. Clarke reflected on the problematic and shifting relation of SF visions of Mars to the latest discoveries, an issue that he later expressed in his introduction to Jack Williamson's 1992 novel of a Mars mission, *Beachhead*. Clarke pays Bradbury the ambiguous compliment of placing him in old-school SF and recognizes the impact of the latest discoveries: "It's quite a challenge . . . to write an exciting story about the exploration of Mars without inventing implausibilities that may be refuted in a few years' time."[106] Clarke's position is revisionist rather than negative, because he saw the surge of scientific knowledge about Mars as fueling new fantasies about the planet. Even in his afterthoughts on the 1971 discussion, however, Bradbury remained unperturbed by the new discoveries, describing the photographs of Mars as "pictures of your next home."[107] And two years later he admitted that his Mars fiction would be reconceived "from Possible Future to mythological but Immediate Past."[108]

Bradbury recalled watching the landing of Viking 1 on Mars on July 20, 1976, at the NASA Jet Propulsion Laboratory in Pasadena in the company of Carl Sagan, Wernher von Braun, and others.[109] When a reporter from ABC television asked him where the Martian cities and beings were, Bradbury reasserted the final image of *The Martian Chronicles* by retorting: "You idiot! You fool! There is life on Mars—look at us! Look at us! We are the Martians!"[110] Despite generational and career differences, the astrophysicist Carl Sagan shared a common background with Bradbury. By 1976 Sagan had been a long-standing supporter of the Search for Extra-Terrestrial Intelligence (SETI) project, the early phase of which Bradbury described in "A Serious Search" (1960). His 1979 best-selling study of science, *Broca's Brain*, devotes a whole chapter to Science Fiction, where he describes, like Bradbury, his early childhood enthusiasm for Burroughs's Mars novels, which offered an "inhabited extraterrestrial world breathtakingly fleshed out." A seasoned reader by the late 1940s, Sagan never abandoned this enthusiasm, arguing that SF complements science because "it can convey bits and pieces, hints and phrases, of knowledge unknown or inaccessible to the reader."[111] In his brief roll call of the genre he includes "many of the works of Ray Bradbury." Like Bradbury,

Sagan saw the developing use of spaceships as a continuation of the grand narrative of exploration that would continue into the future.[112]

SPACE COLONIES

It is a sign of Bradbury's continuing commitment to the space program that in 1978 he contributed an enthusiastic introduction to the aerospace engineer T. A. Heppenheimer's *Colonies in Space*, whom he had helped in the preparation of the manuscript. A campaigner for space research and a planetary scientist, Heppenheimer clearly viewed his book as a belated tribute to John F. Kennedy, its dedicatee, for opening up the concept of the high frontier, extending the national tradition of exploration into near space.[113] Bradbury similarly was fascinated by the notion, further popularized after 1966 by the *Star Trek* slogan "space—the final frontier." Indeed, at one point Gene Roddenberry invited Bradbury to write for *Star Trek*, but he declined on the grounds that he could not write other people's characters, although he liked the series.[114] Introducing a symposium on the frontier theme in SF, Gary Westfahl has pointed to two unavoidable problems in the concept. First, within our revised consciousness of U.S. history, the frontier has come to mean genocide and brutal suppression, a shift that Bradbury had already written into *The Martian Chronicles* in his allusions to the Native Americans. And second, the more sophisticated space exploration has become, the more difficult it has been to cling to the hope for humanity finding a possible habitat on another planet.[115]

Colonies in Space was illustrated by Chesley Bonestell, whose art work was featured on the covers of *Galaxy* magazine, and in the text Heppenheimer engages in a lively commentary on the relation between scientific discovery and Science Fiction, particularly since the 1950s. Thus he takes Rudolph Maté's 1951 film *When Worlds Collide* as one of the last naive works to be produced in the period before the establishment of the National Aeronautics and Space Administration (NASA) in 1958, but nevertheless an important articulation of humanity's "hope of finding new lands," which Heppenheimer takes as a constant in history. The film, based on the 1933 novel by Philip Wylie and Edwin Balmer, describes the construction of a spaceship as a latter-day Noah's Ark to carry survivors to safety after the planet Zyra collides with the Earth. For the action to carry any kind of credibility, we have to assume that there is at least one nearby planet that could sustain human life, but, as Heppenheimer stresses, this is a huge assumption because "the probability of finding life on another planet is inverse to the amount of data we have on that planet."[116] The more we know, the less likely extraterrestrial races become.

Despite his recognition of budgetary restrictions and other practical factors, Heppenheimer never loses his faith in space exploration, speculating that the first settlements will "resemble the American West, with its vast promise for those who would win its land." This vision even leads him to speculate on a rectification of the fate that befell Native Americans: "we may see the return of the Cherokee or Arapaho nation—not necessarily with a revival of the culture of prairie, horse, and buffalo, but in the founding of self-governing communities which reflect the distinctly Arapaho or Cherokee customs and attitudes toward man and nature."[117] Heppenheimer's optimistic vision suggests that the wrongs of American history can be rectified, in marked contrast to Bradbury's ironic historical allusions in *The Martian Chronicles*.

Bradbury was drawn to Heppenheimer's ideas for broadly mythical reasons, seeing the cause of space colonies as an expression of the life force, in other words of a positive impulse to develop human potential as against the deadly rituals being played out by the superpowers in the arms race. The space program for him offered a possible counter to the self-destructive impulse in humanity, arguing: "so much more reason then to cultivate our gardens in space, invite ourselves back in through the gates of time and travel, and establish ourselves not just beyond the Moon but beyond Mars and beyond Pluto and, finally, beyond Death."[118] Bradbury's trajectory works simultaneously backward into mythic time to reverse the Fall, and also forward, out into space. His introduction gains its inspirational force from his use of tropes of liberation, whereby space travel offers us the chance to become "citizens of the Universe."

CODA: SPACE VISIONARY

It should already have become evident that for Bradbury space was an article of faith supporting national ideals. In a 1972 contribution to the Perry Rhodan series, Bradbury commemorates the Moon landing as the "special day when, after three billion years of genetic waiting, genetic dreaming, Man reached up to Touch Space, Touch Moon, Touch Eternity."[119] In short, the landing marked the beginning of the Age of Apollo.[120] Bradbury saw the allocation of funds for the Vietnam War as a betrayal of this promise and repeatedly offered to make films for NASA promoting the space program.

By 1964, Bradbury later explained, his presentation at the New York World's Fair linked Melville, Verne, and space rockets:

> I saw the history of the United States as a history of the three wildernesses: the wilderness of the sea that we crossed to come here, the wilderness of the land that we nailed down to stay here, and the wilderness of the stars to which we move to live forever. So, we have the symbol of the white whale and the symbol of the *Nautilus* submarine, the machine. Within that, we have the symbol of the rocket ship, all the same size and shape.

And then he comes to his key assertion: "space travel is a religious movement—not political or military."[121] Bradbury later explained that in this and similar presentations he was trying to "fuse poetry and fact" in ways that extend the methods of his fiction into other contexts.[122] Like Loren Eiseley, whose works he admired for their intellectual breadth, Bradbury saw no opposition between science and religion. In his address to a 1972 series on Cosmic Evolution, he predicted that the gap between the two would close up.

In his 1980 essay "The God in Science Fiction," Bradbury speculates on the creative energy of the human imagination: "Are we ourselves in some miraculous fashion the Holy Ghost that will haunt the cosmic dusts and call them alive? Will we conjure dead matter on Martian thresholds and Christ-like summon it up into intelligence and immortal life as we pass?" Looking back on his career, Bradbury describes writing the script for *Moby-Dick* as a "born again" experience and gives a strikingly spiritual gloss on two of his Martian stories. "The Rocket" is described as a "parable of faith" and he explains the Martians in "The Fire Balloons" as "spirits without our earthly encumbrances and temptations," in other words as creatures "without sin."[123] Bradbury rounds off his essay by stressing what an inspirational figure Shaw was: he "spoke from pulpits long before our time." Bradbury draws these works and figures together in the trope of a collective quest: "We all go on the same Search, looking to solve the old Mystery."[124]

Since Bradbury was articulating his faith in space through spiritual tropes rather than discursive argument, it was consistent for him to use poetry as a medium for expression. His 1976 poem "Why the Viking Lander? Why Mars?"

characteristically doesn't appeal to material or scientific aims but turns to Bernard Shaw for an answer. Bradbury finds it in the Life Force put forward by Juan in *Man and Superman*, where it denotes a collective willed purpose. He respiritualized it into a quest with "Mars but a beginning / Real Heaven our end."[125] After a visit to Cape Canaveral, Bradbury wrote a poem celebrating the sublime dimension to the space program as the will made flesh, setting up a countervoice to the official notices that supplied his title, "Abandon in Place." J. G. Ballard would focus on the irony of contemporary technology becoming the new ruins, but Bradbury resolutely turns against the past in his final lines calling on the "old ghosts of rocketmen" to arise: "fling up your ships, your souls, your flesh, your blood / our blinding dreams" to fill once again the skies.[126] The focus on human agency rather than technology, the rallying call for vigorous symbolic action, is a consistent priority throughout Bradbury's career.

In their 2001 volume *Imagining Space*, the NASA historians Roger D. Launius and Howard E. McCurdy pay tribute to the visionaries without whom the program would not have existed, visionaries including the SF writers Arthur C. Clarke (especially for *The Exploration of Space*), Isaac Asimov for his *Foundation* series, and of course Bradbury himself. In his foreword, Bradbury re-creates the prophetic voice of "Christus Apollo," recasting a creation narrative to suggest that dream emerges from the terrain of Earth itself: "out of primitive thought and motion and sustenance, it came forth on Earth; we know not where or when, but we inherit the why. We have arrived to audience the wonders, to speak the miracles. We are shadow and substance; shadow which cloaks itself in substance and calls itself Life."[127] Here, the rhetoric takes on a formal level (syntactic repetition and parallelism, archaisms like "we know not," and so forth) to reflect the perceived grandeur of the local subject. Bradbury closes up the gap between spirit and matter to suggest that the life force is somehow embedded in the Earth and quite distinct from an individual consciousness. The rhetorical and allusive density of these lines underpin Bradbury's larger claim that a new age has come into being with the beginnings of space exploration. However declamatory, Bradbury's words harmonize completely with the grand narrative of *Imagining Space*, which is given a specifically American emphasis by, among other comparisons, the analogy drawn with the Lewis and Clark Expedition into the West and by the whole rhetoric of space as the ultimate frontier.

Throughout his career Bradbury saw Science Fiction, the visual arts, and science as interacting with each other. One of his last prose pieces was an afterword to a 2008 retrospective volume on the NASA art program, where he praised the grand vision of the organization. In effect, he uses NASA as a means of embodying a collective witness to the sublimity of space:

> We stand with NASA in response to the incredible miracle of impossible life on an insensate world.
>
> We move back to a Moon that we wish we had never deserted.
>
> We move onward to Mars to establish a base and then a community and finally a miniature civilization on its enigmatic soil.
>
> All this will be done not as a technological fear [sic], a military exercise, or as a display of human vanity . . .
>
> NASA's activities are our activities. The purpose of life on Earth is to see, to know, and to tell what the Cosmos has to offer.[128]

It reflected the status of Bradbury's writing that the 2007 Phoenix lander to Mars took with it a DVD called *Visions of Mars* containing writings by Carl Sagan, Arthur C. Clarke, and not least Bradbury. It is difficult to overstate Bradbury's historical importance. He had a formative influence on a whole generation of SF writers, who continue to produce volumes of tribute stories, and his works are at last gaining recognition for their narration of speculative themes through sophisticated scenic methods.

FICTION BY BRADBURY (SELECTED)

Unattributed references throughout are to Bradbury's works. Bradbury references to first editions unless otherwise stated. The reader is referred to Eller and Touponce's appendixes (*Ray Bradbury: The Life of Fiction*, 437–514) for a listing of Bradbury's stories, published and unpublished, which gives full details of their appearances, revisions, title changes, and so forth.

Ahmed and the Oblivion Machines: A Fable. New York: Morrow, 1998.

The Autumn People. New York: Ballantine, 1965.

Bradbury Stories: 100 of His Most Celebrated Tales. New York: Morrow, 2003. Reprinted as Vol. 2 of *Stories*, 2008.

The Cat's Pyjamas: Stories. New York: Morrow, 2004.

Classic Stories 1: Selections from The Golden Apples of the Sun and R Is for Rocket. New York: Bantam, 1990.

Classic Stories 2: Selections from A Medicine for Melancholy and S Is for Space. New York: Bantam, 1990.

The Collected Stories of Ray Bradbury: A Critical Edition. Volume 1: 1938–1943. Ed. William F. Touponce and Jonathan R. Eller. Kent, Ohio: Kent State University Press, 2010.

Dark Carnival. Sauk City, Wis.: Arkham House, 1947; expanded edition, Springfield, Pa.: Gauntlet Press, 2001.

Death Is a Lonely Business. New York: Knopf, 1985.

Dinosaur Tales. New York: Bantam, 1984.

The Dragon Who Ate His Tail. Colorado Springs: Gauntlet Press, 2007.

Driving Blind. New York: Avon, 1997.

Fahrenheit 451. New York: Ballantine, 1953; 60th Anniversary Edition, New York: Simon and Schuster, 2013; contains additional material.

Farewell Summer. New York: Morrow, 2006.

Fever Dream. New York: St. Martin's Press / Night Lights, 1987.

The Fog Horn and Other Stories. Tokyo: Kinseido, 1981.

Forever and the Earth: Yesterday and Tomorrow Stories. Hornsea, U.K.: PS Publishing, 2006.

From the Dust Returned: A Family Remembrance. New York: Morrow, 2001.

The Golden Apples of the Sun. Garden City, N.Y.: Doubleday, 1953.

A Graveyard for Lunatics: Another Tale of Two Cities. New York: Knopf, 1990.

Green Shadows, White Whale. New York: Knopf, 1992.

The Halloween Tree. New York: Knopf, 1972.

The Halloween Tree. Ed. Jon Eller. Colorado Springs: Gauntlet Press, 2005. Restored text with screenplay.

The Illustrated Man. Garden City, N.Y.: Doubleday, 1951; 45th anniversary edition, Springfield, Pa.: Gauntlet Press, 1996.

I Sing the Body Electric! New York: Knopf, 1969; expanded edition, New York: Avon, 1998.

Is That You, Herb? Colorado Springs: Gauntlet Press, 2003.

The Last Circus and the Electrocution. Northridge, Calif.: Lord John Press, 1980.

Let's All Kill Constance: A Novel. New York: Morrow/HarperCollins, 2003.

Long after Midnight. New York: Knopf, 1976; expanded edition, Hornsea, U.K.: PS Publishing, 2010.

The Machineries of Joy. New York: Simon and Schuster, 1964.

Marionettes, Inc. Burton, Mich.: Subterranean Press, 2009.

The Martian Chronicles. Garden City, N.Y.: Doubleday, 1950.

The Martian Chronicles: The Complete Edition. Burton, Mich.: Subterranean Press, 2009.

Match to Flame: The Fictional Paths to Fahrenheit 451. Ed. Donn Albright and Jon Eller. Colorado Springs: Gauntlet Publications, 2006.

A Medicine for Melancholy. New York: Doubleday, 1959.

A Memory of Murder. New York: Dell, 1984.

The Novels of Ray Bradbury. London: Granada, 1984. Omnibus of *Fahrenheit 451, Dandelion Wine,* and *Something Wicked.*

Now and Forever: Somewhere a Band Is Playing and Leviathan '99. New York: Morrow, 2007.

The October Country. New York: Ballantine, 1955; expanded edition, Springfield, Pa.: Gauntlet Press, 1997.

One More for the Road. New York: Morrow, 2002.

One Timeless Spring. New York: Aeonian Press, 1980.

The Parrot Who Met Papa. Rochester, Mich.: Pretentious Press, 1991.

The Pedestrian. Glendale, Calif.: Roy Squires, 1964.

A Pleasure to Burn: Fahrenheit 451 Stories. Ed. Donn Albright and Jon Eller. Burton, Mich.: Subterranean Press, 2010.

Quicker than the Eye. New York: Avon, 1996.

Ray Bradbury. Ed. Anthony Adams. New York: Harrap, 1975.

R Is for Rocket. Garden City, N.Y.: Doubleday, 1962.

The Shop of Mechanical Insects. Burton, Mich.: Subterranean Press, 2009.

S Is for Space. Garden City, N.Y.: Doubleday, 1966.

Skeletons. Burton, Mich.: Subterranean Press, 2008.

The Small Assassin. London: Ace, 1962.

Something Wicked This Way Comes. New York: Simon and Schuster, 1962.

A Sound of Thunder. Genova: Cideb, 1994.

Stories. 2 vols. London: HarperCollins, 2008.

The Stories of Ray Bradbury. New York: Knopf, 1980. Vol. 1 of the collection listed earlier.

Summer Morning, Summer Night. Ed. Donn Albright and Jon Eller. Burton, Mich.: Subterranean Press, 2010.

There Will Come Soft Rains. Logan, Ind.: Perfection Form, 1989.

Time Intervening. Springfield, Pa.: Gauntlet Press, 2001.

To Sing Strange Songs. Exeter, U.K.: Arnold-Wheaton, 1979.

The Toynbee Convector. New York: Knopf, 1988.

Twice 22. Garden City, N.Y.: Doubleday, 1966. Combines *The Golden Apples* and *A Medicine.*

The Veldt. Logan, Ind.: Perfection Form, 1982.

The Vintage Bradbury: Ray Bradbury's Own Selection of His Best Stories. New York: Vintage, 1965.

Where Everything Ends. Burton, Mich.: Subterranean Press, 2003. Omnibus including *Death Is a Lonely Business* and *A Graveyard for Lunatics.*

POETRY, PLAYS, SCREENPLAYS, AND EDITED COLLECTIONS (SELECTED)

The Anthem Sprinters, and Other Antics. New York: Dial Press, 1963. Collected in *Ray Bradbury on Stage.*

"Bradbury's Comic Adaptation of Edgar Rice Burroughs." *New Ray Bradbury Review* 1 (2008): 174–175. Juvenilia.

Bullet Trick: A Collection of Unpublished Teleplays and Short Stories. Colorado Springs: Gauntlet Press, 2009.

A Chapbook for Burnt-Out Priests, Rabbis and Ministers. Abingdon, Md.: Cemetery Dance Publications, 2001. Miscellany.

"'The Chrysalis': A Bradbury Screenplay Fragment." Ed. Jon Eller. *New Ray Bradbury Review* 2 (2010): 67–73.

Ed. *The Circus of Dr. Lao and Other Improbable Stories.* New York: Bantam, 1956.

The Climate of Palettes. Northridge, Calif.: Lord John Press, 1989. Poetry.

The Complete Poems of Ray Bradbury. New York: Ballantine, 1982.

Dawn to Dusk: Cautionary Travels. Ed. Donn Albright. Colorado Springs: Gauntlet Publications, 2011. Screenplays.

The Day It Rained Forever: A Comedy in One Act. New York: Samuel French, 1966.

The Day the Earth Stood Still II. The Evening of the Second Day. March 10, 1981; screen outline, at http://www.scifiscripts.com/scripts/treatment_1.htm (accessed March 3, 2014).

Death Has Lost Its Charm for Me. Northridge, Calif.: Lord John Press, 1987. Poetry.

Fahrenheit 451. Woodstock, Ill.: Dramatic Publishing Co., 1986.

Falling Upward. Woodstock, Ill.: The Dramatic Publishing Company, 1988.

The First Book of Dichotomy, the Second Book of Symbiosis. Santa Barbara, Calif.: Joshua Odell, 1995. Miscellany re-titled *A Chapbook for Burnt-Out Priests,* 2001.

"From the Archives: A Selection of Ray Bradbury's Fragments." Ed. with commentary William F. Touponce. *New Ray Bradbury Review* 3 (2012): 10–84.

Ed. *Futuria Fantasia* (4 issues, 1939–1940). Issues for Summer 1939, Fall 1939, Spring 1940, and Winter 1940, at http://www.gutenberg.org/ebooks/search/?query=futuria+fantasia/ (accessed March 3, 2014). Reprinted, Seattle, Wash.: CreateSpace, 2012.

The Ghosts of Forever. Buenos Aires: Ediciones Libreria la Ciudad, 1980; New York: Rizzoli, 1981. Poems and essays.

Gotcha! Ed. William F. Touponce. *New Ray Bradbury Review* 1 (2008): 127–162. 1988 teleplay.

The Haunted Computer and the Android Pope. New York: Knopf, 1981.

I Live By the Invisible. Cliffs of Moher, Ireland: Salmon Publishing Company, 2002. Poetry.

It Came from Outer Space. Ed. Donn Albright. Colorado Springs: Gauntlet Press, 2004. Screenplay and related material.

The Love Affair. Northridge, Calif.: Lord John Press, 1982. Poetry and story.

The Martian Chronicles. Woodstock, Ill.: Dramatic Publishing Co., 1986.

Moby Dick: A Screenplay. Burton, Mich.: Subterranean Press, 2008.

The Nefertiti-Tut Express: A Story in Screenplay. Glendale, Calif.: RAS Press, 2012.

Nemo! Burton, Mich.: Subterranean Press, 2012. Screenplay.

Old Ahab's Friend, and Friend to Noah, Speak His Piece. Glendale, Calif.: Roy A Squires, 1971. Poem chapbook.

The Pedestrian: A Fantasy in One Act. New York: Samuel French, 1966.

Pillar of Fire and Other Plays. New York: Bantam, 1975. Collected in *Ray Bradbury on Stage.*

Ray Bradbury on Stage: A Chrestomathy of His Plays. New York: Donald I. Fine, 1991.

They Have Not Seen the Stars: The Collected Poetry of Ray Bradbury. Lancaster, Pa.: Stealth Press, 2002.

This Attic Where the Meadow Greens. Northridge, Calif.: Lord John Press, 1979. Poetry.

Ed. *Timeless Stories for Today and Tomorrow.* New York: Bantam, 1952.

Twin Hieroglyphs That Swim the River Dus. Northridge, Calif.: Lord John Press, 1978. Poetry.

The Veldt. Woodstock, Ill.: The Dramatic Publishing Company, 1988.

When Elephants Last in the Dooryard Bloomed: Celebrations for Almost Any Day in the Year. New York: Knopf, 1973. Poems.

Where Robot Mice and Robot Men Run Round in Robot Towns. New York: Knopf, 1977. Poems.

The Wonderful Ice Cream Suit and Other Plays for Today, Tomorrow and Beyond Tomorrow. New York: Bantam, 1972. Collected in *Ray Bradbury on Stage.*

NONFICTION (SELECTED)

"20,000 Leagues beneath the Imagination of Jules Verne." *Los Angeles Times* (September 26, 1976): M1, 12. Review of Jean Jules Verne, *Jules Verne: A Biography.*

"240-Page Poem of Simmering Life Vibrations." *Los Angeles Times* (December 12, 1971). Review of Loren Eiseley, *The Night Country.*

Afterword and Coda. *Fahrenheit 451: The 50th Anniversary Edition.* New York: Ballantine, 1991, 167–173, 175–179, and at http://www.american-buddha.com/fahren-ray.4.htm (accessed March 3, 2014).

"The American Journey." Script for Federal Pavilion at New York World's Fair 1964/5), at http://www.nywf64.com/unista09.shtml/ (accessed March 3, 2014).

"Anthropologist's Magic Vision of Nature." *Los Angeles Times* (December 14, 1969). Review of Loren Eiseley, *The Unexpected Universe.*

"Apollo Murdered: The Sun Goes Out." *Los Angeles Times* (May 17, 1972). *Perry Rhodan 18: The Menace of the Mutant Master,* by Kurt Mahr. New York: Ace, 1972, 8–10.

"The Ardent Blasphemers." Introduction to Verne, *20,000 Leagues under the Sea,* 1962. Collected in *Bradbury Speaks.*

"An Artist's-Eye View of Space Renaissance." *Los Angeles Times* (October 24, 1971). Review of H. L. Cook and James H. Dean, *Eyewitness to Space.*

At What Temperature Do Books Burn?" *New York Times* (November 13, 1966); *Writer* (July 1967): 18–20. As introduction to *Fahrenheit 451*. New York: Simon and Schuster, 1967.

"Author, Author: Ray Bradbury." *The Fanscient* 6 (Winter 1949): 18–24. Collected in *Fanscient Omnibus* 2 (all issues from 1949).

"Author's Afterword." *Fahrenheit 451*. New York: Ballantine, 1981.

"Beyond Eden." *Omni* (April 1980): 88–89, 114–116.

"Book Burning without Striking a Match." *Los Angeles Times* (May 27, 1979).

"The Bradbury—Berenson Correspondence." Ed. Jon Eller. *New Ray Bradbury Review* 2 (2010): 28–66.

Bradbury Speaks: Too Soon from the Cave, Too Far from the Stars. New York: Morrow, 2005.

"Burning Bright: A Foreword." *Fahrenheit 451: 40th Anniversary Edition*. New York: Simon and Schuster, 1993.

"Confederation Guest of Honor Speech." *Science Fiction Chronicle* 8.iii (December 1986): 22–34.

"Creativity in the Space Age." *Engineering and Science* 26.ix (June 1963): 10–15.

"Cry the Cosmos: A Provocative Essay." *Life* 53.xi (September 14, 1962): 86–94.

"Death Warmed Over." *Playboy* (January 1968): 100–102, 252–253. Introduction to Haining (1972).

"Dusk in the Robot Museums: The Rebirth of Imagination." *Mosaic* 13.iii–iv (Spring–Summer 1980): v–x. Collected in Bloom 2001b. Collected as "On the Shoulders of Giants" in *Zen in the Art of Writing*.

"The Fahrenheit Chronicles." *Spacemen* 8 (June 1964): 30–34, at http://home.wlv.ac.uk/~in5379/films/spacemen_mag/spacemen_mag.htm (accessed March 3, 2014).

"Fahrenheit on Film." *Los Angeles Times* (November 20, 1966): M1, 16.

"A Few Notes on *The Martian Chronicles*." *Rhodomagnetic Digest* (May 1950): 21.

"Films." *Psychology Today* 2.i (June 1968): 10. Review of *2001: Space Odyssey*.

"From Stonehenge to Tranquillity Base." *Playboy* (December 1972): 149, 322, 324. Foreword to Flindt.

"G.B.S. Refurbishing the Tin Woodman: Science Fiction with a Heart, a Brain, and the Nerve!" *Shaw and Science Fiction: Annual of Bernard Shaw Studies* 17 (1997): 11–18. Ed. Milton T. Wolf. Collected in *Bradbury Speaks*.

"The God in Science Fiction." *Saturday Review of Literature* (December 10, 1977): 36–43; Northridge, Calif.: Santa Susana Press, 1978; *Omni* (October 1980): 108–112.

"Horrors! Films That Are Frightful? Delightful!" Salt Lake City *Deseret News* (October 24, 1979): C1.8; and at http://news.google.com/newspapers?nid=Aul-kAQHnToC&dat=19791024&printsec=frontpage&hl=en (website currently unavailable).

"How, instead of Being Educated in College, I Was Graduated from Libraries, or Thoughts from a Chap Who Landed on the Moon in 1932." *Wilson Library Bulletin* 45.ix (May 1971): 842–851.

"How I Was Always Rich and Too Dumb to Know It." *Producer's Journal* (January 1975); *Pages: The World of Books, Writers and Writing* 1. Detroit: Gale, 1976, 189–193.

"How Not to Burn a Book; or, 1984 Will Not Arrive." *Soundings: Collections of the University Library* 7.i (Summer 1975): 4–32. University of California, Santa Barbara.

"How to Be Madder than Captain Ahab or, Writing Explained." *Literary Cavalcade* (October 1973). *The Writer's Guide to Fantasy Literature*. Ed. Philip Martin. Waukesha, Wis.: Writer Books, 2002, 225–228.

"An Impatient Gulliver above Our Roofs." *Life* (November 24, 1967): 3, 22, 31, 32, 34–36.

Introduction. *Fahrenheit 451. 50th Anniversary Edition*. New York: Simon and Schuster, 2003, 23–30; contains "A New Introduction," 5–9.

"I Was There the Day the World Ended, I Was There the Day the World Began." *Magazine of Fantasy and Science Fiction* 97.iv/v (October/November 1999): 10–16.

"John Collier Probes the Darker Regions." *Los Angeles Times* (December 10, 1972). Review of *The John Collier Reader*.

"Journey to a Far Metaphor." *Washington Post Book World* (September 11, 1994). Introduction to Weist.

"Kuttner Recalled." *Conversations with the Weird Tales Circle*. Ed. John Pelan and Jerard Walters. Lake Wood, Colo.: Centipede Press, 2009, 423–425.

"LA's Future Is Up in the Air." *Los Angeles Times* (February 5, 2006), at http://articles .latimes.com/2006/feb/05/opinion/op-bradbury5 (accessed March 3, 2014).

"Letter on Clark Ashton Smith." Donald Sidney-Fryer, *Emperor of Dreams: A Clark Ashton Smith Bibliography*. West Kingston, R.I.: Donald M. Grant, 1978, 108.

"Literature in the Space Age." *California Librarian* (July 1960): 159–164.

"Looking into the Future—Good or Bad." *Los Angeles Times* (October 25, 1970): J1, 6. Review of Ray Brosseau, ed., *Looking Forward*.

"The Machine-Tooled Happyland." *Holiday* (October 1965), 100, 102, 104, at http:// holidaymag.wordpress.com/2012/01/20/the-machine-tooled-happyland-by-ray -bradbury-october-1965 (accessed April 24, 2014).

"Magic, Magicians, Carnival and Fantasy." *Ray Bradbury Review* (1952): 7–10.

"Man and His Spaceship Earth: Theme Show for EPCOT Center/Future World." WED Enterprises, 1977, at http://www.scribd.com/doc/97383243/Ray-Bradbury-Man-and-His -Spaceship-Earth-1977/ (accessed March 3, 2014).

"The Man Who Tried Everything." *Life* 60.vi (February 11, 1966): 12. Review of Julian Huxley, ed., *Aldous Huxley, 1894–1963*.

"Mars and the Mind of Man." With Arthur C. Clarke et al. *Engineering and Science* 35.iii (January 1972): 17–19. Incorporated in *Mars and the Mind of Man*. New York: Harper & Row, 1973.

"Marvels and Miracles—Pass It On." *New York Times Magazine* (March 20, 1955): 26–27, 56, 58.

"Memories Shape the Voice." *The Voice of the Narrator in Children's Literature*. Ed. Charlotte F. Otten and Gary D. Schmidt. Westport, Conn.: Greenwood Press, 1989, 132–138.

"My Mars." *National Geographic Magazine* (October 2008): 3, at http://ngm. nationalgeographic.com/2008/10/space-special/bradbury-text/3 (accessed March 3, 2014).

"New Perspectives on the Dawning of the Age of Apollo." *Los Angeles Times* (May 10, 1970): D1, 16. Review of Neil Armstrong, *First on the Moon*.

"Novelist Appraises Himself, His Craft." *Los Angeles Times* (December 11, 1950): G6.

"On a Book Burning." *Algol* 19 (November 15, 1972): 13–14.

"The Opening Speaker of the 'Cosmic Evolution' lecture series, Ray Bradbury, on July 10, 1972." Transcript at http://www.donaldedavis.com/2012%20new/BRADBURY.html (accessed April 24, 2014).

"Opening the Beautiful Door of True Immortality." *Los Angeles Times* Calendar (November 20, 1977). Review of *Close Encounters of the Third Kind*.

"Percipient Witness." *Heinlein Journal* 11 (July 2002): 3.

"Ray Bradbury." *National Book Awards Acceptance Speeches* (2002), at http://www
.nationalbook.org/nbaacceptspeech_rbradbury.html (accessed March 3, 2014).

"Ray Bradbury: Confederation Guest of Honor Speech." *Science Fiction Chronicle* 8.iii
(December 1986): 22, 24, 31–32, 34.

"Ray Bradbury on Close Encounters." *Starburst* 1.iii (March 1978): 20–23.

"Ray Bradbury Speaks on 'Film in the Space Age.'" *American Cinematographer* 48.I (January
1967): 34–35.

"Ray Bradbury Takes the Stage." *Heinlein Journal* 8 (January 2001): 6.

"Ray Bradbury: Views of a Grand Master." *Locus* 37.viii (August 1996): 6, 73–74.

"Ray Bradbury's Letters to Rupert Hart-Davis." *Missouri Review* 27.iii (Winter 2004):
119–163.

"Reflections from the Man Who Landed on the Moon in 1929." *Engineering and Science* 34.i
(October 1970): 14–19.

"Remembrance of Things Future." *Playboy* (January 1965), 99, 102, 191. Collected in *Beyond
1984*.

"A Salute to Superman," *Superman* 400 (1984), at http://theages.ac/400/bradbury.html
(accessed March 3, 2014).

"Science and Science Fiction." *Ray Bradbury Review* (1952): 25–26.

"Science Fiction before Christ and after 2001." *Science, Fact/Fiction*. Ed. Edmund J. Farrell.
Glenview, Ill.: Scott Foresman, 1974, ix–xv; *International Film Exposition*. Los Angeles:
Filmex, 1975.

"A Serious Search for Weird Worlds." *Life* 47.xviii (October 24, 1960): 116–118, 120, 123–126,
128, 130.

"Shaw as Influence, Laughton as Teacher." *Shaw Review* 18.ii (May 1973): 98–99.

"Space Flights Called Religious by Bradbury." *Los Angeles Times* (December 4, 1967): B14.

"Take Me Home." *New Yorker* (June 4, 2012), at http://www.newyorker.com/
reporting/2012/06/04/120604fa_fact_bradbury (accessed April 24, 2014). "Trailing the
Clouds of Glory into the Age of Apollo." *Los Angeles Times* (January 24, 1971): X1, 14.
Review of David Thomas, *Moon: Man's Greatest Adventure*.

"Unthinking Man and His Thinking Machines." *American Documentation* 19.iv (October
1968): 371–374.

"Walt Disney, His Beauties and Beasts." *Los Angeles Times* (October 21, 1973). Review of
Christopher Finch, *The Art of Walt Disney*.

"We Are Aristotle's Children." *New York Times* (February 9, 1977).

"Wells: His Crystal Ball Was Crystal Clear." *Los Angeles Times* (July 1, 1979): L7. Review of
Peter Haining, ed., *The H.G. Wells Scrapbook*.

"Where Are the Golden-Eyed Martians?" *Perry Rhodan 61: Death Waits in Semispace*, by
Kurt Mahr. New York: Ace, 1973, 146–150.

"Where DO I Get My Ideas?" *Journal of Science Fiction* 1.i (Fall 1951): 8.

"Where Do You Get Your Ideas?" *Ray Bradbury Review* (1952): 43–44.

"Where Is the Madman Who'll Take Us to Mars?" *Wall Street Journal* (November 18, 2004):
A18.

Why Man Explores. With James A. Michener, Norman Cousins, Philip Morrison, and
Jacques Cousteau, Washington D.C.: U.S. Government Publishing Office, 1976. NASA
Educational Publication 125, at http://history.nasa.gov/EP-125/ep125.htm (accessed
March 3, 2014).

"Why Space Age Theatre." *Playgoer* (October 1964).

"Writer Takes Long Look into Space." *Los Angeles Times* (January 10, 1960): E7.

Yestermorrow: Obvious Answers to Impossible Futures. Santa Barbara, Calif.: Capra Press, 1991.

"Zen and the Art of Writing." *Writer* (October 1958). Collected as title essay in *Zen and the Art of Writing and The Joy of Writing: Two Essays.* Santa Barbara, Calif.: Capra Press, 1973.

Zen in the Art of Writing: Essays on Creativity. Santa Barbara, Calif.: Borgo Press, 1990; expanded edition, Santa Barbara, Calif.: Joshua Odell, 1994. Includes the two essays in the previous listing.

INTRODUCTIONS, FOREWORDS, AND AFTERWORDS (SELECTED)

Abbott, Edwin A. *Flatland.* San Francisco: Arion Press, 1980.

Ackerman, Forrest J., ed. *Boris Karloff: The Frankenscience Monster.* New York: Ace, 1969.

Alexander, David. *Star Trek Creator: The Authorized Biography of Gene Rodenberry.* New York: ROC, 1994.

Anon. *Comic-Con: 40 Years of Arts, Writers, Fans, and Friends.* San Francisco: Chronicle Books, 2009.

Anon. *Food for Demons: The E. Everett Evans Memorial Volume.* San Diego: Kenneth J. Krueger, 1971.

Aurness, Craig. *Los Angeles.* Toronto: Skyline Press / Oxford University Press, 1984.

Austin, Terry, et al. *Superman Anniversary Issue No. 400.* New York: DC Comics, 1984.

Baum, Frank L. *The Wizard of Oz: Kansas Centennial Edition.* Lawrence: University Press of Kansas, 2001.

———. *The Wonderful Wizard of Oz.* New York: Modern Library, 2003.

Beaumont, Charles. *Best of Beaumont.* New York: Bantam, 1982.

———. *The Howling Man.* Ed. Roger Anker. New York: TOR, 1992.

———. *The Magic Man.* New York: Gold Medal, 1965.

———. *Selected Stories.* Arlington Heights, Calif.: Dark Harvest, 1988.

Bellows, Jim, ed. *Anyone Who Enters Here Must Celebrate Maggie.* Los Angeles: Ward Ritchie Press, 1971.

Blackstone, Harry. *The Blackstone Book of Magic and Illusion.* Scranton, Pa.: Newmarket Press, 1985.

Bloch, Robert. *Fever Dreams and other Fantasies.* London: Sphere, 1970.

Bogdanoff, Igor, and Grichka Bogdanoff. *Clefs pour la Science Fiction.* Paris: Seghers, 1976.

Borst, Ronald V., ed. *Graven Images: The Best of Horror, Fantasy and Science Fiction Art from the Collection of Ronald V. Borst.* New York: Grove Press, 1992.

Brackett, Leigh. *Lorelei of the Red Mist: Planetary Romances.* Royal Oak, Mich.: Haffner Press, 2008.

———. *No Good from a Corpse.* Tucson, Ariz.: Dennis McMillan Publications, 1999.

———. *Shannach the Last: Farewell to Mars.* Royal Oak, Mich.: Haffner Press, 2011.

Bradbury, Ray, et al. *13 for Corwin: Estimates of Norman Corwin, the No. 1 Writer-Producer-Director during Radio's Golden Age.* Los Angeles: Perpetua Press, 1985.

Brown, Forman. *Small Wonder: The Story of the Yale Puppeteers and the Turnabout Theatre.* Metuchen, N.J.: Scarecrow Press, 1980.

Burroughs, Edgar Rice. *A Princess of Mars.* New York: Modern Library, 2003.

Burrows, William E. *The Infinite Journey: Eyewitness Accounts of NASA and the Age of Space.* New York: Discovery Books, 2001.

Butcher, William. *Verne's Journey to the Centre of the Self: Space and Time in the Voyages Extraordinaires.* New York: St. Martin's Press, 1991.

Chalker, Jack, ed. *In Memoriam: Clark Ashton Smith.* Baltimore: Chalker, 1962.

Champlin, Charles. *Back There Where the Past Was: A Small-Town Boyhood.* Syracuse, N.Y.: Syracuse University Press, 1989.

Christian, James L., ed. *Extraterrestrial Intelligence: The First Encounter.* Buffalo: Prometheus Books, 1976.

Collier, John. *Fancies and Goodnights.* New York: New York Review of Books, 2003.

Crowther, Peter, ed. *Forbidden Planets.* New York: DAW, 2006.

Davidson, Avram. *The Avram Davidson Treasury.* New York: Tom Doherty Associates, 1998.
———. *Strange Seas and Shores.* New York: Doubleday, 1971.

Dean, James, and Bertram Ulrich. *NASA/Art: 50 Years of Exploration.* New York: Abrams, 2008.

Dille, Robert C., ed. *The Collected Works of Buck Rogers in the 25th Century.* New York: Chelsea House, 1969; *Buck Rogers: The First 60 Years in the 25th Century.* Lake Geneva, Wis.: TSR, 1988.

Doherty, Paul. *The Arrival of Halley's Comet.* Woodbury, N.Y.: Barron's Educational, 1985.

Durwood, Thomas, ed. *Close Encounters of the Third Kind: A Document of the Film.* New York: Ariel-Ballantine Books, 1978.

Eichner, Henry H. *The Atlantean Chronicles.* Alhambra, Calif.: Fantasy Publishing, 1971.

Eiseley, Loren. *The Loren Eiseley Reader.* Lincoln, Neb.: Abbatia Press/Loren Eiseley Society, 2009.

Em, David. *David Em at OCCA.* Santa Ana, Calif.: Orange County Center for Contemporary Art, 1984, at http://www.siggraph.org/artdesign/profile/David_Em/ (accessed March 3, 2014).

Etchison, Denis, ed. *Lord John Ten.* Northridge, Calif.: Lord John Press, 1988.
———. *Masters of Darkness.* New York: TOR, 1986.

Evans, E. Everett. *Food for Demons.* San Diego: Shroud, 1971; North Hollywood, Calif.: Fantasy House, 1974.

Farrell, Edmund J., ed. *Science Fact/Fiction.* Glenview, Ill.: Scott Foresman, 1974.

Flanagan, Graeme. *Robert Bloch: A Bio-Bibliography.* Canberra: Graeme Flanagan, 1979.

Flindt, Max H. *Between the Apes and the Angels.* e-book: The Fiction Works, 2004.

Folon, Jean-Michel. *Folon's Folons.* New York: Metropolitan Museum of Art, 1990; *Recent Works.* Monaco: Marisa Del Rey Gallery New York, 1994.

Francis, Bruce, ed. *Literature, Art and Artefacts That Will Forever Remain among the Undead: The Book Sail 16th Anniversary Catalogue.* Orange, Calif.: McLaughlin Press, 1984.

Garci, Jose Luis. *Ray Bradbury, Humanista Del Futuro.* Madrid: Helios, 1971.

Glicksman, Hal, et al., eds. *The Cartoon Show: Original Works by 150 Outstanding American Cartoonists Selected from the Jerome K. Muller Collection.* Costa Mesa, Calif.: University of California, 1974.

Green, Howard E., and Amy Boothe. *Remembering Walt: Favorite Memories of Walt Disney.* Burbank, Calif.: Disney Editions, 2002.

Greenberg, Martin H., ed. *Foundation's Friends: Stories in Honour of Isaac Asimov.* New York: TOR, 1989.

Haber, Karen, ed. *Kong Unbound: The Cultural Impact, Pop Mythos, and Scientific Plausibility of a Cinematic Legend.* New York: Pocket Books, 2005.

Haining, Peter, ed. *The Hollywood Nightmare: Tales of Fantasy and Horror from the Film World.* New York: Taplinger, 1972.

———. *Irish Tales of Terror.* New York: Wings Books, 1988.

———. *Ray Bradbury Introduces Tales of Dungeons and Dragons.* London: Guild/Book Club, 1986.

———. *The Wild Night Company: Tales of Fantasy and Horror from the Film World.* London: Gollancz, 1970.

Hamilton, Edmund. *Kaldar: World of Antares.* Royal Oak, Mich.: Haffner Press, 1998.

Harryhausen, Ray. *An Animated Life.* London: Aurum Press, 2003.

———. *Film Fantasy Scrapbook.* New York: A. S. Barnes, 1972.

Heppenheimer, T. A. *Colonies in Space.* Mechanicsburg, Pa.: Stackpole Books, 1977; New York: Warner Books, 1978.

Hutchinson, Tom. *Rod Steiger: Memoirs of a Friendship.* New York: Fromm International, 2000.

Kane, Brian. *The Definitive Prince Valiant Companion.* Seattle: Fantagraphics, 2009.

Knight, Charles R. *Autobiography of an Artist: Selections from the Autobiography of Charles R. Knight.* Ann Arbor, Mich.: G. T. Labs, 2005.

Korshak, Stephen D., ed. *A Hannes Bok Treasury.* Novato, Calif.: Underwood-Miller, 1993.

Kuttner, Henry. *The Best of Henry Kuttner.* New York: Ballantine, 1975.

———. *The Startling Worlds of Henry Kuttner.* New York: Questor/Popular Library, 1987.

Laemmle, Carla, and Daniel Kinske. *Growing Up with Monsters.* Duncan, Okla.: Bear Manor Media, 2009.

Luce, Claire Booth. *The City of Our Lady Queen of the Angels: A Bicentennial Celebrational Environment.* Los Angeles: Anthony and Elizabeth Duquette Foundation for the Living Arts/L.A. County Museum of Science and Industry, 1980.

Manguel, Alberto. *Logotopia: The Library in Architecture, Art and the Imagination.* Cambridge, Ont.: Cambridge Galleries/ABC Art Books, 2008.

Manning, Sean. *Bound to Last: 30 Writers on Their Most Cherished Book.* Cambridge, Mass.: Da Capo Press, 2010.

Matheson, Richard. *Collected Stories.* Ed. Stanley Wiater. Colorado Springs: Gauntlet Press, 2003.

———. *Duel: Terror Stories.* New York: TOR, 2003.

Melville, Douglas, and Robert Reginald. *Things to Come: An Illustrated History of the Science Fiction Film.* New York: Times Books, 1977.

Moore, Raylyn. *Wonderful Wizard, Marvelous Land.* Bowling Green, Ohio: Bowling Green University Popular Press, 1974.

Mugnaini, Joseph. *Drawings and Graphics.* Metuchen, N.J.: Scarecrow Press, 1982.

Murcury, Miron. *Willis O'Brien: The Oaklander Who Created King Kong.* Oakland, Calif.: Kaiser Center Art Gallery, 1984.

Murray, Bruce C., ed. *Mars and the Mind of Man.* New York: Harper & Row, 1973.

Nolan, William F. *Impact-20.* New York: Paperback Library, 1963.

———, ed. *The Ray Bradbury Companion.* Detroit: Gale Research, 1975.

Nolan, William F., and Martin H. Greenberg, eds. *The Bradbury Chronicles.* New York: ROC, 1991.

Nollen, Scott Allen. *Boris Karloff: A Critical Account of His Screen, Stage, Radio, Television and Recording Work.* Jefferson, N.C.: McFarland, 2008.

Olfson, Lewy. *A Teacher's Guide to Science Fiction.* New York: Bantam, 1968.

Penney, Edmund. *A Dictionary of Media Terms.* New York: Putnam, 1984.

Petaja, Emil, ed. *The Hannes Bok Memorial Showcase of Fantasy Art.* San Francisco: SISU Publishers, 1974.

Playboy. *The Art of Playboy.* New York: Van der Marck Editions, 1985.

Porges, Irwin. *Edgar Rice Burroughs: The Man Who Created Tarzan.* New York: Ballantine, 1975.

Rathbun, Mark. *Richard Matheson: He Is Legend. An Illustrated Bio-Bibliography.* Chico, Calif.: Mark Rathbun, 1984.

Rhymer, Paul. *The Small House Halfway Up in the Next Block.* New York: McGraw-Hill, 1972.

Rice, Dorothy. *Los Angeles with Love.* Los Angeles: Glen House Communications, 1984.

Ross, Bill. *Orange County.* Chicago: Chicago Review Press, 1988.

Schneider, Steve. *That's All Folks! The Art of Warner Bros. Animation.* New York: Henry Holt, 1988.

Sessa, Aldo. *Aldo Sessa: El Arte de la Fotografía.* Mexico City: Museo Nacional de Bellas Artes, 1989.

Singer, Kurt, ed. *Tales of the Macabre.* London: New English Library, 1969.

Skeeters, Paul, comp. *Sidney H. Sime: Master of Fantasy.* Pasadena, Calif.: Ward Ritchie Press, 1978.

Smith, Clark Ashton. *Appointment in Averoigne.* Sauk City, Wis.: Arkham House, 2003.

Stine, Hank, ed. *Forrest J. Ackerman Presents Mr. Monster's Movie Gold: A Treasure-Trove of Imagi-Movies.* Virginia Beach: Donning, 1981.

Sturgeon, Theodore. *The Ultimate Egoist. The Complete Stories of Theodore Sturgeon Vol. 1.* Ed. Paul Williams. Berkeley, Calif.: North Atlantic Books, 1994.

———. *Without Sorcery.* Philadelphia: Prime Press, 1948.

Teunissen, John J., ed. *Other Worlds: Fantasy and Science Fiction since 1939.* Winnipeg: University of Manitoba Press, 1980.

Tibbetts, John C., and James M. Welsh. *American Classic Screen Profiles.* Lanham, Md.: Scarecrow Press, 2010.

Turner, George E. *Spawn of Skull Island.* Vail, Ariz.: Luminary Press, 2002.

Verne, Jules. *20,000 Leagues under the Sea.* Trans. Anthony Bonner. "The Ardent Blasphemers." New York: Bantam, 1962. Collected in *Bradbury Speaks.*

———. *Around the World in 80 Days.* New York: Heritage Press, 1962.

———. *The Mysterious Island.* New York: Heritage Press, 1959.

Waugh, Charles G., and Martin H. Greenberg, eds. *The Arbor House Celebrity Book of Horror Stories.* New York: Arbor House, 1982.

West, William W., ed. *On Writing by Writers.* Boston: Ginn, 1966.

Williamson, J. H. *How to Write Tales of Horror, Fantasy and Science Fiction.* Cincinnati, Ohio: Writers Digest Books, 1987.

Williamson, Jack. *Wizard's Isle: The Collected Stories of Jack Williamson Vol. 3.* Royal Oaks, Mich.: Haffner Press, 2000.

Wrzos, Joseph, ed. *Hannes Bok: A Life in Illustration.* Lakewood, Colo.: Centipede Press, 2012.

Wynorski, Jim, ed. *They Came from Outer Space: 12 Classic Science Fiction Tales That Became Major Motion Pictures.* Garden City, N.Y.: Doubleday, 1980.

INTERVIEWS (SELECTED)

Aggelis, Steven B., ed. *Conversations with Ray Bradbury*. Jackson: University Press of Mississippi, 2004.

———. "Conversations with Ray Bradbury." Thesis, Florida State University, 2003 (contains three interviews not in published collection), at http://diginole.lib.fsu.edu/cgi/viewcontent.cgi?article=1000&context=etd (accessed April 24, 2014).

Anon. "Interview with Ray Bradbury." *Fahrenheit 451: The 50th Anniversary Edition*. New York: Ballantine, 1991, 180–190.

Anon. "Something Wicked This Way Comes (1983): Interview with Ray Bradbury and Jack Clayton." *The Dreamweavers: Interviews with Fantasy Film-makers of the 1980s*. Ed. Lee Goldberg. Jefferson, N.C.: McFarland, 1995, 241–278.

Atkins, Thomas, R. "The Illustrated Man: An Interview with Ray Bradbury." *Sight and Sound* 43.ii (Spring 1974): 96–100; excerpted in *The Classic American Novel and the Movies*. Ed. Gerard Peary and Roger Shatzin. New York: Ungar, 1977, 42–51.

Berton, Pierre. "Ray Bradbury: Cassandra on a Bicycle." *Voices from the Sixties: Twenty-Two Views of a Revolutionary Decade*. Garden City, N.Y.: Doubleday, 1967, 1–10.

Biodrowski, Steve. "MOBY DICK: Ray Bradbury on Adapting Melville's Allegorical Sea Monster." *Script Analyst* (2002), at http://thescriptanalyst.com/interviews/bradbury (accessed March 3, 2014).

Bond, Jeff. "A Classic Encounter: Ray Bradbury Recounts How It Came From Outer Space." *Cinefantastique* 36.iii (June/July 2004): 14–15, 67.

Bradley, Matthew R. "The Illustrative Man: An Interview with SF Legend Ray Bradbury." *Outré* Vol. 1.4 (Fall 1995); reprinted as "Someone Wonderful This Way Came." *Filmfax* 131–132 (Summer 2012/Winter 2012–2013).

Breit, Harvey. "Ray Bradbury." *Writer Observed*. London: Alvin Rodman, 1957, 207–209 (1951 interview).

Buller, Richard. "An Interview with Ray Bradbury." *Northridge Review* 5.i (Spring 1987): 74–80.

Chandler, David. "A Writer's Symposium." *Television Quarterly* 2.ii (Spring 1963): 7–20.

Cunningham, Craig. Transcript of 1961 interview with Bradbury for Oral History Department, UCLA.

Diehl, Digby. *Supertalk*. Garden City, N.Y.: Doubleday, 1974, 62–71.

DiLucchio, Patrizia. *PEOPLE Online*. "Science Fiction/Fantasy Writer Ray Bradbury" (1997), at http://dir.groups.yahoo.com/group/raybradburyoctoberclub/message/1069 (accessed March 3, 2014).

Eller, Jonathan, and William F. Touponce. "A Conversation with Ray Bradbury." *Ray Bradbury: The Life of Fiction*. Kent, Ohio: Kent State University Press, 2004, 433–435.

Elliot, J. M. "An Interview with Ray Bradbury." *Science Fiction Review* 6.iv (November 1977): 48–50.

Ezard, John. "The Tender Advocate of Wonder." *Guardian* (London) (August 24, 1990), at http://www.guardian.co.uk/theguardian/2012/jun/07/archive-1990-ray-bradbury-buck-rogers (accessed March 3, 2014).

French, Lawrence. "Ray Bradbury's Lost TV Show with Orson Welles and His Unused Ending for King of Kings," (1983), at http://www.wellesnet.com/?p=197 (accessed March 3, 2014).

Gehman, Geoff. "Ray Bradbury Sees the Future in Books, Not in Cyberspace." *Morning Call* 31 (October 1999), at http://articles.mcall.com/1999-10-31/entertainment/3278605_1_ray-bradbury-books-jules-verne (accessed March 3, 2014).

Geirland, John. "Bradbury's Tomorrowland." *Wired* 6.x (October 1998), at http://www.wired.com/wired/archive/6.10/bradbury.html (accessed March 3, 2014).

Hall, Mary Harrington. "The Fantasy Makers: A Conversation with Ray Bradbury and Chuck Jones." *Chuck Jones: Conversations*. Ed. Maureen Furniss. Jackson: University Press of Mississippi, 2005, 3–19.

Herndon, Ben. "The Ray Bradbury Theatre: Bradbury Talks about the Return of His Award-Winning Anthology Series for HBO." *Cinephantastique* 16.ii (May 1986): 4–7, 53.

Jacobs, Robert. "The Writer's Digest Interview: Bradbury." *Writer's Digest* 56.ii (February 1976): 18–25. *Fiction Writer's Market*. Ed. John Brady and Jean M. Fredette. Cincinnati, Ohio: Writer's Digest Books, 1981, 88–100.

Jacobs, Robert, et al. "An Interview with Ray Bradbury." *Tangent* 5 (Summer 1976), at http://www.tangentonline.com/interviews-columnsmenu-166/1864-classic-ray-bradbury-interview (accessed March 3, 2014).

Johnston, Amy E. Boyle. "Ray Bradbury: Fahrenheit 451 Misinterpreted." *L.A. Weekly* (May 30, 2007), at http://www.laweekly.com/2007-05-31/news/ray-bradbury-fahrenheit-451-misinterpreted/ (accessed March 3, 2014).

Kerns, William. "Bradbury Delivers Fantasy for Half a Century: Experiences Give Him Insight into Why Children No Longer Read for Fun." *Lubbock Avalanche-Journal* 70, 122 (March 28, 1992): B1. Collected in Aggelis 2.

Lambert, Chad. "Ray Bradbury, Quicker than the Eye." *Everybody's News* (1996), at http://comicrelated.com/news/16482/ray-bradbury-interview (accessed March 3, 2014).

Lewis, Barbara. "Starlog Interview: Ray Bradbury, the Martian Chronicler." *Starlog* 25 (August 1979): 28–30, 55.

Lofficier, Randy, and Jean-Marc Lofficier. "Starlog Interview: Ray Bradbury." *Starlog* 72 (July 1983): 66–68, at http://archive.org/stream/starlog_magazine-110/110_djvu.text (accessed April 24, 2014).

Lovell, Glen. "Classic, Caustic Ray Bradbury on *Fahrenheit 451* Redo." (1983) Santa Cruz Patch, at http://santacruz.patch.com/groups/glenn-lovells-blog/p/bp—classic-caustic-ray-bradbury-on-fahrenheit-451-redo (accessed March 3, 2014).

McCarty, Michael. "Ray Bradbury." *Giants of the Genre*. Ed. Michael McCarty. Holicong, Pa.: Wildside Press, 2003, 152–155.

McDonnell, David, et al. "Starlog Interview: Ray Bradbury." *Starlog* 110 (September 1986): 23–25, 72.

Mogen, David. "Ray Bradbury Interview with Mogen and Siegel (1980)." *New Ray Bradbury Review* 1 (2008): 106–126.

Moore, Everett T. "A Rationale for Bookburners: A Further Word from Ray Bradbury." *American Library Association Bulletin* 55.v (May 1961): 403–404.

Newcomb, Barbara. "It's Up, On, and Away." *Christian Science Monitor* 72, 73 (March 10, 1980): 2021.

Nicholls, Stan. "Ray Bradbury." *Wordsmiths of Wonder: Fifty Interviews with Writers of the Fantastic*. London: Orbit, 1993, 125–136.

O'Leary, Devin. "*Alibi* Flashback: An Interview with Ray Bradbury." (1999), at http://alibi
.com/feature/s/archive/42010/Alibi-Flashback-An-interview-with-Ray-Bradbury.html
(accessed March 3, 2014).

Platt, Charles. *Dream Makers: Science Fiction and Fantasy Writers at Work.* New York: Ungar,
1987, 161–171.

"The Playboy Panel: 1984 and Beyond." *Playboy* (July 1963): 25–37; (August 1963): 31–35, 108,
112, 114, 116–118, at http://www.scribd.com/doc/31248383/Playboy-1984-Panel-of-the
-Future/ (accessed March 3, 2014).

"Ray Bradbury on *Close Encounters of the Third Kind.*" *The Vote* (February 6, 2008), at
http://www.variety.com/article/VR1117980326?refcatid=2795 (accessed March 3, 2014).

"Ray Bradbury: Views of a Grand Master." *Locus* (August 1996): 6, 73–74.

Roberts, Frank. "An Exclusive Interview with Ray Bradbury, Parts 1 and 2." *Writers Digest*
47.ii (February 1961): 39–44, 94–96; 47.iii (March 1967): 41–44, 87.

Rose, Norman. "Ticket to the Moon." NBC Radio (December 4, 1956), at http://www.tor
.com/blogs/2012/04/voices-of-1956-hear-asimov-bradbury-and-campbell-on-the-state-of
-science-fiction/ (accessed March 3, 2014). Includes participation by Isaac Asimov and John
W. Campbell Jr.

Shevey, Sandra. "The Playgirl Interview: Ray Bradbury." *Playgirl* (January 1976): 56–59, 127.

Slusser, George. "To Write the Dream in the Centre of Science: Mars and the Science
Fiction Heritage." *Visions of Mars: Essays on the Red Planet in Fiction and Science.*
Jefferson, N.C.: McFarland, 2011, 185–189.

Spring, Mike. "Ray Bradbury: A Conversation with the Master of Science Fiction," Parts 1
and 2. *Literary Cavalcade* (March 1980): 14–15; (November 1980): 6–7.

Stevens, George, ed. "Ray Bradbury." *Conversations with the Great Moviemakers of
Hollywood's Golden Age at the American Film Institute.* New York: Knopf, 2006, 363–384.

Strick, Philip. "The Illustrated Man." *Sight and Sound* 38.iv (Autumn 1969): 181–182.

Szalay, Jeff. "Starlog Interview: Ray Bradbury." *Starlog* 53 (December 1981): 35–39.

Tibbetts, John C. "'Martian Chronicler' Reflects." *Christian Science Monitor* 83.79 (March
20, 1991): 16–17.

Tuchman, Mitch. "Bradbury: Shooting Haiku in a Barrel." *Film Comment* 18.vi
(November–December, 1982): 39–41.

Turner, Paul, and Dorothy Simon. "Interview with Ray Bradbury." *Vertex* 1.i (April 1973):
24–27, 92–94.

Unger, Arthur. "Exploring the Universe to Understand Ourselves." *Christian Science
Monitor* 72.44(E) (January 28, 1980): 19.

———. "Ray Bradbury: The Science of Science Fiction." *Christian Science Monitor* 73.i(E)
(November 25, 1980): B20–21. Collected in Aggelis; also at http://www.csmonitor.com/
1980/1113/111356.html (accessed March 3, 2014).

Weller, Sam. "The Art of Fiction No. 203: Ray Bradbury." *Paris Review* 192 (Spring 2010):
181–210.

———. "I Am My Grandfather, My Grandfather Is Me." *New Ray Bradbury Review* 3 (2012):
9. Interview excerpt.

———, ed. *Listen to the Echoes: The Ray Bradbury Interviews.* Brooklyn, N.Y.: Melville
House, 2010.

Worden, Leon. "Ray Bradbury on Mars." *SCV Newsmaker* (August 23, 2003), at http://www
.scvhistory.com/scvhistory/signal/newsmaker/sg082303.htm (accessed March 3, 2014).

Zebrowski, George. "Ray Bradbury, Looking Back on a Lifetime of Science Fiction, Says that for Better or Worse, the Future Is Now." *Sci Fi Weekly* (June 21, 2004), at ftp://asavage.dyndns.org/Literature/scifi.com/www.scifi.com/sfw/interviews/sfw11128.html (accessed March 3, 2014).

CRITICAL AND BIOGRAPHICAL WRITING ON BRADBURY

Adams, John Joseph. "Sci-Fi Scribes on Ray Bradbury: 'Storyteller, Showman and Alchemist.'" *Wired* (June 6, 2012), at http://www.wired.com/underwire/2012/06/ray-bradbury-writer-memories/ (accessed March 3, 2014).

Albright, Donn, Jon Eller, and Diana Dial Reynolds. "The Albright Collection: Bradbury Story Fragments." *New Ray Bradbury Review* 3 (2012): 85–131.

Anderson, James. *The Illustrated Bradbury: A Structuralist Reading of Bradbury's* The Illustrated Man. Rockville, Md.: Wildside Press, 2013.

Andreyev, Kirill. "Ray Bradbury." *Soviet Literature Monthly* 5 (1968): 176–180.

Anon. "Ray Bradbury." *Contemporary Authors. New Revision Series 30.* Detroit: Gale Research, 1990, 37–43.

Anon. "Ray Bradbury." *Science Fiction Writers of the Golden Age.* Ed. Harold Bloom. New York: Chelsea House, 1995, 78–93.

Atwood, Margaret. "Straight from the Heartland." *Guardian* (London) (June 9, 2012): 2.

Bailey, K. V. "Mars Is a District of Sheffield." *Foundation* 68 (Autumn 1996): 81–87.

Baker, Brian. "Ray Bradbury: *Fahrenheit 451*." *A Companion to Science Fiction.* Ed. David Seed. Oxford: Blackwell, 2005, 489–499.

Bankston, John. *Ray Bradbury.* New York: Chelsea House, 2011.

Barnish, Valerie A. *Notes on Ray Bradbury's Science Fiction.* London: Methuen, 1978.

Barrett, Amanda Kay. "Fahrenheit 451: A Descriptive Bibliography." MA Dissertation, Indiana University, 2011, at https://scholarworks.iupui.edu/bitstream/handle/1805/2677/Barrett%20-%20Combined%20Thesis.pdf?sequence=1 (accessed March 3, 2014).

Baxter, John. "The Parade's Gone By: Some Recent Ray Bradbury." *Australian Science Fiction Review* 4.iii (June 1989): 9–11.

———. "Ray Bradbury." *Starburst: The Magazine of Cinema and Television Fantasy* 3.iii (1980): 42–46.

Beley, Gene. *Ray Bradbury Uncensored!* New York: iUniverse, 2007.

Bennett, Ronald M. "Ray Bradbury." *Burroughsiana* 1.viii (September 1956): 10–14.

Bick, Ilsa J. "Aliens among Us: A Representation of Children in Science Fiction." *Journal of the American Psychoanalytic Association* 37.iii (1989): 737–760.

Biddison, L. T. "Ray Bradbury's Song of Experience." *New Orleans Review* 1.iii (Spring 1969): 226–229.

Bledig, Joan D., and Gregory Phillips. "Of Burroughs and Bradbury." *Burroughs Bulletin* 67 (2006): 28–32.

Bloom, Harold, ed. *Bloom's Guides: Ray Bradbury's "Fahrenheit 451."* New York: Chelsea House, 2007.

———. *Modern Critical Interpretations: Ray Bradbury's "Fahrenheit 451."* Philadelphia: Chelsea House, 2001.

———. *Modern Critical Views: Ray Bradbury.* New York: Chelsea House, 2001.

————. *Modern Critical Views: Ray Bradbury*. New ed. New York: Bloom's Literary Criticism, 2010.

Bluestone, George. "The Fire and the Future." *Film Quarterly* 20.iv (Summer 1967): 3–10.

Booker, M. Keith. "Compare/Contrast: Media Culture, Conformism and Commodification in Ray Bradbury's *Fahrenheit 451* and M. T. Anderson's *Feed*." *Critical Insights: Dystopia*. Ed. M. Keith Booker. Ipswich, Mass.: Salem Press, 2012, 73–87.

Borges, Jorge Luis. "Prologue to Ray Bradbury, *The Martian Chronicles*." *Selected Non-Fictions*. Ed. Eliot Weinberger; trans. Esther Allen, Suzanne Jill Levine, and Eliot Weinberger. New York: Viking, 1999, 418–419.

Bould, Mark. "Burning Too: Consuming *Fahrenheit 451*." *Essays and Studies 2005: Literature and the Visual Media*. Ed. David Seed. Rochester, N.Y.: Boydell and Brewer, 2005, 96–122.

Braniff, Beverly S. "Ray Bradbury: Hieroglyphics of the Future." *Eureka Studies in Teaching Short Fiction* 3.i (Fall 2002): 95–100.

Brown, Joseph F. "As the Constitution Says: Distinguishing Documents in Ray Bradbury's *Fahrenheit 451*." *Explicator* 67.i (Fall 2008): 55–58.

Burleson, Donald R. "Connings: Bradbury/Oates." *Studies in Weird Fiction* 11 (1992): 24–29.

Burt, Donald C. "Poe, Bradbury, and the Science Fiction Tale of Terror." *Mankato State College Studies* 3 (1968): 76–84.

Carpenter, Markus Arno. "Fleeing from the 'Ghost Machines': Patterns of Resistance in *The Pedestrian* and *The Murderer*." *New Ray Bradbury Review* 1 (2008): 11–34.

Carroll, Laura. "Pages on Fire: *Fahrenheit 451* as Adaptation." *The Shadow of the Precursor*. Ed. Dianna Glenn et al. Newcastle-upon-Tyne, U.K.: Cambridge Scholars Publishing, 2012, 202–217.

Carter, Douglas. "Researching with Original Sources in Culture Studies." *Inquiry* 1.ii (Fall 1997): 35–39, at http://www.vccaedu.org/inquiry/inquiry-fall97/i12-cart.html (accessed March 3, 2014).

Connor, George E. "Spelunking with Ray Bradbury: The Allegory of the Cave in *Fahrenheit 451*." *Extrapolation* 45.iv (Winter 2004): 408–418.

Cordesse, Leon. "La Science-fiction de Ray Bradbury." *Caliban* 5.i (January 1969): 77–83.

Darling, Petra Rae. *Midwest Towns and Martian Colonies: The Midwest and Nostalgia in Ray Bradbury's "The Martian Chronicles."* Charleston, S.C.: BiblioBazaar, 2011.

De Koster, Katie, ed. *Readings on "Fahrenheit 451."* San Diego: Greenhaven Press, 2000.

Dimeo, Richard S. "Ray Bradbury: Prose Painter of the Mind." *Perihelion* (Fall 1970).

Dominianni, Robert. "Ray Bradbury's 2026: A Year with a Current Value." *English Journal* 73.vii (1984): 49–51.

Drew, Barnard A. "Ray Bradbury." *100 Most Popular Genre Fiction Authors*. Westport, Conn.: Libraries Unlimited, 2005, 58–68.

Eller, Jonathan R. "Adapting Melville for the Screen: The *Moby Dick* Screenplay." *New Ray Bradbury Review* 1 (2008): 35–60.

————. *Becoming Ray Bradbury*. Urbana: University of Illinois Press, 2011.

————. "The Body Eclectic: Sources of Ray Bradbury's *The Martian Chronicles*." *University of Mississippi Studies in English* 11–12 (1993): 376–410. Collected in Bloom 2010.

————. "'Floreat!': Ray Bradbury and Bernard Berenson." *New Ray Bradbury Review* 2 (2010): 13–27.

————. "How Science Shaped the Stories of Ray Bradbury." *New Scientist* 211.2828 (August 31, 2011): 46.

———. "Ray Bradbury: Adaptations in Other Media." *New Ray Bradbury Review* 1 (2008): 178–214.

———. "The Stories of Ray Bradbury: An Annotated Finding List (1938–1991)." *Bulletin of Bibliography* 49.i (March 1992): 27–51.

———, ed. *New Ray Bradbury Review 3 (2012)*. Kent, Ohio: Kent State University Press.

Eller, Jonathan E., and William Touponce. *Ray Bradbury: The Life of Fiction*. Kent, Ohio: Kent State University Press, 2004.

Feneja, Fernanda Luisa. "Promethean Rebellion in Ray Bradbury's *Fahrenheit 451*: The Protagonist's Quest." *Amaltea: Revista de Mitocritica* 4 (1012): 1–20, and at http://pendientedemigracion.ucm.es/info/amaltea/revista/num4/feneja.pdf (accessed March 3, 2014).

Foertsch, Jacqueline. "The Bomb Next Door: Four Postwar Alterapocalyptics." *Genre* 30.iv (Winter 1997): 333–358. Collected in Bloom 2010.

Forrester, Kent. "The Dangers of Being Earnest: Ray Bradbury and *The Martian Chronicles*." *Journal of General Education* 28.i (Spring 1976): 50–54.

Freudenthal, Charles. "The Illustrative Man." *Journal of Science Fiction* 1.ii (Fall 1952): 18–21, 23.

Garcia, Frank, and Mark Phillips. "Ray Bradbury Theatre." *Science Fiction and Television Series*. Ed. Garcia and Phillips. Jefferson, N.C.: McFarland, 1996, 299–313.

Gardner, Martin. "The Martian Chronicles." *Gardner's Whys and Wherefores*. Chicago: University of Chicago Press, 1989, 37–43.

Gosling, John. "Ray Bradbury's Chronicles." *SFX Magazine* (May 2000): 2, 65–69.

Greenberg, Martin Harry, and Joseph D. Olander, eds. *Ray Bradbury*. Edinburgh: Paul Harris, 1980. Contents:

Willis E. McNelly and A. James Stupple, "Two Views" (17–32).
Gary K. Wolfe, "The Frontier Myth in Ray Bradbury" (33–54).
Edward J. Gallagher, "The Thematic Structure of *The Martian Chronicles*" (55–82).
Marvin E. Mengeling, "The Machineries of Joy and Despair: Bradbury's Attitudes toward Science and Technology" (83–109).
Eric S. Rabkin, "To Fairyland by Rocket: Bradbury's *The Martian Chronicles*" (110–126).
Lahna Diskin, "Bradbury on Children" (127–155).
Steven Dimeo, "Man and Apollo: Religion in Bradbury's Science Fantasies" (156–164).
Hazel Pierce, "Ray Bradbury and the Gothic Tradition" (165–185).
Sarah-Warner J. Pell, "Style Is the Man: Imagery in Bradbury's Fiction" (186–194).
Donald Watt, "Burning Bright: *Fahrenheit 451* as Symbolic Dystopia" (195–213).

Grimsley, Juliet. "*The Martian Chronicles*: A Provocative Study." *English Journal* 59.ix (December 1970): 1239–1242.

Griskey, Michele. *Ray Bradbury*. Hockessin, Del.: Mitchell Lane Publishers, 2006.

Guffey, George R. "*Fahrenheit 451* and the 'Cubby-Hole' Editors of Ballantine Books." *Coordinates: Placing Science Fiction and Fantasy*. Ed. George E. Slusser, Eric S. Rabkin, and Robert Scholes. Carbondale, Ill.: Southern Illinois University Press, 1983, 99–106.

———. "The Unconscious, Fantasy and Science Fiction: Transformations in Bradbury's *Martian Chronicles* and Lem's *Solaris*." *Bridges to Fantasy*. Ed. George E. Slusser. Carbondale, Ill.: Southern Illinois University Press, 1982, 142–159. Collected in Bloom 2010.

Hamblen, Charles F. "Bradbury's *Fahrenheit 451* in the Classroom." *English Journal* 57.iv (September 1968): 818–819, 824.

Harlow, Morgan. "Critical Commentary: Ray Bradbury's *The Martian Chronicles*." *WLA Journal* 17.i–ii (2005): 311–314.

Heaphy, Maura. "Ray Bradbury." *100 Most Popular Science-Fiction Authors*. Westport, Conn.: Libraries Unlimited, 2010, 81–86.

Hoskinson, Kevin. "*The Martian Chronicles* and *Fahrenheit 451*: Ray Bradbury's Cold War Novels." *Extrapolation* 36.iv (1995): 345–359. Bloom 2001.

Indick, Ben P. *Ray Bradbury, Dramatist*. San Bernardino, Calif.: Borgo Press, 1989.

Isherwood, Christopher. "Christopher Isherwood Reviews." *Tomorrow* 10 (October 1950): 56–58.

———. "Migration to Mars." *Observer* (September 16, 1951[a]): 7.

———. "Young American Writers." *Observer* (May 13, 1951[b]): 7.

Johnson, Wayne L. "The Invasion Stories of Ray Bradbury." *Critical Encounters: Writers and Themes in Science Fiction*. Ed. Dick Riley. New York: Ungar, 1978, 23–40.

———. *Ray Bradbury*. New York: Ungar, 1980.

Kagle, Steven E. "Homage to Melville: Ray Bradbury and the Nineteenth-Century Romance." *The Celebration of the Fantastic: Selected Papers from the Tenth Anniversary International Conference on the Fantastic in the Arts*. Ed. Donald E. Morse. Westport, Conn.: Greenwood Press, 1992, 279–289.

Kahveci, Sirin. *Metaphorical Death of the Character and the Text's Consuming Power. Comparison of Ray Bradbury's "Fahrenheit 451" and Paul Auster's "The Book of Illusions."* Saarbrucken: Lambert Academic Publishing, 2011.

Kirk, Russell. "The Fantasy World of Ray Bradbury." *Enemies of the Permanent Things: Observations of Abnormity in Literature and Politics*. New Rochelle, N.Y.: Arlington House, 1969, 109–124.

Langlet, Irene. "L'Ecart futuriste comme donnee metalitteraire. Une lecture des Chroniques martiennes de Ray Bradbury." *Poetique* 109 (February 1997): 83–103. Collected in *La Science-fiction, Lecture et poetique d'un genre litteraire*. Paris: Armand Colin, 2006.

Lay, Roger, Jr. "Adapting Bradbury for the Screen: 'A Piece of Wood' and 'Chrysalis.'" *New Ray Bradbury Review* 2 (2010): 74–82.

Linkfield, Thomas P. "The Fiction of Ray Bradbury: Universal Themes in Midwestern Settings." *Midwestern Miscellany* 8 (1980): 94–101.

Logsdon, Loren. "Ray Bradbury's 'The Kilimanjaro Device': The Need to Correct the Errors of Time." *Midwestern Miscellany* 20 (1992): 28–39; *Eureka Studies in Teaching Short Fiction* 3.i (Fall 2002): 83–94.

Mancini, Candice L., ed. *Censorship in Ray Bradbury's "Fahrenheit 451."* Farmington Hills, Mich.: Greenhaven Press, 2011.

Maziarczyk, Grzegorz. "Huxley/Orwell/Bradbury Reloaded; or, The Campy Art of Bricolage." *Imperfect Worlds and Dystopian Narratives in Contemporary Cinema*. Ed. Artur Blaim and Ludmila Gruszewska-Blaim. New York: Lang, 2011, 45–61.

McGiveron, Rafeeq O. "Bradbury's *Fahrenheit 451*." *Explicator* 54.iii (1996): 177–180.

———. "'Do You Know the Legend of Hercules and Antaeus?' The Wilderness in Ray Bradbury's *Fahrenheit 451*." *Extrapolation* 39.ii (1997): 102–109.

———. "'They Got Me a Long Time Ago': The Sympathetic Villain in *Nineteen Eighty-Four*, *Brave New World*, and *Fahrenheit 451*." *Critical Insights: Dystopia*. Ed. M. Keith Booker. Ipswich, Mass.: Salem Press, 2012, 125–141.

———. "To Build a Mirror Factory: The Mirror and Self-Examination in Ray Bradbury's *Fahrenheit 451.*" *Critique* 39.iii (Spring 1998): 282–287.

———. "What 'Carried the Trick'? Mass Exploitation and the Decline of thought in Ray Bradbury's *Fahrenheit 451.*" *Extrapolation* 37.iii (1996): 245–256.

———, ed. *Critical Insights: Fahrenheit 451.* Hackensack, N.J.: Salem Press, 2014.

McGuirk, Carol. "Bradbury, Heinlein and Hobo Heaven." *Science Fiction Studies* 28.ii (July 2001): 319–321.

McMillan, Gloria, ed. *Orbiting Ray Bradbury's Mars: Biographical, Anthropological, Literary, Scientific and Other Perspectives.* Jefferson, N.C.: McFarland, 2013.

McNelly, Willis E. "Bradbury Revisited." *Vector* 56 (Summer 1970): 3–5.

———. "Ray Bradbury." *Science Fiction Writers.* Ed. E. F. Bleiler. New York: Scribner's, 1982, 171–178.

———. "Ray Bradbury." *Supernatural Fiction Writers.* Ed. E. F. Bleiler. New York: Scribner's, 1985, 917–924.

———. "Ray Bradbury: Past, Present, and Future." *Voices for the Future: Essays on Major Science Fiction Writers.* Ed. Thomas D. Clareson. Bowling Green, Ohio: Bowling Green University Popular Press, 1976, 167–175.

McNelly, Willis E., and Keith Neilson. "Fahrenheit 451." *Survey of Science Fiction Literature Vol. 2.* Ed. Frank N. Magill. Englewood Cliffs, N.J.: Salem Press, 1979, 749–755.

McReynolds, D. J. "The Short Fiction of Ray Bradbury." *Survey of Modern Fantasy Literature Vol. 3.* Ed. Frank N. Magill. Englewood Cliffs, N.J.: Salem Press, 1983, 1471–1481.

Meier, Marcia. *A Tribute to Ray Bradbury: Thirty-Three Years of Inspiration at the Santa Barbara Writers Conference.* Santa Barbara, Calif.: Santa Barbara Writers Conference, 2005.

Menefee, Christine C. "Imagining Mars: New Chronicles." *School Library Journal* 40.xii (December 1994): 38–39.

Mengeling, Marvin E. "Ray Bradbury's *Dandelion Wine*: Themes, Sources, and Style." *English Journal* 60.7 (October 1971): 877–887.

———. *Red Planet, Flaming Phoenix, Green Town: Some Early Bradbury Revisited.* Bloomington, Ind.: 1st Books Library, 2002.

Miller, Calvin. "Ray Bradbury: Hope in a Doubtful Age." *Reality and the Vision.* Ed. Philip Yancey. Dallas: Word Publishing, 1990, 92–101.

Mogen, David. "Meeting Bradbury: Adaptations, Transformations, and Tributes." *New Ray Bradbury Review* 1 (2008): 91–98.

———. *Ray Bradbury.* Boston: Twayne, 1986.

Moorcock, Michael. Introduction. *Fahrenheit 451.* London: Folio Society, 2011.

Morrissey, Thomas J. "Ready or Not, Here We Come: Metaphors of the Martian Megatext from Wells to Robinson." *Journal of the Fantastic in the Arts* 10.iv (2000): 372–394.

Morseberger, Robert E. "The Illustrated Man." *Survey of Science Fiction Literature Vol. 2.* Ed. Frank N. McGill. Englewood Cliffs, N.J.: Salem Press, 1979, 1008–1013.

Moskowitz, Sam. "Ray Bradbury in France." *Riverside Quarterly* 3.iii (August 1968): 226–228.

Mucher, Walter J. "Being Martian: Spatiotemporal Self in Ray Bradbury's *The Martian Chronicles.*" *Extrapolation* 43.ii (Summer 2002): 171–187. Collected in Bloom 2010.

Naha, Ed. "The Martian Chronicles." *Future Life* 14 (November 1979): 18–21, 42, 63.

Nichols, Phil. "Echoes across a Half-Century: Ray Bradbury's *Leviathan '99*." *When Genres Collide: Selected Essays from the 37th Annual Meeting of the Science Fiction Research Association*. Ed. Thomas J. Morrissey and Oscar De Los Santos. Waterbury, Conn.: Fine Tooth Press, 2007, 203–209.

———. "Ray Bradbury and BBC Radio: 1971 to 2007." *New Ray Bradbury Review* 1 (2008): 79–90.

———. "Re-Presenting Mars: Bradbury's Martian Stories in Media Adaptation." Hendrix et al., 2011, 95–104.

———. "A Sympathy with Sounds: Ray Bradbury and BBC Radio, 1951–1970." *Radio Journal* 4.i–iii (2006, i.e., 2007): 111–123.

Nolan, William F. *Nolan on Bradbury*. Ed. S. T. Joshi. New York: Hippocampus Press, 2013.

———. *The Ray Bradbury Companion*. Detroit: Gale Research, 1975.

———, ed. *The Ray Bradbury Review*. San Diego: William F. Nolan, 1952; Los Angeles: Graham Press, 1988.

O'Kelly, Michael. Dir. *Live Forever. The Ray Bradbury Odyssey*. Documentary film. Aquaviva Productions, 2012.

Pagetti, Carlo. "Ray Bradbury e la Fantascienza Americana." *Studi Americani* 11 (1965): 409–429.

Paradowski, Robert J. "Ray Bradbury." *Critical Survey of Long Fiction*. Ed. Carl Rollyson. Vol. 1. Pasadena, Calif.: Salem Press, 2010, 539–549.

Parkinson, Bob. "Ray Bradbury: A Short Critique." *Vector* 39 (April 1966): 2–6.

Patrouch, Joseph F. "Symbolic Settings in Science Fiction: H. G. Wells, Ray Bradbury, and Harlan Ellison." *Journal of the Fantastic in the Arts* 1.iii (1988): 37–45.

Peary, Gerald. "*Fahrenheit 451*: From Novel to Film." *Omni's Screen Flights / Screen Fantasies: The Future According to Science Fiction Cinema*. Ed. Danny Peary. Garden City, N.Y.: Doubleday, 1984, 127–132.

Pfeiffer, John R. "Ray Bradbury's Bernard Shaw." *Shaw Vol. 17: Shaw and Science Fiction*. Ed. Milton T. Wolf (1997): 119–132.

Piddock, Charles. *Ray Bradbury, Legendary Fantasy Writer*. Pleasantville, N.Y.: Gareth Stevens Publishing, 2009.

Plank, Robert. "Expedition to the Planet of Paranoia." *Extrapolation* 22.ii (Summer 1981): 171–185. Collected in Bloom 2010.

Platt, Charles. "Ray Bradbury." *Who Writes Science Fiction?* London: Savoy Books, 1980, 189–200.

Prosser, H. L. "Teaching Sociology with *The Martian Chronicles*." *Social Education* 47 (March 1983): 212–215, 221.

Rabkin, Eric S. "Is Mars Heaven? *The Martian Chronicles*, *Fahrenheit 451*, and Ray Bradbury's Landscape of Longing." Hendrix et al., 2011, 95–104.

———. "Science and the Human Image in Recent Science Fiction." *Michigan Quarterly Review* 24.ii (Spring 1985): 251–264.

Raybin, Ronald. "Ray Bradbury's *The Illustrated Man*: Reality Extrapolated." *Wisconsin English Journal* 18.iii (April 1976): 8, 15–18.

Reid, Robin Anne. *Ray Bradbury: A Critical Companion*. Westport, Conn.: Greenwood Press, 2000.

Reilly, Robert. "The Artistry of Ray Bradbury." *Extrapolation* 13.i (December 1971): 64–74.

Robinson, Kim Stanley. Preface. *The Martian Chronicles*. New York: Book of the Month Club, 2001, vii–xi.

Rosenman, John B. "The Heaven and Hell Archetype in Faulkner's 'That Evening Sun' and Bradbury's *Dandelion Wine*." *South Atlantic Bulletin* 43.ii (May 1978): 12–16.

Sandercombe, W. Fraser. "Ray Bradbury." *Masters of SF*. Ontario: Collector's Guide Publishing, 2010, 121–143.

Schweitzer, Darrell. "Tales of Childhood and the Grave: Ray Bradbury's Horror Fiction." *Discovering Modern Horror Fiction II*. Ed. Schweitzer. Mercer Island, Wash.: Starmont, 1988, 29–42.

Seed, David. "The Flight from the Good Life: *Fahrenheit 451* in the Context of Postwar American Dystopias." *Journal of American Studies* 28.ii (1994): 225–240.

Sisario, Peter. "A Study of the Allusions in Bradbury's *Fahrenheit 451*." *English Journal* 59.ii (February 1970): 201–205.

Slusser, George E. *The Bradbury Chronicles*. San Bernardino, Calif.: Borgo Press, 1977.

Smith, Jeremy. "The Failure of *Fahrenheit 451*." *Strange Horizons* (13 October 2003), at http://www.strangehorizons.com/2003/20031013/fahrenheit.shtml (accessed March 3, 2014).

Smolla, R. A. "The Life of the Mind and a Life of Meaning: Reflections on Fahrenheit 451." *Michigan Law Review* 107(6): 895–912, at http://www.michiganlawreview.org/assets/pdfs/107/6/smolla.pdf (accessed March 3, 2014).

Spencer, Susan. "The Post-Apocalyptic Library: Oral and Literate Culture in *Fahrenheit 451* and *A Canticle for Leibowitz*." *Extrapolation* 32.iv (1991): 331–342. Collected in Bloom 2010.

Stockwell, Peter. "Language, Knowledge, and the Stylistics of Science Fiction." Subjectivity and Literature from the Romantics to the Present Day. Ed. Philip Shaw and Peter Stockwell. London: Pinter, 1991, 101–112.

Stupple, A. J. "The Martian Chronicles." *Survey of Science Fiction Literature Vol. 3*. Ed. Frank N. Magill. Englewood Cliffs, N.J.: Salem Press, 1979, 1348–1352.

———. "Two Views: The Past, the Future, and Ray Bradbury." Voices for the Future: Essays on Major Science Fiction Writers. Ed. Thomas D. Clareson. Bowling Green, Ohio: Bowling Green University Popular Press, 1976, 175–184.

Sullivan, Anita T. "Ray Bradbury and Fantasy." *English Journal* 61 (1972): 1309–1314.

Teicher, Morton I. "Ray Bradbury and Thomas Wolfe: Fantasy and the Fantastic." *Thomas Wolfe Review* 12.iii (Fall 1988): 17–19.

Tibbetts, John C. "The Illustrating Man: The Screenplays of Ray Bradbury." *Creative Screenwriting* 6.i (January–February 1999): 45–54; *New Ray Bradbury Review* 1 (2008): 61–78.

Touponce, William F. "Art and Aesthetics in the 'Age of the Chrysalis.'" *New Ray Bradbury Review* 2 (2010): 7–12.

———. "The Existential Fabulous: A Reading of Ray Bradbury's 'The Golden Apples of the Sun.'" *Mosaic: A Journal for the Interdisciplinary Study of Literature* 13.iii–iv (1980): 203–218.

———. "Introduction: Situating Bradbury in the 'Reign of Adaptations.'" *New Ray Bradbury Review* 1 (2008): 7–10.

———. "Laughter and Freedom in Ray Bradbury's *Something Wicked This Way Comes*." *Children's Literature Association Quarterly* 13.i (Spring 1988): 17–21.

————. *New Ray Bradbury Review 2 (2010)*. Kent, Ohio: Kent State University Press.

————. *Ray Bradbury*. Mercer Island, Wash.: Starmont House, 1989.

————. *Ray Bradbury and the Poetics of Reverie*. San Bernardino, Calif.: Borgo Press, 1997.

————. *Ray Bradbury and the Poetics of Reverie: Fantasy, Science Fiction, and the Reader*. Ann Arbor, Mich.: UMI Research Press, 1984.

————. "Some Aspects of Surrealism in the Works of Ray Bradbury." *Extrapolation* 25.iii (1984): 228–238.

————. "A Theologian of the Beautiful and the Sublime: Ray Bradbury's *Now and Forever*." *New Ray Bradbury Review* 2 (2010): 83–89.

————, ed. *New Ray Bradbury Review 1 (2008)*. Kent, Ohio: Kent State University Press.

Trout, Paul A. "*Fahrenheit 451*: The Temperature at Which Critics Chill." *Cresset* 57.i (November 1993): 6–10.

Valis, Noel M. "*The Martian Chronicles* and Jorge Luis Borges." *Extrapolation* 20.i (1979): 50–59.

Verley, Claude. "Etude narrative et thematique de 'The Pedestrian' de Ray Bradbury: Le cycle rompu." *Caliban* 22 (1985): 101–117.

Vollmer, Clay P. "Ray Bradbury on Creativity in the Future" (April 10, 2000), at http://www.cl.uh.edu/futureweb/bradbury.html (accessed March 3, 2014).

Warren, Bill. "At Play in the Business of Metaphors." *Starlog* 153 (April 1990): 29–32, 58.

Weiner, Lauren. "The Dark and Starry Eyes of Ray Bradbury." *New Atlantis* 36 (Summer 2012): 79–91.

Weist, Jerry. *Ray Bradbury: An Illustrated Life: A Journey to Far Metaphor*. New York: William Morrow, 2002.

Weller, Sam. *The Bradbury Chronicles*. New York: Harper Perennial, 2006.

————. "Five Bradbury Projects You Didn't Know About." *Listen to the Echoes* (December 23, 2012), at http://listentotheechoes.com/?paged=2 (accessed May 1, 2014).

White House Press Office, "Statement by the President on the Passing of Ray Bradbury," at http://www.whitehouse.gov/the-press-office/2012/06/06/statement-president-passing-ray-bradbury (accessed March 3, 2014).

Wolfe, Gary K. "Ray Bradbury," *Dictionary of Literary Biography Volume 8: Twentieth-Century American Science Fiction Writers*. Ed. David Cowart. Detroit: Gale Research, 1981, 61–76.

Wolper, David L. *Ray Bradbury: Story of a Writer*. TV documentary 1963, at http://archive.org/details/RayBradburyStoryOfAWriterByDavidL.Wolper (accessed March 3, 2014).

Wood, Diane S. "Bradbury and Atwood: Exile as Rational Decision." *The Literature of Emigration and Exile*. Ed. James Whitlark and Wendell Aycock. Lubbock: Texas Tech University Press, 1992, 131–142.

Wood, Edward. "The Case against Bradbury." *Journal of Science Fiction* 1.i (Fall 1951): 9–12.

Zipes, Jack. "Mass Degradation of Humanity and Massive Contradictions in *Fahrenheit 451*." *No Place Else*. Ed. Eric S. Rabkin et al. Carbondale, Ill.: Southern Illinois University Press, 1983, 182–198.

OTHER MATERIAL

Agel, Jerome, ed. *The Making of Kubrick's "2001."* New York: Signet, 1970.

Aldiss, Brian W., with David Wingrove. *Trillion Year Spree: The History of Science Fiction*. New York: Avon Books, 1988.

Allen, William Rodney, ed. *Conversations with Kurt Vonnegut.* Jackson: University Press of Mississippi, 1988.

Amis, Kingsley. *New Maps of Hell: A Survey of Science Fiction.* London: Gollancz, 1961.

Armour, Richard. "How to Burn a Book." *California Librarian* (December 1953); *A Safari into Satire.* Los Angeles: California Library Association, 1961, 9–11.

Asimov, Isaac. *Asimov on Science Fiction.* London: Granada, 1984.

———. *The Martian Way and Other Stories.* Garden City, N.Y.: Doubleday, 1955.

———. *Robot Visions.* London: Victor Gollancz, 1990.

Berger, Albert I. *The Magic That Works: John W. Campbell and the American Response to Technology.* San Bernadino, Calif.: Borgo Press, 1993.

———. "Science-Fiction Critiques of the American Space Program, 1945–1958." *Science Fiction Studies* 5.ii (July 1978): 99–109.

Bishop, Ellen. "Race and Subjectivity in Science Fiction." *Into Darkness Peering: Race and Colour in the Fantastic.* Ed. Elisabeth A. Leonard. Westport, Conn.: Greenwood Press, 1997, 85–104.

Booker, M. Keith. *The Dystopian Impulse in Modern Literature: Fiction as Social Criticism.* Westport, Conn.: Greenwood Press, 1994.

Brackett, Leigh. *The Best of Leigh Brackett.* Ed. Edmond Hamilton. New York: Ballantine, 1977.

———. *The Coming of the Terrans.* New York: Ace, 1967.

———. *The Long Tomorrow.* Garden City, N.Y.: Doubleday, 1955.

———. *Martian Quest: The Early Brackett.* Royal Oak, Mich.: Haffner Press, 2002.

Bradley, Matthew R. *Richard Matheson on Screen: A History of the Filmed Works.* Jefferson, N.C.: McFarland, 2010.

Bretnor, Reginald, ed. *Modern Science Fiction: Its Meaning and Its Future.* 2nd ed. Chicago: Advent, 1979.

Brians, Paul. *Nuclear Holocausts: Atomic War in Fiction, 1895–1984.* Kent, Ohio: Kent State University Press, 1987.

Burns, Eric. *Invasion of the Mind Snatchers: Television's Conquest of America in the Fifties.* Philadelphia, Pa.: Temple University Press, 2010.

Burroughs, Edgar Rice. *A Princess of Mars.* New York: Ballantine, 1980.

Campbell, John W., Jr. *The John W. Campbell Letters. Volume 1.* Ed. Perry A. Chapdelaine Sr. et al. Franklin, Tenn.: AC Projects, 1985.

———. *The Planeteers.* New York: Ace, 1966.

Chaikin, Andrew. "Live from the Moon: The Societal Impact of Apollo," at http://history .nasa.gov/sp4801-chapter4.pdf (accessed March 3, 2014).

Cheng, John. *Astounding Wonder: Imagining Science and Science Fiction in Interwar America.* Philadelphia: University of Pennsylvania Press, 2012.

Clarke, Arthur C. *2001: A Space Odyssey.* London: Legend, 1990.

———. *The Exploration of Space.* Revised ed. Harmondsworth, U.K.: Penguin, 1958.

———. *Greetings, Carbon-Based Bipeds!* London: HarperCollins, 2000.

———. *Profiles of the Future.* London: Scientific Book Club, 1962.

———. *The Sands of Mars.* London: Sphere, 1973.

Crossley, Robert. *Imagining Mars: A Literary History.* Middletown, Conn.: Wesleyan University Press, 2011.

De Baecque, Antoine, and Serge Toubiana. *Francois Truffaut.* Paris: Gallimard, 1996.

Denney, Reuel. "Reactors of the Imagination." *Bulletin of the Atomic Scientists* 9.vi (July 1953): 206–210, 224.

Disch, Thomas M. *On SF*. Ann Arbor, Mich.: University of Michigan Press, 2005.

Dunn, Maggie, and Ann Morris. *The Composite Novel: The Short Story Cycle in Transition*. New York: Twayne, 1995.

Eiseley, Loren C. "The Fire Apes." *Harper's Monthly* (September 1949): 47–54.

———. *The Invisible Pyramid*. New York: Scribner's, 1971.

———. *The Star Thrower*. London: Wildwood House, 1978.

Eisenhower, Dwight D. "Remarks at the Dartmouth College Commencement Exercises," 1953, at http://www.presidency.ucsb.edu/ws/?pid=9606 (accessed March 3, 2014).

Elliot, Jeffrey M. *Science Fiction Voices 4: Interviews with Modern Science Fiction Masters*. San Bernardino, Calif.: Borgo Press, 1982.

Etxeberria, Juan Gonzalez. "Metamorphosing Worlds in the Cinema of the Fantastic." *CLCWeb: Comparative Literature & Culture* Vol. 10 (December 2008), at http://docs.lib .purdue.edu/clcweb/vol10/iss4/7/ (accessed March 3, 2014).

Fallaci, Oriana. *If the Sun Dies*. Trans. Pamela Swinglehurst. London: Collier's, 1967.

Federman, Donald. "Truffaut and Dickens: *Fahrenheit 451*." *Florida Quarterly* (Summer 1967).

Gold, H. L. "Yardstick for Science Fiction." *Galaxy Science Fiction* 1.v (February 1951): 2–3.

Haley, W. D. "Johnny Appleseed—A Pioneer Hero." *Harper's New Monthly Magazine* 43 (November 1871): 830–837.

Hamilton, Edmond. *The Best of Edmond Hamilton*. New York: Ballantine, 1977.

Hartman, Geoffrey H. *The Fate of Reading and Other Essays*. Chicago: University of Chicago Press, 1975.

Heinlein, Robert A. *Red Planet*. New York: Ballantine, 1977.

Hendrix, Howard V. et al., eds. *Visions of Mars: Essays on the Red Planet in Fiction and Science*. Jefferson, N.C.: McFarland, 2011.

Hoberman, J. *An Army of Phantoms: American Movies and the Making of the Cold War*. New York: New Press, 2011.

Huntington, John. "Utopian and Anti-Utopian Logic: H. G. Wells and His Successors." *Science Fiction Studies* 9.ii (1982): 122–146.

Huxley, Aldous. *Brave New World*. London: HarperCollins, 1994.

———. *Complete Essays. Volume 6: 1956–1963*. Ed. Robert S. Baker and James Sexton. Chicago: Ivan R. Dee, 2002.

Jacob, Gilles, and Claude de Givray, eds. *Francois Truffaut: Correspondence, 1945–1984*. Trans. Gilbert Adair. New York: Farrar, Straus and Giroux, 1989.

Keller, David H. "The Revolt of the Pedestrians." *The Road to Science Fiction. Vol. 2: From Wells to Heinlein*. Ed. James Gunn. Lanham, Md.: Scarecrow Press, 2002, 171–195.

Knight, Damon. *In Search of Wonder: Essays on Modern Science Fiction Writers*. Revised ed. Chicago: Advent, 1967.

Kuttner, Henry. *The Best of Kuttner I*. London: Mayflower Dell, 1975.

Launius, Roger D., and Howard E. McCurdy. *Imagining Space: Achievements, Predictions, Possibilities, 1950–2050*. San Francisco: Chronicle Books, 2001.

Life Editorial. "Toynbee and the Future." *Life* 37.xix (November 8, 1954): 36.

Mandel, Siegfried, and Peter Fingesten. "The Myth of Science Fiction." *Saturday Review* 38 (August 17, 1955): 7–8, 24–25.

Matheson, Richard. *Collected Stories*, Vol. I. Ed. Stanley Wiater. Colorado Springs: Edge Books, 2003.

McAleer, Neil. *Odyssey: The Authorised Biography of Arthur C. Clarke*. London: Victor Gollancz, 1992.

McBride, Joseph. *Steven Spielberg: A Biography*. London: Faber, 1998.

McLuhan, Marshall. *Understanding Media: The Extensions of Man*. London: Routledge and Kegan Paul, 1964.

Mead, Shepherd. *Big Ball of Wax: A Story of Tomorrow's Happy World*. London: T. V. Boardman, 1955.

Miller, Walter M., Jr. *A Canticle for Leibowitz*. Boston: Gregg Press, 1975.

Miller, Walter M., Jr., and Martin H. Greenberg, eds. *Beyond Armageddon: Survivors of the Megawar*. London: Robinson, 1987.

Moskowitz, Sam. *Seekers of Tomorrow: Masters of Modern Science Fiction*. Westport, Conn.: Hyperion Press, 1974.

Moylan, Tom. *Scraps of the Untainted Sky: Science Fiction, Utopia, Dystopia*. Boulder, Colo.: Westview Press, 2000.

Mumford, Lewis. *Technics and Civilization*. London: George Routledge, 1934.

Onosko, Tim. "Tomorrow Lands." *Omni* (September 1982): 69–72, 106–107.

Patterson, William H., Jr. *Robert A. Heinlein: In Dialogue with His Century. Volume I: Learning Curve, 1907–1948*. New York: TOR, 2010.

Pohl, Frederik. *The Way the Future Was: A Memoir*. St. Albans, U.K.: Granada, 1983.

Pohl, Frederik, and C. M. Kornbluth. *The Space Merchants*. New York: Ballantine, 1981.

Pope, Gustavus W. *Journey to Mars*. Rockville, Md.: Wildside Press, 2006.

Pratt, Fletcher. "Time, Space and Literature." *Saturday Review* (July 28, 1951): 16–17, 27–28.

Priestley, J. B. *Thoughts in the Wilderness*. London: Heinemann, 1957.

Rabkin, Eric S. "The Composite Novel in Science Fiction." *Foundation: The Review of Science Fiction* 66 (Spring 1996): 93–100.

———. *Mars: A Tour of the Human Imagination*. Westport, Conn.: Praeger, 2005.

Robinson, Kim Stanley. "Martian Musings and the Miraculous Conjunction." Hendrix et al., 2011, 146–151.

———. *Red Mars*. New York: Bantam, 1993.

Ruddick, Nicholas. *The Fire in the Stone: Prehistoric Fiction from Charles Darwin to Jean M. Auel*. Middletown, Conn.: Wesleyan University Press, 2009.

Sagan, Carl. *Broca's Brain: Reflections on the Romance of Science*. New York: Ballantine, 1980.

Shaw, George Bernard. *Back to Methuselah: A Metabiological Pentateuch*. Revised ed. London: Oxford University Press, 1945.

Sidney-Fryer, Donald. *Emperor of Dreams: A Clark Ashton Smith Bibliography*. West Kingston, R.I.: Donald M. Grant, 1978.

Smith, Clark Ashton. *Tales of Science and Sorcery*. St. Albans, U.K.: Panther, 1976.

Sobchack, Vivian. *The Limits of Infinity: The American Science Fiction Film 1975*. New York: A. S. Barnes, 1980.

Stockwell, Peter. *The Poetics of Science Fiction*. Harlow, U.K.: Pearson Education, 2000.

Sturgeon, Theodore. *Voyage to the Bottom of the Sea*. New York: Pyramid Books, 1961.

Tenn, William. "The Fiction in Science Fiction." *Science Fiction Adventures Magazine* 2.1 (February 1954): 66–78.

Tesla, Nikola. "Talking with Planets." *Collier's Weekly* (9 February 1901), at http://www.tfcbooks.com/tesla/1901-02-09.htm (accessed March 3, 2014).

Toynbee, Arnold J., et al. "Reflections on My Own Death." *Rotarian* 120.v (May 1972): 24–27.

Truesdale, Dave, and Paul McGuire III. "An Interview with Leigh Brackett and Edmond Hamilton." *Tangent* 5 (Summer 1976), at http://www.tangentonline.com/interviews-columnsmenu-166/1270-classic-leigh-brackett-a-edmond-hamilton-interview (accessed March 3, 2014).

Truffaut, Francois. *Correspondence.* Ed. Gilles Jacob and Claude de Givray. Trans. Gilbert Adair. New York: Farrar Straus and Giroux, 1989.

———. "Journal of *Fahrenheit 451.*" *Cahiers du Cinema* 5 (1966): 11–22; Part Two, 6 (1966): 10–23; Part Three, 7 (1967): 8–19.

Vonnegut, Kurt. *Player Piano.* London: Panther, 1977.

Welles, Orson, ed. *Invasion from Mars: Interplanetary Stories.* New York: Dell, 1949.

Wells, H. G. *Mind at the End of Its Tether.* London: Heinemann, 1945.

———. *Things to Come.* London: Cresset Press, 1935.

Westfahl, Gary, ed. *The Mechanics of Wonder: The Creation of the Idea of Science Fiction.* Liverpool: Liverpool University Press, 1998.

———. *Space and Beyond: The Frontier Theme in Science Fiction.* Westport, Conn.: Greenwood Press, 2000.

Whalen, Tom. "The Consequences of Passivity: Re-evaluating Truffaut's *Fahrenheit 451.*" *Literature/Film Quarterly* 35.iii (2007): 181–190.

Whyte, William H., Jr. *The Organization Man.* New York: Simon and Schuster, 1956.

Wiater, Stanley, Matthew R. Bradley, and Paul Stuve, eds. *The Richard Matheson Companion.* Colorado Springs: Gauntlet Publications, 2008.

Williamson, Jack. *The Best of Jack Williamson.* New York: Ballantine, 1978.

Wolfe, Gary K. *The Known and the Unknown: The Iconography of Science Fiction.* Kent, Ohio: Kent State University Press, 1979.

Wolfe, Thomas. *Of Time and the River.* London: Heinemann, 1935.

The Centre for Ray Bradbury Studies was founded at Indiana University in 2007, Director Jonathan R. Eller. Website at http://iat.iupui.edu/bradburycenter/ (accessed March 3, 2014).

CHAPTER 1. OUT OF THE SCIENCE FICTION GHETTO

1. White House Press Office, "Statement by the President," 2012.
2. Disch, "America's Official Science Fiction Writer," 52.
3. Adams, "Sci-Fi Scribes."
4. Weller, 2006, 66.
5. Nicholls, 1993, 128. In a 1953 survey of SF, Bradbury's fiction was singled out as being particularly character-centered; Denney, 208.
6. Pratt, 16.
7. Cunningham, 224.
8. *Yestermorrow*, 23. Unattributed references throughout are to Bradbury's works. Bradbury references to first editions unless otherwise stated.
9. Weller, 2006, 27–28.
10. Aurness, 3; Platt, 1987, 167.
11. Aggelis, 2004, 5, 178.
12. Tibbetts and Welsh, x; Tibbets, 2008, 61.
13. For commentary on the story, see *Collected Stories of Ray Bradbury*, 358–360, 480–481.
14. *Zen and the Art of Writing*, 39.
15. "Percipient Witness," 3.
16. Elliot, *Science Fiction Voices 4*, 19.
17. Aggelis, 2004, 21; Nolan, 2013, 82.
18. Patterson, 253; "Ray Bradbury Takes the Stage," 6.
19. For full information on these early stories, see *Collected Stories of Ray Bradbury*.
20. Eller, *Becoming Ray Bradbury*, 72.
21. Ibid., 68.
22. Nolan, 1963, 9.
23. Eller, *Becoming Ray Bradbury*, 75, 108–109.
24. Editorial comment after "Don't Get Technatal," *Futuria Fantasia* 1 (Summer 1939).
25. Mumford, 341.
26. Bradbury was always impatient with a crudely predictive model of SF and recommended an anthology of futuristic writing from the turn of the nineteenth century because it showed how poor Americans were at projecting their future; "Looking Into the Future," 1970.
27. *A Memory of Murder*, 8.

28. Nolan, 2013, 260.

29. Eller and Touponce, *RB*, 2004, 54, 61.

30. Pohl, 117.

31. Eller and Touponce, *RB*, 2004, 54.

32. *Match to Flame*, 17. *F&SF* for May 1963 was a special Bradbury issue.

33. Eller and Touponce, *RB*, 2004, 90.

34. "Magic, Magicians, Carnival and Fantasy," 9.

35. Eller and Touponce, *RB*, 2004, 70.

36. *Stories* II, 173. References throughout will be to this most comprehensive collection.

37. *From the Dust Returned*, New York: Avon, 2002, 41.

38. For commentary on Bradbury's Gothic writing, see Pierce, in Greenberg and Olander.

39. On the story's genesis, see Eller, *Becoming Ray Bradbury*, 114–115. Bradbury attended the dramatization of *Darkness at Noon* in 1951; Eller, *Becoming Ray Bradbury*, 228.

40. Ruddick, 67–68.

41. For the early version, "The Parallel," see *Collected Stories of Ray Bradbury*, 402–410.

42. *Stories* II, 419.

43. Ibid., 786.

44. Weller, *Listen to the Echoes*, 278; *Zen in the Art of Writing*, 9; Weller, 2006, 92.

45. Bradbury's debt to Wolfe is discussed by Teicher.

46. *Stories* II, 799.

47. *Stories* I, 765.

48. "Magic, Magicians, Carnival and Fantasy," 7. For a more accurate account, see Eller and Touponce, *RB*, 2004, 362.

49. *Stories* II, 367.

50. Anderson, 85.

51. Weller, 2006, 171–172.

52. Eller, *Becoming Ray Bradbury*, 195.

53. Turner, 27. Bradbury originally planned that in the nursery "the ceiling would have this tremendous eye looking down at you"; "Literature in the Space Age," 161.

54. *Stories* I, 216.

55. "Literature in the Space Age," 162.

56. *Stories* I, 158.

57. Anderson, 44.

58. *Stories* I, 192.

59. The issue of *Startling Stories* where the story first appeared (July 1950) also carried Edmond Hamilton's novel of a nuclear strike, *City at World's End*, and Frank Belknap Long's "Invasion."

60. *Stories* II, 15.

61. Ibid., 23.

62. *Stories* I, 343.

63. *Stories* II, 768, 769.

64. Cf. Anderson, 66.

65. *Stories* II, 776.

66. Ibid., 228, 237.

67. *Illustrated Man*, New York: Bantam, 1982, 186.

68. Aggelis, 2004, 73.

69. Nolan, 2013, 148.

70. Moskowitz, 368.

71. Aggelis, 2003, 170. Cf. "I hate cyberspace. I hate the internet," Gehman.

72. Campbell, 1985, 316.

73. "Science and Science Fiction," 26.

74. *Yestermorrow*, 96.

75. "Man Who Tried Everything,"12. In 1963 Bradbury participated with Huxley in a panel discussion on literature and Science Fiction at U.C.L.A.

76. *Stories* I, 269.

77. "Fahrenheit Chronicles."

78. *Marionettes, Inc.*, 112.

79. "Death Warmed Over," 252.

80. *Bullet Trick*, 181–271.

81. *Stories* I, 866.

82. Asimov, *Robot Visions*, 12.

83. Williamson, 1978, 172.

84. *Stories* I, 179.

85. Ibid., 859.

86. *Marionettes, Inc.*, 116.

87. *Stories* II, 510.

88. Weller, 2006, 253–254. "Here There Be Tygers" was rejected; "A Miracle of Rare Device," was accepted but not broadcast, perhaps because of cost; a fourth script from 1962, "Nothing in the Dark," was based on Bradbury's story "Death and the Maiden." The first two scripts are included in *Bullet Trick*.

89. Aggelis, 2004, 70.

90. "Machine-Tooled Happyland," 100. In his 1977 poem "Where Robot Mice and Robot Men Run Round In Robot Towns," Bradbury uses Shaw and Shakespeare as inspirational figures countering the predominance of technology in contemporary society.

91. *Stories* I, 769.

92. Ibid., 777–778.

93. Weller, 2006, 237.

94. *Stories* I, 629.

95. Ibid., 637.

96. "Fahrenheit Chronicles," 1964.

97. *Bullet Trick*, 299–326.

98. "Machine-Tooled Happyland," 100.

99. Ibid., 102.

100. *Stories* II, 492.

101. Porges, 17.

102. *Dinosaur Tales*, 15.

103. Weist, xxi.

104. *Stories* I, 293.

105. Weller, 2006, 189; Eller, *Becoming Ray Bradbury*, 283.

106. Cunningham, 489.

107. Eller, *Becoming Ray Bradbury*, 262–263.

108. *Stories* I, 692.

109. Ibid., 261.

110. Ibid., 257.

111. Weller, "Art of Fiction."

112. Cheng, 203.

113. The story probably dates from the early 1950s.

114. Despite many allusions to him, Bradbury wrote very little on Wells but praised him because, unlike Huxley and Orwell, he "imagined alternatives to doom"; "Wells: His Crystal Ball."

115. *Stories* II, 778.

116. Ibid., 782.

117. Aggelis, 2004, 117.

118. *Yestermorrow*, 173, 174.

119. Jacobs, *Tangent* interview.

120. Aggelis, 2004, 82.

121. Tenn, 67.

122. Weller, 2006, 166.

123. Nolan, 1975, 9.

124. Breit, 208.

125. *Yestermorrow*, 97.

126. Ibid., 103.

127. Farrell, xi, xii.

128. Clarke, 2000, 62.

129. Rose, 1956.

130. Bretnor, 138, 80, 135. In his preface to the 1989 tribute story collection, *Foundation's Friends*, Bradbury praised Asimov's voracious appetite for different forms of literature and areas of Science Fiction.

131. Asimov, 1984, 255.

132. Charles Knight, 108–113 (110).

133. *Timeless Stories*, ix; *Circus of Dr. Lao*, vii.

134. Bradbury, ed. *Circus of Dr. Lao*, vii, viii.

135. Abbot, 7.

136. Porges, 21; "A Salute to Superman."

137. Baum, xv.

138. *Dandelion Wine*, 101.

139. *Farewell Summer*, 208.

140. *Something Wicked*, New York: Ballantine, 1963, 11.

141. Aggelis, 2004, 18.

142. "Marvels and Miracles," 27.

143. *A Graveyard for Lunatics*, 14.

144. Discussed in chapter 4.

145. "Man and His Spaceship Earth," 11.

146. Onosko, 107.

147. *One More for the Road*, New York: Avon, 2003, 27.

148. *Quicker than the Eye*, London: Earthlight, 1998, 20.

1. Reprinted as "Bradbury's Comic Adaptation of Edgar Rice Burroughs," *New Ray Bradbury Review* 1 (2008).

2. Aggelis, 2004, 96.

3. Eller, *Becoming Ray Bradbury*, 17.

4. Porges, 18–19.

5. Rabkin, "Is Mars Heaven?" 95.

6. "Where DO I Get My Ideas?" 8.

7. Bretnor, 84.

8. Clark Ashton Smith, *Tales*, 20.

9. "Letter on Clark Ashton Smith," 108. The second story was "City of the Singing Flame" (1931).

10. Hendrix, 73; Brackett, 1967, 1.

11. An acknowledged inspiration for Bradbury's "Asleep in Armageddon" ("Perchance to Dream"): Eller, *Becoming Ray Bradbury*, 69.

12. Brackett, 1977, 88. Related stories collected in Brackett, *Martian Quest* (2002).

13. *Collected Stories of Ray Bradbury*, 277.

14. Eller and Touponce, *RB*, 507.

15. "Million-Year Picnic," *Planet Stories* 3, iii (Summer 1946), 98.

16. Eller, *Becoming Ray Bradbury*, 190–191.

17. Weller, *Listen to the Echoes*, 214. For a definitive account of the volume's composition, see Eller and Touponce, *RB*, 105–122.

18. *Martian Chronicles*, Garden City, N.Y.: Doubleday, 1958, 94. Subsequent page references in text. Mars stories not in *Martian Chronicles* signaled in text as "separate."

19. Dunn and Morris, 1. Cf. Rabkin, 1996.

20. Tibbetts, 1991, 17.

21. Bloom, 2010, 141–171.

22. Greenberg and Olander, 55–82.

23. For George Slusser, the bridge passages "provide lyrical contrast and thematic counterpoint"; Slusser, 1977, 55.

24. *Martian Chronicles*, 1986, 9.

25. "Few Notes on *Martian Chronicles*,"21. In a 1999 interview Bradbury denied that the book was SF at all, insisting that it was "fantasy" based on Greek myth: O'Leary, 1999.

26. "How I Wrote My Book," *Martian Chronicles*, 2009, 203–204. Bradbury's essay is dated October 17, 1950.

27. Clarke, 2000, 62. The stories are "And the Moon Be Still as Bright" and "Million-Year Picnic."

28. Clarke, 1973, 49. For a valuable discussion of this novel, see Crossley, 208–211.

29. Clarke, 1973, 149.

30. Burroughs, 21–22.

31. Pope, 136.

32. The name *Ylla* is also used in "Disease," a reverie sequence by possibly the last Martian dying from Earthborne disease: *Martian Chronicles*, 2009, 239–240.

33. Crossley, 128–148.

34. Bradbury et al., *Mars and the Mind of Man*, 1973, 19.

35. *Stories* I, 200. Original title "Fathers."

36. Nolan, 2013, 65.

37. Bradbury later insisted that any dramatization of *Martian Chronicles* should evoke a "fantastic dreamworld of shadows and lights" rather than attempt a quasirealist representation of Mars: Mogen, 2008, 118.

38. French, 1983.

39. *Stories* II, 268.

40. *Stories* I, 684. The title echoes the promise of deliverance in the Book of Daniel 12:12. On Bradbury's use of compounds to give the Martians a poetical language, see Stockwell, 2000, 129.

41. "Where DO I Get My Ideas?" 8.

42. Introduction, *Timeless Stories*, ix–x.

43. *Illustrated Man*, New York: Bantam, 1982, 142. The concrete mixer has been described as "Bradbury's symbol for American materialism"; Slusser, 1977, 30.

44. *Illustrated Man*, 150.

45. Ibid., 155.

46. Rabkin, "Composite Novel," 96.

47. Mogen, 1986, 88. Mogen's whole discussion of the tension between the sacred and profane in Bradbury's Mars as continuing the American frontier tradition remains very helpful (63–81). See also McMillan, 122–130.

48. "Beautiful Ohio" on a romanticized past. "Beautiful Dreamer" and "Roamin' in the Gloamin'" on the romantic loss of reality.

49. *We'll Always Have Paris*, London: Harper Voyager, 2009, 130.

50. Bloom, 2010, 54.

51. Borges, 419.

52. Campbell, 1966, 11. The story originally appeared in *Thrilling Wonder Stories*, which carried a number of Bradbury's stories in 1949–1950.

53. Eller describes them as "masters of illusion": Bloom, 2010, 155.

54. Eller and Touponce, *RB*, 28.

55. "Where DO I Get My Ideas," 8. Cf. "Lonely Ones" (1949), where two campers on Mars are tantalized by the sight of small, apparently feminine, footsteps in the sand.

56. Original title "I, Mars." The preamble from an "old poem" on the sentience within a telephone system was added later to the text.

57. Wells, 1935, 141. Italics in original. Wells's script was followed closely in the film.

58. Hamilton, 1977, 50.

59. Weller, *Bradbury Chronicles*, 101; Eller, *Becoming Ray Bradbury*, 13, 43, 65. In 1946 Hamilton married Bradbury's long-term mentor Leigh Brackett.

60. The imagery of the story stresses the fragility of the "settlement" which "seemed no more than a motion-picture set far on ahead of them on a vast, empty stage": *Stories* I, 526.

61. Hendrix, 107; Hendrix also discusses the influence of Joseph Wood Krutch's *Modern Temper*, on which see Eller, *Becoming Ray Bradbury*, 174–175.

62. "Love Affair" (1982, written ca. 1948) also describes settlers as carrying disease, where one of the last surviving Martians, named Sio, falls in love with a young woman from Earth.

63. "How I Wrote My Book," *Martian Chronicles*, 2009, 205.

64. Heinlein, 188. Emphasis in original.

65. Crossley, 2011, 196.

66. *Stories* I, 248.

67. Ibid., 247.

68. The story was withdrawn from *Martian Chronicles* before copy could be set up: Eller and Touponce, *RB*, 513.

69. *Martian Chronicles*, 2009, 249.

70. Ibid., 338.

71. Greenberg and Olander, 43.

72. Cf. The role of the blind poet Rhysling in Heinlein's 1947 story "Green Hills of Earth." This story was collected with Bradbury's "Zero Hour" and "Million-Year Picnic" in Orson Welles's 1949 anthology *Invasion from Mars*.

73. Originally entitled "Naming of Names," but not to be confused with the bridge passage in *Martian Chronicles* with that title. Gary Wolfe argues that, if included, the story would have negated "Million-Year Picnic": Greenberg and Olander, 47.

74. *Stories* I, 510.

75. Ibid., 512.

76. "Death Warmed Over," 102.

77. Eller, *Becoming Ray Bradbury*, 236. Bradbury had misgivings about retaining "Way in the Middle" because it had no supporting story: Weller, 2006, 182. For Bradbury's own comments on both stories, see "Literature in the Space Age," 163–164. "Other Foot" also had as title "Last White Man."

78. Greenberg and Olander, 112; Mogen, 1986, 82; Weller, *Bradbury Chronicles*, 158; Dunn and Morris, 35.

79. *Stories* I, 873.

80. "Few Notes on *Martian Chronicles*," 21.

81. Haley, 830.

82. Robinson, "Martian Musings and the Miraculous Conjunction," in Hendrix, 147–148.

83. The term *terraforming* is an SF coinage, first appearing in Jack Williamson's story "Collision Orbit," published in *Astounding Science Fiction* (July 1942).

84. Chosen to avoid reference to Mars and therefore SF in its title; see Eller, *Becoming Ray Bradbury*, 213.

85. Robinson, 2001, viii–ix. Robinson's companion volume to his Mars trilogy, *Martians* (1999), may have been inspired by *Martian Chronicles* for its assembly of different narratives unified by location.

86. There are districts in California named Allendale and also at least six townships in other American states with that name.

87. Bradbury's inspiration was a photograph of Hiroshima: Weller, 2010.

88. These symbolic details were added to the original text in composition: Bloom, 2010, 156–158.

89. "Garbage Collector" (in *Golden Apples of the Sun*, 1953), "Highway" (in *Illustrated Man*, 1951), and "To the Chicago Abyss" (in *Machineries of Joy*, 1964), respectively.

90. Isherwood, 1950, 56, 57. In his British review he describes Bradbury as a "philosopher-poet": Isherwood, 1951a, 7. The review in the *Magazine of Fantasy and Science*

Fiction explicitly took its cue from Isherwood and praised Bradbury for achieving a "poet's interpretation of future history beyond the limits of any fictional form": "Recommended Reading," *F&SF* 2.ii (April 1951): 112.

91. Eller, *Becoming Ray Bradbury*, 262; Weller, 2006, 300–301.

92. Bradley, 2010, 213, 218. Of Anderson, Bradley commented: "his timing was all off" (Nicholls, 131). Bradbury's own screenplays of 1983 and 1997 are included in *Martian Chronicles: The Complete Edition*. For commentary on the adaptations, see Gosling.

93. *I Sing the Body Electric!*

94. Ibid. The concept may have been suggested by Philip K. Dick's *Eye in the Sky* (1957).

95. "Where Is the Madman?" A18.

96. "My Mars," 3.

97. Eller and Touponce, *RB*, 125.

CHAPTER 3. *FAHRENHEIT 451* IN CONTEXTS

1. The title possibly is suggested by Henry Kuttner's "Clash By Night" (1943), evoking a neofeudal society. On the novel's genesis, see Eller, "Story of *Fahrenheit 451*" in *Fahrenheit 451*, 60th Anniversary Edition, 167–187.

2. *Match to Flame*, 299.

3. Ibid., 322.

4. Ibid., 336.

5. Cunningham, 194.

6. *Stories* II, 569.

7. Ibid., 570. The composite daily TV fare of this period is summarized in Burns, 34–35.

8. Keller, 173. Cf. Eller, *Becoming Ray Bradbury*, 13, 238.

9. Eller and Touponce, *RB*, 176–180.

10. *Match to Flame*, 427.

11. Cunningham, 185, 186.

12. Gold, 2.

13. Matheson, *Collected Stories Vol. 1*, 40. Original title "Waker Dreams."

14. *Match to Flame*, 16, 19. See Eller, *Becoming Ray Bradbury*, 245–246.

15. Weller, 2006, 196. By the 1960s Bradbury's political allegiances had shifted, thanks partly to his hostility toward Lyndon Johnson.

16. "Literature in the Space Age," 159; Jacobs, 1976.

17. FBI File June 8, 1959, 9, *Ray Bradbury File*.

18. *Match to Flame*, 141.

19. *Stories* II, 700.

20. *Match to Flame*, 106–107.

21. Eller and Touponce, *RB*, 400.

22. *Match to Flame*, 121.

23. Ibid., 136.

24. *Ray Bradbury on Stage*, 283.

25. See Hall, 12.

26. *Ray Bradbury on Stage*, 292, 322.

27. Eller, *Becoming Ray Bradbury*, 82–83.

28. Weller, 2006, 171; Aggelis, 2004, 156.

29. "Man Who Tried Everything," 12. In 2005 Bradbury dedicated his collection of essays, *Bradbury Speaks*, to Loren Eiseley and Huxley, "whose essays showed me the way."

30. Huxley, 2002, 243.

31. Huxley, 1994, 81.

32. Ibid., 163.

33. *Day It Rained Forever*, London: Hart-Davis, 1959, 74, 75.

34. *Yestermorrow*, 101.

35. Letter to author from Bradbury, September 2, 1992. Center for Ray Bradbury Studies.

36. *Bradbury Speaks*, 161. His second 1982 essay, collected in *Yestermorrow*, proposes designing user-friendly neighborhoods within the city.

37. Amis, 87, 109–110. Cf. Bradbury's frequently self-quoted assertions that he did not aim to predict futures but to *prevent* them.

38. Aggelis, 2004, 157. Vonnegut admits that he "ripped off" the subject of *Player Piano* from Huxley: Allen, 93.

39. Vonnegut, 38.

40. Pohl and Kornbluth, 7.

41. Moylan, 169.

42. Whyte's argument was endorsed by Huxley. The novel nearest to Bradbury's that Whyte discusses is *Nineteen Eighty-Four*.

43. Bloom, *Modern Critical Interpretations*, 100.

44. *Yestermorrow*, 93.

45. "Burning Bright"; see "At What Temperature Do Books Burn?" 19.

46. Eisenhower.

47. Armour, 10. His sketch first appeared in the *California Librarian* in December 1953.

48. *Fahrenheit 451*, 60th Anniversary Edition, 83. Subsequent references in text.

49. Weller, *Listen to the Echoes*, 124.

50. Paul advises in I Corinthians 7:ix, "it is better to marry than to burn." Bradbury's dramatization makes immediate gratification and satisfaction explicit in this scene: "Answers to everything. Solutions": *Fahrenheit 451*, 186, 5.

51. Bloom, *Modern Critical Interpretations*, 22.

52. Bluestone, 10.

53. Eller and Touponce, *RB*, 191–192.

54. Eller, *Becoming Ray Bradbury*, 294.

55. Bloom, *Modern Critical Interpretations*, 2001, 113. On the centrality of commercialism to the dystopian tradition, see Booker, 1994, 110.

56. Sisario, 202.

57. Whyte, 10.

58. "America on the Move: City and Suburb," at http://amhistory.si.edu/onthemove/exhibition/exhibition_15_2.html (accessed March 19, 2014).

59. Mead, 16. In the second edition Mead described his novel as a "logical extension" of the rating system and commercial TV (10).

60. *Match to Flame*, 450.

61. Eller and Touponce, *RB*, 188.

62. *Match to Flame*, 357.

63. Stockwell, 2000, 214.

64. *Match to Flame*, 415.

65. Eller, *Becoming Ray Bradbury*, 218, 270.

66. *Day It Rained Forever*, 219.

67. Cunningham, 444. On the difficulties of getting the story published, see Eller, *Becoming Ray Bradbury*, 238. On Bradbury's Latino subjects, see McMillan, 39–56.

68. Brians, 2.

69. *Match to Flame*, 205.

70. *Machineries of Joy*, New York: Bantam, 1983, 228.

71. In his notes for the stage adaptation, Bradbury presents the man as more pathological, "just living in another day, another time": *Ray Bradbury on Stage*, 255–256.

72. *Illustrated Man*, 120.

73. "To the Future," *Collier's Weekly* (May 13, 1950): 14.

74. Brackett, 1955, 174.

75. The same trope is used in Fredric Brown's 1949 story "Letter to a Phoenix," which is narrated by a human who has lived for thousands of years after being exposed to radiation.

76. Eller and Touponce, *RB*, 177. Conversely John Huntington argues that Bradbury evokes the idea of books at the expense of their material production; Huntington, 138.

77. Moylan, 149.

78. Hartman, 255.

79. McGuirk, 321.

80. Huntington, 137.

81. W. M. Miller Jr., 1975, 255.

82. Ibid., 68–69.

83. Bloom, *Modern Critical Interpretations*, 2001, 72.

84. Miller and Greenberg, 7, 12, 13.

85. *Revelations* 22:ii.

86. Cf. Watt in Bloom, *Modern Critical Interpretations*, 2001, 37.

87. *Bullet Trick*, 275. Bradbury's 1961 teleplay "The Jail" (collected in *Bullet Trick*) similarly describes a totally mechanized trial process and a state technology which can "transplant" selves into other bodies.

88. *Bullet Trick*, 275.

89. Cf. McGiveron, 1998.

90. Truffaut, 1989, 203; Truffaut, 1966, I, 13. Truffaut's secretary Helen Scott explained to Bradbury that in the final film "extravagance is barred from this science-fiction": letter, February 22, 1966, Center for Ray Bradbury Studies.

91. Truffaut, 1989, 203, 287.

92. Letter to Truffaut, August 31, 1966. Center for Ray Bradbury Studies.

93. "*Fahrenheit* on Film," M1.

94. Adams.

95. Whalen.

96. Truffaut, 1966, I, 17.

97. De Baecque and Toubiana, 314–315.

98. Aggelis, 2004, 146.

99. Bradbury found the school scene "too explanatory": Aggelis, 2004, 75.

100. Bould, 101, 115.

101. Bluestone, 6.

102. Truffaut, 1967, III, 19.

103. Carroll, 211–212.

104. Ibid., 211.

105. Truffaut, 1967, III, 13.

106. Bosley Crowther, review, *New York Times* (November 15, 1966), at http://movies
.nytimes.com/movie/review?res=9D02E6D91330E43BBC4D52DFB767838D679EDE
(accessed March 19, 2014).

107. Aggelis, 2004, 146.

108. *Fahrenheit 451*, 1986, 89.

109. *Yestermorrow*, 114.

110. Weller, 2006, 269.

111. *Zen in the Art of Writing*, 71, 73. The whole scene is published in Weist, 162–165.

112. *Zen in the Art of Writing*, 78.

113. Lovell.

114. *Match to Flame*, 16.

115. Geirland.

116. Johnston.

117. See Guffey.

CHAPTER 4. BRADBURY ON SPACE

1. Weller, "Five Bradbury Projects," 2012.

2. Fallaci, 26.

3. *Yestermorrow*, 99.

4. Durwood, 15.

5. Weller, 2006, 277; Murray, 143.

6. Wells, 1935, 141. Bradbury cites Wells's screenplay in "From Stonehenge to
Tranquillity Base."

7. "Ray Bradbury's Letters to Rupert Hart-Davis," 144.

8. Aggelis, 2004, 150.

9. *R Is for Rocket*, London: Pan, 1972, 11.

10. *Stories* I, 954.

11. Ibid., 164.

12. Ibid., 169, 172. There may be an ironic allusion in his father's warning to the 1954
movie *Rocket Man*, where a boy comes into possession of a ray gun which compels people
to tell the truth.

13. *R Is for Rocket*, 148, 150.

14. *Cup of Gold* was the title of the 1929 novel by Steinbeck, one of Bradbury's favorite
writers.

15. Clarke, 1962, 109.

16. *Stories* I, 314.

17. "Ray Bradbury's Letters to Rupert Hart-Davis," 126.

18. *Stories* II, 759.

19. Ibid., 248.

20. Ibid., 256–257.

21. *Day It Rained Forever*, London: Hart-Davis, 1959, 180.

22. *Stories* II, 412. Bradbury described Shaw's collected prefaces as his "bible": Weller, *Listen to the Echoes*, 162.

23. *Stories* II, 413, 416.

24. Shaw, xix. On Bradbury's fascination with Shaw, see Pfeiffer, 1997.

25. Shaw, xxiii.

26. Ibid., 170.

27. "Beyond Eden," 114.

28. Shaw, 293.

29. "Beyond Eden," 116.

30. *Bradbury Speaks*, 80.

31. Ibid., 107.

32. Ibid., 109, 110.

33. Wells, 1945, 6.

34. *Bradbury Speaks*, 112–113.

35. Sobchack, 113.

36. Bradbury delivered the first George Pal lecture for the Academy of Motion Pictures in 1980 and contributed to the 1987 documentary *Fantasy Worlds of George Pal*.

37. *Cat's Pyjamas*, 192. On spiders, see Eller, "Bradbury's Web of Fear," *It Came from Outer Space*, 32–33.

38. Weller, 2006, 191.

39. *It Came from Outer Space*, 104.

40. Ibid., 106.

41. Hoberman, 226.

42. *It Came from Outer Space*, 92.

43. *S Is for Space*, London: Pan, 1972, 35. In his introduction Bradbury adopts the role of a boy-magician whose ancestry included Verne and Wells.

44. Aggelis, 2004, 103.

45. Letters from Essex to Bradbury and an opening section of his screenplay are collected in *It Came from Outer Space*.

46. "Ray Bradbury Speaks on Film," 34.

47. McAleer, 215.

48. Clarke, 1990, 222. The novel was written during the making of the film.

49. An image also used by Bradbury in the 1947 dystopian story "Pillar of Fire," collected in *S Is for Space*.

50. On the complex story of the film's reception, see "2001: A Space Odyssey Internet Resource Archive," at http://www.palantir.net/2001/meanings/essay05.html (accessed March 3, 2014).

51. "Films," 10. Cf. "It's the single most beautiful film ever made. The camera work is absolutely incredible. But when you've said that, you've almost said the whole thing": Jacobs, 1976.

52. Agel, 299.

53. Weller, *Listen to the Echoes*, 230.

54. Durwood, 14. Cf. "Ray Bradbury on *Close Encounters*," 1978. On similar grounds, Bradbury has expressed enthusiasm for the second Star Wars film (*Empire Strikes Back*,

1980, coscripted by Bradbury's former mentor Leigh Brackett) because it contains Zen Buddhism: Weller, *Listen to the Echoes*, 235.

55. "Ray Bradbury on *Close Encounters*."

56. Durwood, 15. Bradbury later asserted that the film showed a direction for SF in projecting a "religious relationship with the universe": *Bradbury Speaks*, 40.

57. Weller, *Listen to the Echoes*, 234. Two of Spielberg's favorite SF authors were Arthur C. Clarke and Bradbury: McBride, 79.

58. "God in Science Fiction," 37.

59. In that sense Bradbury is reviving the religious significance of SF imagery. A 1955 survey of SF's new mythology argued that the priest had been replaced by the scientist and the church by the spaceship; Mandel and Fingesten, 25.

60. The inclusion of Truffaut as a French scientist could hardly help but trigger associations with *Fahrenheit 451*.

61. "Fahrenheit Chronicles," 1964.

62. *Day the Earth Stood Still II*, Finale E. Bradbury described the promise of the ending as a "celebration also," a sign of the "usual Bradbury optimism": Lofficier and Lofficier, 1983.

63. *Dinosaur Tales*, 20; Turner, 24.

64. Atkins, 46–47.

65. *Green Shadows, White Whale*, New York: Avon, 152.

66. Corwin was a formative figure in 1940s radio drama and instrumental in Bradbury's early career: *Zen in the Art*, 91–92. In the mid-1960s Irwin Allen's television series *Voyage to the Bottom of the Sea* ran a number of episodes which drew explicitly or implicitly on Melville's novel, notably "Ghost of Moby Dick" (1964) and "Jonah and the Whale" and "Leviathan" (both 1965). Theodore Sturgeon wrote the 1961 novelization of the original film and Allen brought in Ray Harryhausen for some of the special effects.

67. Full details of composition in Nichols, "Sympathy with Sounds." On variations between adaptations, see Carter.

68. *Bradbury Speaks*, 184. Bradbury elsewhere describes Nemo as out to "sink War" (Beaumont, 1982, xi); and Verne as the "verb that moves us to Space": Butcher, xiii. In 1976 Bradbury described Verne as the "most American writer in the last 100 years"; 20,000 Leagues beneath the Imagination," M1.

69. Aggelis, 2004, 104.

70. "Space Flights," B14.

71. *Now and Forever*, 160. Bradbury has dated the action at 2199, perhaps an anagram of 1929: "Reflections from the Man," 17.

72. *Now and Forever*, 151.

73. *Bradbury Speaks*, 164–165.

74. *Now and Forever*, 124. The floodgate image is taken from "Ardent Blasphemers": *Bradbury Speaks*, 173.

75. An innovation in the 1972 script; Carter.

76. *Now and Forever*, 176.

77. Ibid., 139.

78. Ibid., 133, 152.

79. Ibid., 184, 202.

80. *Why Man Explores*, 1976.

81. "Writer Takes Long Look," E7.

82. Berger, 1978.

83. *Unexpected Universe* (1969), *Night Country* (1971), and *Another Kind of Autumn* (1977). Bradbury also provided a publicity statement for *Star Thrower* (1978) and introduced the *Loren Eiseley Reader* (2009). Cf. Eller, *Becoming Ray Bradbury*, 202.

84. Eiseley, 1971, 1. Eiseley regularly uses SF examples in his writing, in a 1968 introduction to David Lindsay's *A Voyage to Arcturus* praising the latter's projection of ecological diversity.

85. Like Bradbury, Eiseley saw Melville's Ahab as a Faustian figure challenging Nature, whose actions anticipate those of the "atom breakers"; Eiseley, 1978, 199.

86. Clarke, 1958, 17.

87. McAleer, 90–91.

88. Clarke, 2000, 213.

89. Ibid., 208.

90. "Writer Takes Long Look," E7.

91. "Serious Search," 120, 123, 130.

92. Ibid., 126, 128. The last image forms the coda to his story "Matter of Taste."

93. "Cry the Cosmos," 89. In the 1963 *Playboy* panel Bradbury returned to this issue of extraterrestrial "bizarre life forms." The panel included Asimov, Blish, Clarke, Pohl, Sturgeon, and Van Vogt.

94. Ibid., 90, 92.

95. *Stories* II, 698. For Bradbury's comments on science and blasphemy, see "Creativity in the Space Age," 11.

96. "Impatient Gulliver," 31–32.

97. Ibid., 22, 32. Bradbury repeated the charge of scale reduction in TV in the 1976 NASA forum *Why Man Explores*.

98. Weller, 2006, 277. Cf. Bradbury's 1984 view of space travel as cultural retention: "space and the planets in it . . . will resemble the back lot of a motion picture studio" (*Yestermorrow*, 230).

99. "Impatient Gulliver," 34, 35.

100. Ibid., 35, 36.

101. *I Sing the Body Electric!*

102. "Trailing the Clouds of Glory," 14.

103. Chaikin, 56.

104. Murray, xi.

105. Ibid., xii–xiii.

106. Clarke, 2000, 419.

107. Murray, 135.

108. "Where Are the Golden-Eyed Martians?" 148.

109. Von Braun's only work of SF was his novel *Project Mars: A Technical Tale*, written 1949, published 2006.

110. Aggelis, 2004, 154. Much quoted by Bradbury, with variations.

111. Sagan, 163, 167.

112. Sagan's only novel *Contact* (1985) describes the pursuit of extraterrestrial beings through transmitted messages.

113. Heppenheimer explicitly acknowledged his inspiration from Gerard K. O'Neill's *High Frontier: Human Colonies in Space* (1976), which considers directions for the American space program after Apollo. Among SF works applying his theories is Jerry Pournelle and John E. Carr's *Endless Frontier* (1979).

114. Aggelis, 2004, 168. Despite this refusal, Bradbury and Roddenberry became close friends and Bradbury paid tribute to him in an address at the latter's funeral.

115. Westfahl, 2000, 3.

116. Heppenheimer, 6, 16.

117. Ibid., 278–280, 302.

118. Ibid., 4.

119. "Apollo Murdered," 8.

120. Cf. "New Perspectives." Bradbury enthusiastically endorsed Clarke's declaration in his epilogue to *First on the Moon* that the landing had triggered a major shift outward of the human imagination.

121. Beley, 11, 12. For a restatement of Bradbury's "triple wildernesses," see "Unthinking Man," 372.

122. Aggelis, 2004, 153.

123. "God in Science Fiction," 110.

124. Ibid., 111, 112.

125. *Complete Poems*, 24.

126. Ibid., 84–85.

127. Launius and McCurdy, 15.

128. Dean and Ulrich, 174, 175.

Bradbury, Ray (Works) (*continued*): "The Blue Bottle," 13, 74–75; "Bonfire," 106; "Bright Phoenix," 88, 95; "Changeling," 26; "Christus Apollo," 150–151, 156; "Chrysalis," 6, 136; "The City," 17–18; "The Concrete Mixer,"59–60; "Corpse Carnival," 8; "Cry the Cosmos," 147–148; *Dandelion Wine*, 1, 41; *Dark Carnival*, 9–10; "Dark They Were and Golden-Eyed," 72–73, 151; "Day After Tomorrow," 38; *Death Is a Lonely Business*, 42; "Death Warmed Over," 23–24; "Downwind from Gettysburg," 29–30; "The Dragon Who Ate His Tail," 34; *The Earthmen* (TV drama), 32; "The Earth Men," 54, 64–65; *The Evening of the Second Day*, 140; "The Exiles," 81; *Fahrenheit 451*, 2, 11, 23, 81, 83–121; *Farewell Summer*, 41; "The Fire Balloons," 56–57, 155; "The Fireman,"85–86, 101–104; "Fly Away Home," 62; "The Flying Machine," 127; "The Foghorn," 30–31; "Forever and the Earth," 12–13; "The Fox and the Forest," 107; *From the Dust Returned*, 10; "Frost and Fire," 11; "G.B.S.—Mark V," 13, 129–130, 131–132; "The Gift," 126; "The God in Science Fiction," 139, 155; "The Golden Apples of the Sun," 126–127; *A Graveyard for Lunatics*, 42; "The Green Morning," 75–76; *Green Shadows, White Whale*, 130, 141; "The Highway," 17, 18, 105; "I, Rocket," 13–14, 125; "Icarus Montgolfier Wright," 127–128, 129; *The Illustrated Man*, 2, 15–21, 59, 150; "An Impatient Gulliver above Our Roofs," 148–150, "I Sing the Body Electric," 27–28; *I Sing the Body Electric*, 150; *The Jail*, 24; "Kaleidoscope," 16–17; "King of the Grey Spaces," 124; "The Last Night of the World," 105; "The Laurel and Hardy Alpha Centauri Tour," 43; *Let's All Kill Constance*, 42; *Leviathan '99*, 141–144; "The Library," 87–88; "The Long Rain," 17, 20–21; "The Long Years," 77–78; "The Lost City of Mars," 80; "The Machineries of Joy," 148; "The Man," 17, 128; "Marionettes, Inc." 18, 25; *Mars Is Heaven*, 33; "The Martian," 66; *The Martian Chronicles*, 2, 13, 15, 45–82, 103, 125, 132, 135, 146–147, 152–155; *The Masks*, 65; "A Matter of Taste," 134; *A Memory of Murder*, 8; "The Messiah," 57–58; "The Million-Year Picnic," 20, 50, 60–61; "The Murderer," 23; "My Mars," 80–81; "The Naming of Names," 71–72; "Next Stop the Stars,"125; "Night Call, Collect," 67; "Night Meeting," 55; *Now and Forever*, 141; *The October Country*, 10; "The Off Season," 65–66; "The One Who Waits," 59; "The Other Foot," 17, 73–74; "The Other Highway," 44; "The Pedestrian,"84–85, 98; "Pendulum," 4–5; "Perchance to Dream," 128–129; "A Piece of Wood," 24; "Pillar of Fire," 88–90; "The Piper,"49–50; "The Playground," 19; "Punishment without Crime," 25–26; "Referent," 92; *R Is for Rocket*, 124–127; "The Rocket," 18–19, 150, 155; "The Rocket Man," 17, 125–126; "The Scythe," 6; "A Serious Search for Weird Worlds," 146–147; "The Silent Towns," 27, 66–67; *S Is for Space*, 124, 127, 128, 136; "The Small Assassin," 8; *Something Wicked This Way Comes*, 41, 65; "A Sound of Thunder," 31, 32–34; "Spaceship Earth," 42–43; "The Strawberry Window," 68; *Summer Morning, Summer Night*, 40–41; "The Taxpayer," 71; "There Will Come Soft Rains," 15, 78–79, 103; "They All Had Grandfathers," 70–71; "The Third Expedition," 62–64; "Thought and Space," 122; "Tomorrow and Tomorrow," 6; "Tomorrow's Child," 14; "To the Chicago Abyss," 106–107; "To the Future," 34, 107; "A Touch of Petulance,"32; "The Toyn-

David Seed is a professor of American literature at Liverpool University. He is author of *Brainwashing: The Fictions of Mind Control* and *Science Fiction: A Very Short Introduction*.

MODERN MASTERS OF SCIENCE FICTION

John Brunner   *Jad Smith*

William Gibson   *Gary Westfahl*

Gregory Benford   *George Slusser*

Greg Egan   *Karen Burnham*

Ray Bradbury   *David Seed*

THE UNIVERSITY OF ILLINOIS PRESS

is a founding member of the

Association of American University Presses.

Designed by Kelly Gray

Composed in 10.75/14.5 Dante

with Univers display

by Lisa Connery

at the University of Illinois Press

Manufactured by Sheridan Books, Inc.

University of Illinois Press

1325 South Oak Street

Champaign, IL 61820-6903

www.press.uillinois.edu